Additional Praise for Daniel Patrick Forrester's CONSIDER

"THINK and be spared—egregious mistakes, widespread second guessing, and embarrassing contrition. That is the simple and powerful message from Daniel Forrester who has extensively probed the sturm and drang of management. Our cultural bias toward action limits critical thinking to less than 10 percent of our day's activity. Yet thoughtful analysis can spawn great ideas and prevent bad things from happening."
—John F. Budd, Chairman and Chief
Executive Officer, Omega Group

"Daniel Forrester singles out what is potentially the largest opportunity for corporations and governments of our time: the power of deep reflection at all levels of the organization. Anyone in the corporate world should read this book; it may transform your company."
—Sergio A. Pernice, MBA Director and Professor of
Organizational Design and Financial Engineering and
Risk Management, UCEMA Business School, Argentina

"In a very readable interesting book Daniel Forrester captures the essence of an organization's power to grow and prosper in both good and bad times. If you are serious about growing your organization in these turbulent times do yourself a favor: Buy, read and act on Daniel Forrester's recommendations."
—Peggie O'Neill Co Founder and Former Director of Loyalty Management
University, Host of *Passionate Leaders Powerful
People* (TV Show), and Director of Prayer Power Worldwide

"A great book for a time in which too many of us pull back from the data deluge, clinging to unshakable beliefs instead of exercising our minds. Bottom line: free your time and the rest will follow."
—Thomas P.M. Barnett, author and strategist

Consider

Consider

Harnessing the Power of Reflective Thinking in Your Organization

Daniel Patrick Forrester

CONSIDER

Copyright © Daniel Patrick Forrester, 2011.

First published in 2011 by
PALGRAVE MACMILLAN®
in the United States—a division of St. Martin's Press LLC,
175 Fifth Avenue, New York, NY 10010.

Where this book is distributed in the UK, Europe and the rest of the world,
this is by Palgrave Macmillan, a division of Macmillan Publishers Limited,
registered in England, company number 785998, of Houndmills,
Basingstoke, Hampshire RG21 6XS.

Palgrave Macmillan is the global academic imprint of the above companies
and has companies and representatives throughout the world.

Palgrave® and Macmillan® are registered trademarks in the United States,
the United Kingdom, Europe and other countries.

ISBN: 978–0–230–10607–9

Library of Congress Cataloging-in-Publication Data is available from the
Library of Congress.

A catalogue record of the book is available from the British Library.

Design by Newgen Imaging Systems (P) Ltd., Chennai, India.

First edition: January 2011

10 9 8 7 6 5 4 3 2 1

Printed in the United States of America.

For Nancy Harvier Forrester
You are my north, south, east, and west.
Thank you for teaching me the meaning of reflection.
I love you.

Contents

Acknowledgments

The origins of this book can be traced back to a few key moments. In 2005, Rob Guth of the *Wall Street Journal* wrote a feature story about the fabled "Think Weeks" of Bill Gates that I describe in chapter 2. That story made me ask myself: Why can't think time happen when Gates is actually at the office? A few years later, I was working with my talented coach and friend, Alice Rutkowski of Speakeasy in New York. It was during one of my many moments within the group talks that I framed what became the driving force behind this book: That it's only when we slow down, even for a moment, that data gives rise to meaning.

"Thank you" does not begin to describe the depth of my feelings and respect for the dozens of people who took their time to think with me, coach me, guide me, teach me, and humble me on a topic as vast and important as reflective thinking. I ask forgiveness from anyone I have omitted. This book is the sum of the vast experiences and knowledge gained only by marinating in the wisdom of others.

Darryl Vernon Poole and Van Wishard have mentored me throughout every kernel of thinking that became this book. Darryl, you took over where my dad and John Dalton left off and have enabled me to see my life in a context that always grounds me. You never ask for anything yet you give and give until you decide to give again. I have learned more from you than any book or teacher I have ever read or known. Van, your keen mind and intellectual prowess are only matched by your humility and humanity. Most men walk this earth with but a few people who tell them the truth and see in them more than they can understand; the two of you literally held my hands and guided me to bring forth the first book of my life. At this point, all I can do is pay forward the wisdom, kindness, and knowledge that I have been blessed to experience because both of you are in my life.

More than five years ago, Preston Bradford asked me a question while we were barbequing at his beautiful island home in the Georgian

Bay of Ontario, Canada. He said, "So when you are writing a book?" His question was not whether I would write a book, but "when." That sent a powerful signal to me. Thank you for asking that question Preston. Here is your answer.

I want to thank the people I interviewed for this book. This is their story. The following extraordinary people were willing to be interviewed either in person, over the phone, or via questions posed in email. I am also thankful to those who took the time to review my writing in context and offer upgrades and feedback. My sincere thanks and continued good wishes go to:

Admiral Thad Allen (retired)
Ken Anderson
Kyle Bass
Robert Bea
Joshua Bell
Andrew Belton
Douglas Bennett
Maria Bezaitis
Brooksley Born
Jim Brickley
Prudence Bushnell
Fred Collopy
Tom Cooley
Conrad Crane
Scott Dockter
Kenneth Feinberg
Richard Floersch
Rob Guth
Tio Hardiman
Harry Hertz
Jeff Hoffman
General Jack Keane (retired)
Rakesh Khurana
Jay Light
Sandy Linver
Diane Lynch
Erin Carlson Mast
General James Mattis

Chris Mercogoliano
Jeb Nadaner
John Nagl
Susan Nolen-Hoeksema
Barbra Pagano
Elizabeth Pagano
General David Petraeus
Matthew Pinsker
Darryl V. Poole
Joe Raelin
Mitchell Reiss
Sister Mary Jean Ryan
Stefan Sagmeister
Sarah Sewall
David Shenk
Robert Shumsky
Jonathan Spira
Arthur Staats
Kristina Sullivan
Carol Tavris
Nancy Tennant
Bill Thompson
David Walker
Edward Watkins
Tom Wheeler
Van Wishard
John Wolpert

In addition to all of the people listed, I have the good fortune to know Stacey Kole of the Chicago Booth School of Business. Without hesitation, Stacey invited me to come to Chicago in 2009 and share my earliest hypotheses around the topic of reflective thinking. Harry Davis and Linda Ginzel graciously arranged for one of the Booth School's legendary workshops to take place around my thesis. Over a dozen talented minds came to the session and offered feedback and new angles to explore that changed the trajectory of this book. That workshop gave me tremendous confidence that what I was thinking through was worthy of deeper and more expansive examination. I am indebted to all of you for your feedback and interest in this project.

My Godfather, Paul O'Connell, from Iona College gave me his time and so many ideas that helped form key chapters within this book. Paul also listened to me and helped me think through one of the more difficult writing challenges as I was running out of steam with the manuscript due date looming. Paul, on many occasions you expressed the words that my dad would have said had he lived to see me write this book. Thank you.

Early on in the concept phase of this book I was privileged to work with the very talented Julia Pelosi who helped edit initial thoughts into coherent prose. I also remain thankful to Jeff Seifert for his feedback, edits, and encouragement as I shared pieces of ideas as the book was formulating in my mind. John Kador advised me in all that it takes to create a compelling pitch that would grab a publisher's attention.

I am forever grateful to my colleague and dear friend Benoit Gaucherin who fielded many calls from me as this book was undertaken. Ben was my sounding board and a constant flow of encouragement as he checked in with me during every phase of this project. Ben, you are a coach and mentor who has been a constant source of balance and steady advice for well over a decade.

It was not until I met my agents Kristina Holmes and Michael Ebeling of Ebeling Associates that the goal of writing my first book by the age of 40 became possible. The two of them guided, coached, and pushed me to package my energy and ideas. Kristina, you are a kind and gentle soul with immense talent. I was drawn to work with you from our first conversation. I am honored to be associated with both of you and forever thankful that you took me on as your partner.

My sincere thanks to Kiernan Vieth and Elizabeth Eckert who helped me with transcribing so many hours of interviews and in finding key data points and citations tied to many research angles.

My friend, advisor, and attorney, Ian Portnoy, helped me with every facet of the legalities of writing this book. Ian's talents as a strategic advisor are only exceeded by his kindness, follow through, and constant search to help others achieve their God-given potential. I am blessed to have such a calming presence in my life.

The University of Rochester's William E. Simon Graduate School of Business played a key role in shaping this book. Not only did the school shape my worldview as I had the pleasure of studying there, but during the writing of this book, I was twice asked to lecture and share my findings with large audiences. My sincere thanks to Greg Tilson, Holli Budd, Greg Shaffer, Cliff Smith, Harriett Royer, Ron Schmidt, and Dean Mark Zupan for sharing in my passion and in helping me bring this book to life.

When it came time for writing the first version of the manuscript, I needed a physical location in which to think and write. Lisa and Bill Veith graciously supplied me with their charming home on the beautiful Chesapeake Bay in which to live away from my family for nearly two months. To write a book on reflective thinking in such a setting was ideal. I will never forget your kindness, hospitality, and encouragement. Thank you.

To my dear friend Iain Dale, thank you for your advice and feedback through each stage of writing this book. Your entrepreneurial attitude and passion for reading and writing has influenced me in many ways.

I am indebted to the very talented Chris Carlson, not only for his encouragement with this project, but also for taking time from his schedule to supply the promotional photographs for the book. Stephen Schneider selflessly shared his design talents throughout many stages of this project.

Varun Jain was critical in helping to prepare for the promotion of this book. In addition, the immensely talented Jeff Syfu supplied incredible design work for the website promotion. The incomparable Dan Willis asked me many challenging questions (under hot lights) and shaped the video content portion of the site. My sincere thanks to all of you.

Masako Sho graciously gave of her time and design talents for the diagrams within this book. She also helped me to prepare for the workshop at the University of Chicago. Masako, you define the word excellence.

I was helped by many who offered feedback, encouragement, unique angles, key introductions, case studies, articles, research, suggestions, and genuine interest in my work. My thanks goes to Andrew Belton, David Yang, Raj Shah, Tim Smith, Tim Dunne, Vince O'Neill, Drew Rockwell, Mark Berler, Martin "Big Daddy" Corboy, Tracie Ahern, Alan Wexler, Dennis Wholey, Cindy Gunn, Amy Shah, Chris Davey, Bret Kinsella, Aleks Zelenovic, Martha Cotton, Tim Clemente, Christoph Hinkelmann, Meg Armstrong, Jesse Danzig, Father Thomas Petrillo, Dara Brown, Matt Huber, Matt Winkler, Tom Hutton, Suzy Farren, Marshall Coleman, Lynn Coleman, Frank DeRosa, John Dower, Edward Larson, John Cole, William Riordan, Columb Lytle, Larry

Vogt, Gerry Creamer, Robert Sokol, Raney Zatawski, Chris O'Hara, Bill Issacs, Peter DiGiammarino, Pete Odell, General Barry Knutson, Peggy O'Neill, Thomas Bateman, Austyn Crites, Jack Baumann, Jeff Skalecki, Jennifer Walker, Jerry Porter, Joan and Art Zeizel, Scott Rasor, Stephanie and Mathias Preble, Nathan Zeldes, David Norcross, Saundra Whitlow, Tara Handy, Aldo Bello, Kristy Lewis, Kevin Novak, *Jo Ann Jenkins*, John Kelley, Angela Evans, Donna Paskin, Ravee Kurian, Brent Williams, Tony Bitonti, Joe Connolly, Teresa Bozzelli, Burton McFarland, Christina Frederick, Andy Macey, Matt Lane, Ming Lam, Rich Ross, Bill Annibell, David Denham, Dean McRobie, Nate Brewer, Tim Smith, Casey Connor Minton, Conall O'Cuinn, Katie Luby, Reagan Ramsey, Tim Young, Lauren Staub, Hank Summy, Jane Conver, and Kris McMenamin.

Jerry Greenberg and Stuart Moore impacted my life and the content of this book through the courage and vision that they had in forming Sapient.

A very special thanks to my talented friend and colleague David Whitehouse, who saw some of the earliest chapters of the book and offered feedback, unwavering enthusiasm, and encouragement when I needed it the most.

Frank DiGiammarino constantly reminded me that this was a worthy project and he has been a powerful influence in my life. I am thankful for your guidance and steadfast friendship. Carol DiGiammarino was my shadow editor for this book. She was the first person to read each chapter—even before my publisher had a look. Carol you have no idea how talented you are. Your comments and feedback were honest, clear, and immensely helpful in enabling me to write a coherent text that would connect with many. Thank you.

I had the pleasure of working with my very talented editor Laurie Harting of Palgrave Macmillan. Laurie, you helped me take a concept and turn it into a meaningful manuscript. You are tough and direct and pushed me to go deeper where I could and to leave out details that did not advance my thesis. You have made me a better writer. My special thanks to Tiffany Hufford at Palgrave for keeping me on time with the manuscript and in assisting in executing the roll-out of this book.

A very special word to those serving in the United States military around the world: Your innovation, perseverance, and courage inspired me throughout this journey. My thanks for allowing me to tell about small parts of what you do for the country each day. We have much to learn from all of you. My wife and I will donate to the amazing charity: "No Greater Sacrifice" in your honor.

Along the way, I spent countless hours at several nurturing places that supplied great coffee, company, and free WiFi. My thanks to the kind people of: The Java Stop in Deale, Maryland, The Tombs and Saxby's Coffee in Georgetown, Washington, DC, Quartermaines Coffee in Bethesda, Maryland, and Le Pain Quotidien in Washington, DC.

If there is anyone to whom I want to hand deliver a copy of this book, it would be my dear friend, the late John Dalton. John's voracious appetite for the written word inspired me. He treated me with respect and care when no one else in Washington knew that I existed. He taught me to face fear and have the courage to follow through. He taught me politics through a historic view so far removed from the petty babble that echoes on television today. John, I think you would have been proud of this work. I miss you.

To my brothers and sisters and their spouses, as well as my nieces and nephews, for their continued love and support across all the years of my life. A special thanks to Jacob Sadowski for taking such an interest in my work and in lifting my spirits by interviewing me for your schoolwork—that meant a lot to me.

To our beautiful children, William Edward and Charlotte Jayne Forrester, I want you to know that daddy was away from you for all those months and weekends with a purpose. I love you both beyond any words I can convey. My hope is that some day you will find a quiet corner in which to read all the wisdom of the many people who humbled me with their stories and insights. Reflection is not a fleeting concept—it will sustain you and help you through your most difficult moments.

To my beautiful wife Nancy Forrester, you have afforded me the time to think through all the ideas within this book. The dedication of this book to you says it all. To my mother-in-law and father-in-law, Doris and Howard Harvier, for their encouragement, love, and support. Thank you.

Throughout my life, my mother, Patricia Forrester, pushed me gently and deliberately as only a mom could. Mom, thank you for teaching me to never see fear as an obstacle and to push myself to be more than I thought possible. I love you.

During the hundreds of hours I spent alone writing this book, I felt my dad's calm presence and guidance. I remember as a young man when he would read my writing often in the middle of watching a New York Islander's game at home in his recliner with a cup of iced coffee at his side. He would then mark it up with a red pen and suggest rewrites on a humongous yellow legal pad. I took all that feedback to heart and subconsciously it permeated every paragraph within this book. Each day I discover another facet of what it means to think and act like you, Dad. It's intuitive. Yours was a reference point that will sustain me through everything in this lifetime. You are remembered, loved, and missed.

Finally, my thanks to almighty God for the gift of life and the many blessings he has given me. I seek no validation through this book— except in your eyes as a worthy contribution for others to **consider**.

Bethesda, Maryland
November, 2010

Introduction

The Space between Data and Meaning

"STOP, THINK, AND DON'T DO SOMETHING STUPID!" This is the warning Dr. Robert Bea drills into his Civil and Environmental Engineering students at the University of California in Berkeley. Bea wants to dramatize what he terms the inevitable "Oh, shit" moments that present themselves—sometimes years before an actual engineering calamity occurs. Evidence that procedures may go disastrously wrong can be found in a broken piece of equipment or in failure to thoroughly explore the downsides of unproven, and "buggy," technology platforms. Bea believes that if he can get the students to remember this simple phrase and associate it with the action-driven businesses they will shortly enter, perhaps they can save countless lives and billions of dollars. Disasters have recognizable patterns and indicators. Bea would know, as he has studied the causes and effects of over 600 such events. If engineers have the courage to force things to a stop and take the time to think about the broadest context of what they are observing, it's more likely that major problems can be avoided. Big risks can't be managed in the incessant real-time flow of now; there must be some safe, intellectual white space between all the actions and triggers.[1]

Mike Williams was one of the last crewmen aboard BP Global's (BP) *Deepwater Horizon* oil-exploration platform before it exploded and then descended to the bottom of the Gulf of Mexico. While it will be many months, indeed years, before there is conclusive evidence of the many things that resulted in the disaster, Williams told *60 Minutes* of an accident that happened during a routine test weeks before the actual catastrophe. Nearly 5,000 feet below the surface of water, rubber gaskets were closed within the "blowout preventer," the technology that controls the drilled hole's pressure and keeps oil and natural gas from escaping uncontrollably. The blowout preventor is the technology relied upon to shut down and control the flow of oil, especially when there are potential threats to the operation from below, from weather patterns and tides, or human error. Williams revealed that a crewman on the *Deepwater* in the control tower had "accidentally nudged a joystick, applying hundreds of thousands of pounds of force, and moving 15 feet of drill pipe through the closed blowout preventer." Williams told *60 Minutes* that someone on the deck had "discovered chunks of rubber in the drilling fluid. He thought it was important enough to gather this double handful of chunks of rubber and bring them into the driller shack. [He recalled] asking the supervisor if this was out of the ordinary. [The supervisor responded,] 'Oh, it's no big deal.' And [Williams] thought, 'How can it be not a big deal? There are chunks of our seal now missing.'"[2]

The above moment is exactly the type that Dr. Bea discusses in his lectures as he opens his classes with video clips of major disasters. Bea had anonymously been given the transcripts from on-deck conversations for the *Deepwater Horizon* in the weeks leading up to the disaster. There was mounting evidence that this was like the countless other disasters he had studied, as people did not dissent and take a step back. Bea wants students to recognize a moment like the one described above. They should insist that people stop and rethink what can happen. It sounds so simple. Bea is a realist and understands that, in the context of large companies and confusing government authorities and rule-sets, it's hard to stop the deployment of a multibillion-dollar oil operation. When it costs a company like BP 1 million dollars a day in search of oil, it's nearly impossible to be the engineer who dissents and suggests there's an embedded failure that could mean costly delays, or even suggests walking away from a project. Bea calls it the "blow torch on the ass incentive."[3]

Bea is among a handful of people with a deep understanding of oil rigs, engineering, and the limits of man's capacity to enable technology in pursuit of innovation and profit. He had already interviewed the top 50 people involved in our country's greatest environmental disaster and initially concluded that the *Deepwater Horizon* spill was avoidable. Although now in academia, Bea once worked for Shell Oil and currently consults for companies around the world that are willing to listen to him frame the risks inherent in the design and implementation of the technologies they seek to employ. With an encyclopedic knowledge of engineering failures, including the levees that gave way due to Hurricane Katrina and the aftermath of the space shuttle *Columbia* disaster, Bea is the guy who gets called when the unthinkable becomes reality. He never wants to say, "I told you so." He'd rather the phone calls stop; but they don't.[4]

Before the federal government called a moratorium on all off-shore oil-well drilling projects, Bea had been working with a company for nearly two years as they were deploying even more complex oil-extraction technology than that of the *Deepwater Horizon*. Bea pushed back constantly as plans and prototypes were discussed. He was con-sistently ignored, even as everyone looked at the live television shots of oil spewing from the hole punched into the earth nearly a mile under water. Bea explained: "They are very intelligent people and they have known me for many years." He said the company reminded him of a self-assured toddler attempting to walk alone for the first time down a staircase. "They have an almost child-like focus on: 'I wanna,' 'I can,' and 'I'm gonna.' Then they start down a slippery slope of incrementally bad decisions that lead to disaster; like a child falling head-over-heels down the flight of stairs."[5]

It has been suggested that the *Deepwater Horizon* disaster represents the limitations of man's ability to harness technology for his betterment. I asked Bea if he believed that we had reached such an edge—even if we are too proud to admit it. He thinks that's part of the problem embed-ded within disasters like the *Deepwater Horizon*. He once escorted the CEO of Shell Oil Company out of a building and to an awaiting lim-ousine. As the car pulled away, Bea read the bumper sticker that now sits within his mind as a symbol of the state of technology and man's action-driven ambitions. It read, "If you aren't standing close to the edge, then you are taking up too much room."[6]

We are all standing on the same edge and rarely do we see evidence of people suggesting we should back away. On Wall Street, few dissented and suggested a time-out from deal-making—the downside was ratio-nalized away under the delusions of good times and exuberance. Just as Dr. Bea suggests that his students must learn to stop and think again, so too must every organization. We may not be employees on a sophisti-cated oil rig or Wall Street bankers, but we are all working on problems with speed and ferocious competition that doesn't reward thoughtful dissent and prolonged and expansive inquiry. We are also working with technologies that have changed every facet of our relationships to time, problem solving, and one another. We are living in an age of immediacy that can't be singularly managed with instantaneous responses. For these reasons, stepping away from the problem—and structuring time to think and reflect—just may prove the most powerful differentiator that allows your organization to remain relevant and survive. All risk can't be eliminated and all decisions can't be made in the blink of an eye. But major risks must be managed, especially when there is evidence that the unthinkable is slowly unfolding before your eyes.

What's This Book About?

There's an intangible and invisible marketplace within our lives today, where the products traded are four-fold: attention, distraction, data, and meaning. They are passed around in a frenzied dance that can drain your senses and dilute sound judgment. In this marketplace, there are very few buyers of the more costly products: attention and meaning—especially when distraction and data are incessantly distributed to all of us for free. Yet, we rarely step back to question the pace, personal impact, chaotic information flows, unpredictability, and lack of meaning that swirl within our organizations. We collapse at the end of the day and then get back in the water the next morning. The word that describes what we are all living through is "busyness," a non-stop state of busyness. It makes us feel wanted and useful, but at the same time we feel drained and uncontrolled.

The stories and examples within this book demonstrate that the best decisions, insights, ideas, and outcomes result when we take sufficient time to think and reflect. While technology allows us to act and react more quickly than ever before, we are taking increasingly less time to consider our decisions before we make them. With all the speed and immediate reaction practiced within organizations today, we are witnessing countless real-time examples of the very edge of man's ability to "corral" the same technologies he so proudly deploys. From shocking market fluctuations with no logical explanations to an oil spill in the Gulf of Mexico revealing countless engineering, managerial, and oversight missteps, we are living through the simultaneous conditions of technology enablement of mankind's most profound insights and poorly executed ideas. The difference between these two conditions is in the amount, structure, quality, and discipline given to reflecting and learning—before we reflexively jump into action mode and give an immediate response—on the essence of, and context, surrounding problems.

Organizations are standing on the very narrow edge described above by Dr. Bea. Will we elevate the importance—or dare I suggest the cultural imperative—of consistently adopting think time and reflection, or will we pass it over as our work pace gallops to a new, dizzying speed? The choice in how we behave is ours; so are the consequences that result from such a critical decision.

Data, Meaning, and Change

Over sixty years ago, the late Peter Drucker wrote, "No one born after the turn of the twentieth century has ever known anything but a world uprooting its foundations, overturning its values and toppling its idols."[7] In the early hours of the twenty-first century, we have rapidly toppled many idols in many different markets, and change is now permanent. Change is also unsettling. Constant change doesn't lend itself to instantaneous insights through simple phrases like "too big to fail," and "liquidity crisis." The question we must ask ourselves is this: In the midst of dramatic and extreme change, has decision making devolved into merely informed chaos, or can we imbed reflection and think time into our habits and routines to arrive at better outcomes and understanding?

Librarian of Congress Dr. James Billington stated: "It took two centuries for the Library of Congress to acquire today's analog collection—32 million printed volumes, 12.5 million photographs, 59.5 million manuscripts and other materials—a total of more than 134 million physical items. By contrast, with the explosion of digital information, it now takes only about 15 minutes for the world to produce an equivalent amount of information."[8] This means that in the time it will take you to read my opening thoughts, a Library of Congress has already been created that neither you nor I will ever have the chance to fully understand, let alone rapidly apply to the problems we are trying to solve.

With all the data coming at us, our only choice appears to be "staying on top of it" all day, every day. It also makes you ask: How do we stay on top of "meaning" the same way we do our email and all the other data that surrounds us? Meaning is determined in one's mind while we are away from the data. It is when we are afforded fleeting moments of time to think that we get to a common understanding of a problem and agreed-upon methods to solve them. Meaning involves forcing connections to be made in one's mind, or even in small groups, where posturing gives way to "real dialogue" or to what Massachusetts Institute of Technology's Bill Isaacs calls, "The art of thinking together." Then an email hits our inbox or pulsates within our Blackberry. Our cell phone rings, or we reflexively pop open a favorite website in between or even during meetings. We freely allow our attention to be diverted into the unfiltered and addictive world of what marketing innovator and documentarian, Aldo Bello, described to me as "media snacking." When we snack, we never get full or satisfied. Meaning is a meal consumed in courses, slowly, and with control, even when frenetic data-calls try to derail you just as you sit down and place the napkin on your lap.

When overworked people declare that they "just don't have time to think," leaders have a choice: They can settle for the status quo and declare that it's the way the world works today, or they can insist that reflection is a strategic business enabler. I will demonstrate throughout this book that leaders who fight for the latter choice have better outcomes. And once they lead with thinking and reflection embedded, others will emulate their example until it bleeds into the DNA of the organization.

A Sobering Context

If your attention has not yet been drawn away from this book, or interrupted by a call, email, or instant message, then reflect on the following: Take a step back and pause for a moment around each bullet below. Think about the big ideas and decisions facing your organization amid the following:

- *Longer workdays*, driven in part by accelerating technological connectedness, leading to 50 to 70 million Americans suffering from sleep deprivation and disorders[9] affecting health, careers, personal relationships, and even automotive safety.
- *Drowning in information/data overload* and content creation like a Library of Congress every 15 minutes.
- Inability to decipher quality, authoritative information from suspect, nonauthoritative sources enabled by anyone with a digital camera, computer, and the ability to comment via the Web.
- Increasing international *connectedness as well as friction* amplified by globalization, thus pitting the United States against a slate of emerging, hostile, impatient and often misunderstood actors.

- An *incessant global, 24/7 news cycle*, where mistakes and simple missteps are amplified and transmitted at a speed that drowns out reality, clarity, and true insight.
- A *technologically savvy generation of young people (millenials)* slowly entering a workforce resistant to giving them a seat—a generation with (on average) poor reading, writing, and comprehension skills and which prefers text messaging over any other type of communication style.[10]
- A permanent election cycle that fosters *inadequate, truncated, and hurried debates of transgenerational and systemic issues*, including managing unprecedented national debt, contending with illegal immigration, and managing the implementation and ongoing fallout from health-care reform.
- Medical and technical innovations that enhance, sustain, and alter life and at the same time create *profound and poorly understood and discussed moral and ethical questions.* As this book was written, the first manmade, viable single-cell life form was created.[11]
- The need to reform primary and secondary educational systems that are failing to enable the next generation of leaders to cope with any and all of the concepts listed above.

Bias toward Action Revisited

More than 25 years ago business gurus were extolling the value of "bias towards action,"[12] as American companies searched for new ways to compete with Japan. Yet, layer in complexity and technology and action bias today takes on a whole new meaning. Healthy action bias results in people taking risks, experimenting, being accountable, and having basic follow-through. Destructive action bias now manifests itself in impulsive and instantaneous responsiveness to every request, call, email, and message that's lobbed our way. There is a hierarchy of communication we all practice, in which electronic and immediate data responses reign far above in-person and more time-intensive, dialogue-driven interaction. The trade-off is easy to make: we gain speed, immediate connection, and reactions while giving up richer contexts that emerge only when we take time to think. There are times when the arrival of each new electronic message or data-driven distraction has become a digital proxy for the sound of a bell once used by a doctor named Pavlov.

For the last decade, the global marketplace has been characterized by unprecedented actions, and reactions, in the private and public sectors alike. In this environment, inaction is unthinkable. How many CEOs or politicians have you recently heard speak who did not invoke the ideas of speed and action? Leaders with "action bias," therefore, sound very reasonable until market tumult quickly exposes how little control these leaders have. Yet, with a little forethought, sometimes our best move may be to stay put. Consider professional soccer goalies defending against penalty kicks. What is the best strategy for stopping the ball? Is the goalie better off lunging to the right or the left?

It turns out that staying in the center instead of jumping to the right or left is the best move a goalie can make. A unique analysis by several economists, entitled, "Action Bias Among Elite Soccer Goalkeepers: The Case of Penalty Kicks," showed that goalkeepers who dive right stop the ball 12.6 percent of the time. Goalies who dive left do a little better, 14.2 percent. But goalies who don't move do the best of all. Goalies who stay in the center of the goal have a 33.3 percent chance of stopping the ball. Yet, goalies stay in the center a mere 6.3 percent of the time. The economists concluded that a bias for action—any action—is very difficult to overcome even when it is demonstrably an inferior choice.[13]

Deciding to stay in the center of the goal instead of jumping is also an action. It's a conscious choice that can only be taken after seeing that other alternatives are less effective. Staying in the center takes courage, just as much as to suggest that drilling be stopped when crumbled rubber from an underwater gasket shows up on the deck of an oil rig, as happened on the *Deepwater Horizon*. To stay in the center involves stepping back, questioning assumptions, and then courageously acting counter to conventional wisdom. Only by carving out think time and reflection can we actually understand, in an entirely different context, the actions we take. Why do we miss so many balls? Is there a better approach? Why did that degraded and blackened rubber gasket just show up on the deck of the oil rig? Today, few of us give permission to step back and rethink a problem—or to fundamentally reconsider, below the surface of a problem, the set of assumptions we are making.

What's the Value in Reading This Book?

Organizations that prioritize think time and reflection benefit by ensuring that workers are focused on solving the right problems that matter to the mission and stability of the organization. Such organizations can create early-warning systems for detecting when they are implementing a failing strategy. Having a conversation within your organization around the value of think time and reflection can result in nurturing employees so that they can act with control and thoughtful intent throughout moments of crisis and great uncertainty. Organizations that embed think time and reflection into processes and routines are more likely to generate new ideas, products, services, and solutions.

By reading this book you will discover how organizations like PBD Worldwide Fulfillment are protecting think time and reflection so that daily habits and routines are not disrupted by incessant technological distraction. You will see examples of leaders like Sister Mary Jean Ryan of SSM Health Care Systems in the Midwest, and her team, codify think time and reflection into the fabric of processes and operations so that quality and consistency emerge in patient care. You will go behind the scenes with Grammy Award–winning violinist, Joshua Bell, as he detaches from the day-to-day activities in order to mentally prepare himself for sustained moments of focus and attention around some of the most difficult music ever played. You will discover the habits of atypical thinkers, like attorney Brooksley Born, and global investor Kyle Bass, who both predicted the near collapse of the global economy, within a context few wanted to even discuss. Late, great thinkers like Abraham Lincoln and Jim Henson will teach you that their think time habits are more relevant today than ever. You will also see that while companies like Google powerfully give dedicated think time to whatever an employee wants, organizations like Whirlpool Corporation have taken think time to new levels with outstanding business results. Finally, you will understand better, and find lessons learned, as to how leaders like General David Petraeus and Colin Powell force think time and reflection into what seem like impossibly dense schedules; they allow connections to form in their minds so they can attempt to answer ambiguous questions such as, "Should we go to war?" and "How do we turn around a failing strategy?"

Through over one hundred interviews (formal and informal) with business and military leaders, diplomats, anthropologists, economists, academics, musicians, designers, and even a former gang member from Chicago, I have discovered dozens of ways for you to reclaim what immediacy has taken away: reflection. *This* is the first book to amass a comprehensive view of how readers can:

- Replicate the behaviors of individuals who formally structure think time and reflection in order to solve both simple and complex problems.
- Ensure that technology encourages productivity without creating unwanted distractions that consume organizational think and reflection time.
- Define a new language and set of rules that will enable employees to feel less overwhelmed and more comfortable taking a step back to think through problems.
- Define motivating reward structures and incentives for encouraging think time and its innovative outputs.
- Discover what it means to create an organizational culture where think time and reflection are not a slogan but part of daily routines.
- Understand what it means to create a culture where dissent is valued and the downside risks of a problem are considered with the same rigor as the upside.

Think with Me for a While

This book frames some of the most consequential choices you will make in your career. It's a set of choices that can expose think time and reflection as strategic assets. We can't, nor would we try to, slow down the world, but we can, at times, choose to move counter to the flow. We can choose to allow our minds (even short) bursts of time to assimilate what is coming at us. It's only when we have context and perspective separated from the actual problem that a new idea can form that might solve it. That idea can be lost in the data, or hatched into meaning that transforms what you are working on. Immediate responses have their place, but they will never replace deep thought (and problems that become reframed) through reconsideration of our deepest assumptions and biases. When, inside your organization, evidence presents itself that it's best to take a step back and reconsider the problem, will you have the courage to force moments to stop, think, and not do something stupid? Within the pages and stories that follow you will discover it can be done.

I

The Human Need for
Think Time

Of Business, Interleaving,
and Oil Spills

There is a tempo that envelops us driven by technology, connected-ness, and our bias for action and immediate response. It's a pulsating and often unforgiving pace that swirls when we are awake and even as we sleep. Data flows between us in small digital packets. Asynchronous data exchanges are rapidly unveiled on miniature screens at home, work, and every space in between. From Twitter "tweets" emanating from a desperate populace in Iran to a husband calling his wife on his cell phone as his train is running late, technology connects us in profound and mundane ways. Global trends analyst Van Wishard says, "We live in two worlds; a world of data and a world of meaning." It doesn't matter if you are a president of a country or an average person with a cell phone, "busyness" subsumes what we all crave—time to think.

During the U.S. presidential campaign, Senator Barack Obama traveled through Europe, stopping in London to meet with the then-leader of the UK Conservative Party and now British prime minister, David Cameron. The two were unaware that a powerful microphone was picking up their conversation. Their discussion could be echoed by professionals within hundreds of thousands of organizations today: They expressed concern about losing touch with the larger causes they believe in, which are so often overwhelmed by densely packed sched-ules and urgent matters that need their attention.

Cameron asked if Obama had taken any time off. Obama said, "I have not. I am going to take a week in August. Somebody who had worked in the White House—not Clinton himself, but somebody who had been close to the process—said that should we be successful, the most important thing you need to do is to have big chunks of time during the day when all you're doing is thinking." Obama added that failing to make time to think would mean that the campaign would "start making mistakes," or "lose the big picture." Many months later, the newly inaugurated President Obama was asked when, in his schedule, he finds time to think. He revealed his "night owl" habit of writing about issues that are not immediate and pressing. He said, "If you don't build in some thought time, you end up being pushed aside by the constant churning of events." The campaign results achieved by Obama reveal that his team executed a set of strategies involving contingency, risk management, moxie, and the unprecedented use of technology. The big picture was never lost.[1]

The two leaders have also spoken out against the role technology plays in diverting attention from key issues. During a commencement address, the tech-savvy president, who was keen to keep in touch with his closest advisors via his Blackberry, had this to say: "You're coming of age in a 24/7 media environment that bombards us with all kinds of content and exposes us to all kinds of arguments, some of which don't always rank that high on the truth meter. And with iPods and iPads; and Xboxes and PlayStations—none of which I know how to work—information becomes a distraction, a diversion, a form of entertainment, rather than a tool of empowerment, rather than the means of emancipation."[2] Meanwhile, Prime Minister Cameron, no technology laggard himself, set new rules for his colleagues during his first cabinet meeting. He informed senior ministers that the distraction of mobile devices, both cell phones and Blackberries, would not be welcome.[3] To some laughter, Cameron rebuked a minister who violated the new rule and fielded what would be the last phone call received during a critical meeting.[4] Obama and Cameron are aware of the downside of the immediacy afforded through technology and connectedness. They are trying to promote attention over distraction, and meaning over data.

Context through Think Time

Leaders often refer to "the big picture" as a metaphor for seeing their work and collective actions in context. Within our culture of immediacy, we often fail to look at a problem in anything but the "context of itself," as noted by author and global strategist Thomas P.M. Barnett. Barnett asserts that, given the complexity and global interconnectivity of business and geopolitics, "We must look at problems in the context of everything else."[5] All too often, action bias and distraction creep in just as meaning and context emerge. Few leaders maintain "big picture" focus because problems seem too pressing to take adequate time to think them through. This bias toward action pervades organizations, from the level of systematic practices right down to the individual's behavior. Together with constant distraction, it is nearly impossible for leaders and their employees to maintain focus on the questions that truly matter.

Does This Look Familiar?

You're at your desk, about to open the project plan from last week, when a colleague pops in to see how your weekend went. You turn away from the computer and engage in a minute or two of conversation. That one minute of forgettable banter will cost you ten more refocusing on the project. Information overload analysis firm Basex calls those ten minutes our "recovery time" from an interruption.

Consider the following snapshot of an ongoing study of the major activities performed in the course of an average knowledge (white-collar) worker's day. See if this breakdown resembles your average day in the office:

How a Typical Information Worker's Day is Spent

60% Work

= 25% Productive content creation including writing email messages

+ 20% Meetings in person, by phone, video and online

+ 15% Searching through content including the Web, digital communications and paperwork

12% Thinking and reflecting

28% Interruptions
Interruptions by things that aren't urgent or important (such as unnecessary email messages) and time it takes to get back on track

Source: Basex

This research indicates that critical thinking amounts to only 10 to 12 percent of your working day. Among the dozens of leaders I interviewed for this book, most believed that 10 to 12 percent was a gross overestimate, particularly for the most senior leaders within an organization. What this suggests in terms of work productivity is that current emphasis in most organizations is action-oriented—either responding to interruptions or carrying out decisions, with much less time taken to think and reflect. There are two modes now: *on* and *off.* And when we are on, and the data flows and simultaneous conversations pulse, it's very difficult to get meaning and context. Why do we allow this to occur?

The fallout from the financial crisis resulted in companies and institutions shedding millions of jobs as demand for products and services evaporated within days. Many economists have remarked that "worker productivity" has yet again risen, proving that workers can produce more with less. For those fortunate enough to retain their jobs, this often means they take on much more responsibility. In other words, the tempo has actually speeded up for many. The financial meltdown has put organizations under tremendous pressure to take decisive action in an environment in which we need more, rather than less, time to develop strategic solutions to challenging problems. How can we find time to think when we are taking on more and more responsibility and complexity? In addition, how can we find time to think when time itself becomes a meaningless distinction given the constancy of data and connectedness; our days have no natural beginning or end.

Of Multitasking, Interleaving, and Plastic Time

Thousands of job descriptions feature the term *multitasking.* For example, a simple query on monster.com looking for a manager in the state of Maryland featured this requirement: "Strong computer, project planning and organizational skills in a multi-tasking environment are essential." MacmillanDictionary.com defines multitasking as, "the activity of doing more than one thing at the same time, such as talking on the phone while you are working on a computer." The only problem is that multitasking between two technology-driven tasks is nearly impossible.

Leading researchers, like Stanford's Richard Nass, have determined through multiple experiments, including the use of functional MRIs of the human brain, that our minds function best when pursuing only a single task. For example, when we try to do two technology-facilitated tasks at once, neither is done as well as if we had only one task. Our performance suffers and quality suffers. Nass recently commented: "It turns out multitaskers are terrible at every aspect of multitasking. They're terrible at ignoring irrelevant information; they're terrible at keeping information in their head nicely and neatly organized; and they're terrible at switching from one task to another." Nass and his Stanford team were troubled by their research because younger generations are attempting more multitasking. He concluded, "Ignoring irrelevancy—that seems pretty darn important. Keeping your memory in your head nicely and neatly organized—that's got to be good. And being able to go from one thing to another? Boy, if you're bad at all of those, life looks pretty difficult."[6]

Nass's research did not uncover tiny populations with computer-like minds capable of simultaneously handling the demands of two technology-driven activities. However, a recent study by the University of Utah concluded that 2.5 percent of people are able to perform two attention-driven tasks at the exact same time. Researchers focused on the ability of people to drive an automobile while using a cell phone. The experiment was conducted in a simulator and featured hands-free connectivity. The study noted, "Supertaskers have a strikingly remarkable ability to successfully perform two attention-demanding tasks that over 97 percent of the population cannot perform without incurring substantial costs in performance."[7] The study concluded, "Our results suggest that the overwhelming majority of people suffer significant bidirectional impairment from using a cell phone while driving. Second, our results suggest that there are supertaskers in our midst; rare but intriguing individuals with extraordinary multi-tasking ability. These individual differences are important because they challenge current theory that postulates immutable bottlenecks in dual-task performance." Some will read this paragraph and self-servingly conclude that they are one of the 2.5 percent supertaskers. In reality, you are more likely with the nearly 97 percent of us, for whom multitasking remains a mythical aspiration.

Wireless and multichannel technology has the ability to facilitate nearly continual human connectedness, and contributes to disjointing time itself. We are all feeling busy and stretched, because there are few periods, if any, in which we can sustain a thought, let alone ponder something that requires us to fundamentally question our most basic assumptions. Time for thinking is relegated to the sidelines, and this has consequences. Academic and essayist William Deresiewicz recently wrote an essay based on a lecture he gave to the Plebe class at West Point. He pointedly advised the young soldiers that, "Thinking means concentrating on one thing long enough to develop an idea about it.... In short, thinking for yourself. You simply cannot do that in bursts of 20 seconds at a time, constantly interrupted by Facebook messages or Twitter tweets, or fiddling with your iPod, or watching something on YouTube." He goes on to say, "Here's the other problem with Facebook and Twitter and even the *New York Times*. When you expose yourself to those things, especially in the constant way that people do now—older people as well as younger people—you are continuously bombarding yourself with a stream of other people's thoughts. You are marinating yourself in the conventional wisdom.... You are creating a cacophony in which it is impossible to hear your own voice, whether it's yourself you're thinking about or anything else."[8]

Interleaving

Maria Bezaitis is the director of the People and Practices Research team at Intel Corporation. Her unique research team takes on big and ambiguous topics in an effort to study human behavior and define how Intel can think critically about people and their relationships to technological innovation. One of their recent studies involved observing the behaviors of people, how they experience mobile technology, and what that is doing to their perceptions of time itself. They wondered why people are so busy yet somehow always know the latest post on a favorite website like Facebook? What are we actually doing as we constantly switch between media and tasks?

Their research showed that people are now experiencing what they call "plastic time." Anthropologist Ken Anderson, a member of the Intel team, explained to me that in plastic time, time itself bends in a constant state of interruption and movement between many different tasks. Anderson said, "Plastic time is not part of people's cognitive mental models of their behavior. It 'flies under the radar' occurring in ways people cannot accurately recall." He continued, "Plastic time is unanticipated, unreflexive and fluid. Plastic time is in the negative space of what people refer to as 'busyness.'"[9]

Intel's research reveals that we are not actually multitasking (as it's a nearly impossible human capability and it has a definite connotation), but rather we are all "interleaving." Bezaitis explained to me, "It's the way that people process daily activities to accommodate plastic time. Interleaving activities assume that activities are plastic, or 'bursty,' as they happen. As such, people tend to stack or layer activities going from one to another in relatively short periods of time." She described that interleaving is a strategy of optimization as we try to do more tasks in the same time. Intel arrives at no conclusions about the quality of that time and the efficacy of switching. They simply believe that interleaving is happening and having a profound impact on work and home life. It will take time to discover its impact on relationships. Bezaitis pointed out to me that "reflection" is a relative term and is defined by individuals in the context of new technologies and experiences. Reflection can actually involve allowing one's mind to wander while deep inside a website or social media experience; it need not mean a lone thinker sitting on a hillside. Today, one person's trip down memory lane in a Facebook session is another person's meaningless waste of time.[10]

Within all of this, a few ideas became clear to me. First, there is seemingly no time to think, as we are in a perpetual state of leaving one task for the next or attempting to do the impossible, such as multitasking. Even if we want to think for an elongated period of time, say 30 minutes, our choices in terms of technology and connectivity give instant rise to our desire to leave think time—even though we know we are shortchanging something we believe has value. Second, plastic time symbolizes the fragmentation of our days that allows each of us to move in and out of tasks and conversations on our own terms—there is no referee or coordinator in plastic time. We are all now islands of information, processing new things constantly based on our own preferences and digital desires. Third, the connectivity afforded by technology flowing into our homes and work lives means that plastic time is all the time and not just during our moments at work. We have lost nearly all distinction between home and work, and that has implications we are only now beginning to understand.

Intel's study helped me conclude that think time and reflection have become activities that we have allowed to become fragmented into mini moments situated within a constant stream of other tasks. Yet, I believe that think time and reflection are not activities that can be shortchanged and left to whimsy in order to be valuable, and therein lies the tension. With the problems that organizations must face today, shortchanging think time and reflection and permitting them to be fragmented through plastic time will exact a cost from those who allow it to happen. On the other hand, as you will see throughout this book, think time and reflection can become powerful tools for those who learn to practice and codify them.

I believe that embracing think time and reflection as habits and organizational capabilities will determine the success or rapid failure of organizations in the twenty-first century. So let's define these terms. Think time is *the purposeful elevation of chunks of our work time, forged within densely packed schedules. It forces the consideration of core significant and pending decisions, outside of cursory overviews and immediate response.* Closely related, but requiring more discipline to achieve, is the state of reflection. Reflection is *the deliberate act of stepping back from daily habits and routines (without looming and immediate deadline pressures), either alone or within small and sequestered groups. It's where meaning is derived through reconsideration of fundamental assumptions, the efficacy of past decisions and the consequences including the downside of future actions. It's where space is given for the "totally unexpected" to emerge.*

Devaluing Reflection

Meaning isn't rapidly manufactured given the single-tasking (not multitasking) capabilities of the human mind. Meaning unveils itself over time. Context is richer as we drive farther away and see more and more detail in the rear-view mirror. Not that we shouldn't make rapid decisions; sometimes we should, as immediacy does have its virtues. However, decisions of high consequence can't always be made in the blink of an eye. Ideas are hatched by people granted some time alone with their thoughts. Ideas must then be collaboratively shepherded through group dynamics, where they are allowed to marinate and often emerge as something totally new. The problems facing organizations today are too large in scope to be owned by any one individual. Big ideas are contemplated by few only to be implemented by many. If an organization and its leaders don't value the time necessary to think through a solution to a problem, the organization will likely flounder and prove irrelevant. The world has too many people thinking simultaneously about the same problems. Others will commandeer the idea and its implementation should you fail to step back to properly consider it before jumping into action mode to implement it.

Darryl V. Poole is founder and chief strategist of the Cambridge Institute for Applied Research, Inc. He advises CEOs and leaders around the world on underlying trends in technology and corporate governance and on the implications of the stresses brought upon organizations by globalization. Poole believes the immediate consequence of devaluing reflection is that those individuals who more easily succumb to technology are directed by those who take the time to practice reflection. He says, "Those who do not reflect become subject to the rule of those who do. Reflection is personal and true reflection can be painful. Those who do not reflect allow themselves to become very willing participants in a technology addiction that seemingly relieves them of the responsibility TO reflect."[11]

In our culture of immediacy, we can easily solve the wrong problems with great speed. Solving the wrong problems can take our teams, customers, and partners in directions that make little sense. It often means that we are justifying a set of destructive behaviors. Two disparate examples follow to illustrate the consequences of failing to address the "right" problems.

What Problem Are You Trying to Solve?

Robert Shumsky has spent his entire professional life in search of methods that allow people and organizations to "do their jobs better and create cultures where improvement and quality always get better over time." Shumsky, now a professor at the Tuck School at Dartmouth, believes that technology and automation rapidly force outcomes that may not be the most desirable. "In every company," he said, "I think there is tendency to believe that if you're moving, if you're doing something immediate (or at least it looks like immediate), then you're doing the right thing."[12]

What Shumsky is referring to is an ingrained bias for action. Action bias *can* actually result in positive outcomes, particularly in our globalized world, where change and data are constants and some decisions must be made with speed. But without the necessary ideology and discipline to step back and analyze future decisions, action bias more typically causes waste that slowly degrades the core of an organization.

Shumsky shared a supply chain story to illustrate the point. "I once worked on an assembly line at one of the largest U.S. technology manufacturers," he said. "The people on that line were absolutely convinced that the right thing to do at any time was to build product. Just like the soccer goalie whose purpose is to dive for the oncoming ball, the workers on the assembly line are there to build things. But if you don't step back and take a look at what you're doing in context, then you wind up building the wrong thing, or more often, low quality things. You need to always be thinking not just of the short term, but the actual needs of your customers and the long-term goal of what you are trying to do."[13]

He continued: "We were making components of a high-density hard disk drive and about every tenth or twelfth unit was defective—meaning that the lens in one of the readers was a little out of place. This persistent defect was caught a few work stations down the line from me." The defective units were put on shelves while the line chugged along. In fact, this team went on to build another shelf just to hold more defective units. Shumsky said, "Nobody paused and said, 'Wait a minute! Let's take a step back. Is this the goal? Is this really what we should be doing?'"[14]

Hurricanes and Think Time

Failing to allow for think time and reflection can have much more dire consequences than defective products or lost revenue. Consider the set of events that transpired in the days leading up to Hurricane Katrina in 2005. Michael Brown was the director of the Federal Emergency Management Agency within the Department of Homeland Security. He was responsible for coordinating the federal response to the devastating effects wrought by hurricanes. Yet, for almost seven days the world watched as images emerging from the Gulf region revealed phenomenal devastation and millions of lives at risk. Brown chose to position himself away from the epicenter of the destruction. As a result, he never gained an accurate understanding of the problem that he and many others consistently referred to as the "hurricane response." As public outrage mounted, Brown was forced to resign.

Then U.S. Coast Guard chief of staff and recently retired commandant Admiral Thad Allen was chosen by President Bush to be the new lead for the Katrina response following Michael Brown. Can you imagine getting told that you are in charge of coordinating the recovery after the most devastating hurricane in U.S. history, six days into the crisis with lives on the line and the whole world watching? What's the first thing you would do? What would you say? What, if any, actions would you take within the first 24 hours? How would you find time to think and reflect when the cameras are shoved in your face and people are dying around you? How would you describe the problem?

In my first interview with Allen, he shared that on arriving in the region, he realized he had to buy some time to develop a strategy that would demonstrate a different set of results. In an environment of intense public scrutiny and criticism of government response, this was no easy task. Allen related, "You must be able to build contexts and mental models for problem solving. When I was sent down to be lead federal official during Katrina, the reason that situation was so broken was an inability by government to actually classify the event. For over a week, no one could figure out what was actually going on [the order of magnitude and complexity of the event] and then decide what the objectives were."[15]

Eighteen hours after his arrival in New Orleans, Allen determined the true context of what he and the country were facing. As he shared, this was due in large part to time he took to reflect on the situation. He said, "When I went back to my room at night, I had quiet time. I was isolated and had time to reflect. I also used transit time as some down time when I could think uninterrupted. I moved around in helicopters a lot when I first came to New Orleans. I took swatches of time and invested in asking myself, 'What else am I missing; what am I not thinking about?'"[16]

During one helicopter ride, Allen looked out over the devastation and concluded that he was not there to coordinate a hurricane response. He said, "I had the epiphany that I was dealing with the effect of a weapon of mass destruction used on the City of New Orleans, but without criminality. And up until that point, no one had stepped back and said we are dealing with a different animal here. As I looked down, I realized that we had a loss of continuity of government but there was still a standing mayor. We sent resources in for over a week, all of whom were virtually self-deployed. People poured into New Orleans but they didn't work for anyone."[17]

Through moments of think time and reflection, Allen reclassified a catastrophic event and reframed it within a new and more effective context. Only then was he able to coordinate support for the local, state, and federal response with clarity, direction, and urgency. "I told the president what I was going to do," said Allen. "I didn't have the luxury to float an idea and have it blessed by someone. I needed immediate action, results and effects. I then had to say to the American people that, 'I am here. I am accountable. I am in charge and we will fix this.'"[18]

Oil Spills, Analogies, and Communications

In the final months of his role as commandant of the U.S. Coast Guard, Thad Allen was yet again tapped to become the point person for the federal government as it coordinated and responded to the unprecedented oil release happening 5,000 feet below the water's surface in the Gulf of Mexico. In this instance, Allen used his fleeting moments of reflection (again on planes, helicopter rides, and often in the early morning) to help him frame descriptions of the aftermath of the *Deepwater Horizon* oilrig explosion. The communications challenges he faced involved connecting with vastly different constituencies from the national press corps all the way to local fishermen in the Gulf who watched in shock as their businesses imploded within days and weeks. The demands were constant. The anger was building. Allen also had the daunting challenge of explaining what role the government could and should play in solving a problem that was beyond their competence.

The demands on Allen were building as the media and public focused constantly on the hazy images broadcast via the Internet and live television of oil gushing from the mangled oilrig resting on the ocean floor. Allen shared, "It immediately became very clear when the rig sank that this was going to exceed any plans that were on the shelf for a response. And that this was going to be a major environmental catastrophe." While his retirement from the coast guard was well known and published before the *Deepwater Horizon* exploded, President Obama and Secretary of Homeland Security Janet Napolitano asked Allen to remain the lead federal official in charge of the national incident response.[19]

While few of us will ever be called on to respond to a crisis the scope of which Allen faced, his experience presents lessons for us on the value of deep thinking in order to discover language and analogies to best describe a situation that was far from a simple oil spill. He also showed us that leaders must learn to not take sides and be above the fray even when it's clear where the blame sits. Reflection means balanced thinking and not allowing emotion to blind one to possibilities— even if they are unintuitive to those around you. The way that Allen built trust with BP's leadership remains misunderstood by most. He thought through how he should behave rather then reflexively getting caught up in the public outcry against BP. People wanted the federal government to step in and quickly cap the well. People wanted the government to be more relevant than it could actually be given the limits of the capabilities and technology solutions that it could bring to the situation.

Throughout the crisis, we saw Thad Allen on television each day as he answered thousands of questions. But far from view was his relationship with the President of the United States and what was happening in Allen's personal life. The busyness, pressure, and complexities made maintaining balance in his life simply impossible. The situation was so severe that even Allen was initially at a loss to put a context on the problem and the true impact of the government's response working with BP. He told reporters at a White House press conference, "I've never dealt with a scenario like this. I've been dealing with oil spills for over 30 years. This is an unprecedented anomalous event."[20] The *Deepwater* aftermath was also distinct from what he had experienced with Hurricane Katrina. As he explained, "I was involved from the beginning as it was a search and rescue mission and I was commandant of the coast guard. For 48 hours we were looking for eleven people— ultimately and tragically we lost them."[21]

June 15, 2010, stands out in Thad Allen's mind as a critical day in his relationship with the president and in the ultimate outcomes for the response. On flights between Washington and the Gulf that day he was given precious time to collect his thoughts as the context of what he faced unfolded. He was also given latitude to own the problem in such a way that it altered his thought patterns and fed into his think time the next morning. He recalled one critical conversation with President Obama aboard Air Force One on the way back from the Gulf, which helped frame his thinking about the course of action he should take. The cabin lights were dimmed. Allen was seated alone on a couch and lost in thought. He recalled, "The president sat down next to me and we had about a 40-minute conversation that was probably the pivotal point in the entire response for me."[22]

Obama asked Allen if he had enough resources and whether he needed anything else. The president listened as Allen explained, "Mr. President, BP's got enough corporate resources. The issue is the industrial base, getting boom and getting skimmers." Allen continued, "Quite frankly, Sir, we are having problems with aviation safety over the site as we have had eight near mid-air collisions and what I really need to do is put a military command and control structure over the top of the air space and link surveillance with our vessels of opportunity and our surface units who are trying to find the oil." President Obama looked directly at the 62-year-old Allen and said, "You do whatever you need to do but let me tell you this, there are no do-overs."[23]

Thinking back on this critical exchange, Allen said, "At the moment the president said that, I felt empowered to do what I needed to do. What the president was looking for were effects and accountability." The next morning Allen arose at 4:30 in the morning. He used the time alone to think through and frame a critical two-page e-mail that laid out a major course change in the response.[24]

I asked Allen to explain how to communicate and frame such a complex problem when immediacy and pressure often consume reflective thinking. Allen explained, "The problem sits in my head and then I often try out my initial description with my staff. I will try to come up with a catch phrase or something that I think is descriptive of the problem. I then watch how they respond to what I say." He continued, "I will also talk generally about the problem statement in the press. As it slowly matures, and I think I have a description that works, I will formally roll it out and then say, 'So here is what I think.'" He advises that a useful problem statement should be short, concise, meaningful, and impactful.[25]

Allen told me that things were too complex to put into a single sentence as he had in Katrina. He had to quickly grasp what was unique about this situation, which involved the critical element of a commercial entity being responsible for the disaster itself and for finding its remedy. He had a series of revelations; some that he shared in public and some that he shared after the fact: "One of things that made this unique from Katrina was that there was no human access to source of the problem. And all the access to the source of the problem and all the means to solve the problem at the source did not belong to the U.S. government; they belonged to the private sector." He added, "This caused no small amount of angst with our political leaders as it seemed to question the relevancy of government. The response mechanism that we had been using for the last 20 years didn't anticipate the crisis that would be brought about by the fact that the means to the solution of a problem of national scale would not be owned by the federal government."[26]

In terms of the problem of the hole punctured in the bottom of the ocean that was flowing incessantly with oil, Allen explained, "We were not dealing with an oil spill. This thing flowed for 85 days. And when the oil came to the surface, each day there was a new set of currents and wind directions. What we had was hundreds of thousands of patches of oil." Allen explained that this created an even greater problem because the wind blew from one direction and then another and conditions changed constantly. He continued, "By the time it was done we had put at risk the Florida Panhandle, Alabama, Mississippi, and most of Louisiana—with some tar balls washing up in Texas. Rather than defend a specific coastline we had to acquire enough resources to defend the entire gulf simultaneously—that was way beyond what our prepared response plans called for."[27]

One catalyst that helped him accelerate his thinking and then frame the problem through an analogy he could share with the general public occurred to him shortly after he answered a question posed by the White House press corps. On May 24, 2010, with a live, national audience watching, a reporter asked, "To this point, whether the government can do more, can it push BP out of the way if it feels like that company is not doing the job? What is your response to that?" Allen didn't hesitate and bluntly said "Well, to push BP out of the way would raise the question of replacing them with what."[28]

Allen concluded that there was no federal intervention to remedy the situation, as the public demanded government action and the White House wanted to understand how they could be relevant in finding solutions. He needed to give the public and the administration an analogy that would allow them to grasp the complexity and reality of what he had concluded. Allen shared, "I said that this is more like Apollo 13[29] than the *Exxon Valdez*. The reason it was more like Apollo 13 is that we were dealing with the source of the oil, which was 5,000 feet down on the sea floor and there was no apparent means to stop it once it happened. No infrastructure existed in the Gulf of Mexico to bring oil to the surface because it is all controlled by pipelines that normally bring it back to shore." He continued, "So we had a huge technological problem with no human access. This required BP engineers and federal scientists to get into a room and throw everything on the table and come up with a solution."[30]

Beyond the oil gushing into the ocean, Allen realized that there was another problem he was facing with both political leaders and the American people. There was deep distrust of BP, its senior leadership, and the remedies that they proposed given their involvement in the disaster and financial responsibilities to its shareholders. Had Allen reacted in haste and reflexively put the government in charge of the well, he would have exacerbated the problem. He quickly realized that the well-established national plans for responding to such disasters had never considered that the remedy could sit almost entirely in the hands of the commercial sector. It was a major lesson learned. Allen had to interact with BP without anger or animosity, as it would have done nothing to remedy the situation. He concluded that the national contingency response plan was, "socially and politically nullified." He had to build and maintain an integrated, innovative, and problem-solving relationship with both the catalyst of and the cure for the problem. Allen explained, "I considered it my personal responsibility to establish that relationship with the senior leaders of BP. I got asked all the time whether I trusted BP—the real problem was that BP had to trust me."

He frames the most significant lesson to be learned from this disaster this way: "There has to be a whole of government, whole of nation, and whole of community response to events like this. I don't think we will ever have a disaster response in this country again, whether it's a hurricane or an oil spill, that won't involve the private sector, the public at large, the government, nongovernmental organizations, and faith-based organizations." He believes that it's critical to ensure that the general public and the private sector remain engaged, informed, and part of solving the problem. He concluded, "The public demands participation and the private sector is needed. We need to find a way to assimilate all the resources, passion, and commitment to try and solve problems like this. This will include things like social media and the ability of the public to organize, as they will be involved whether you like it or not."

Of Siestas and Kaleidoscopes

What Admiral Allen describes above is his discovery that he needs time to see the larger context of what he is working on, even when he could take massive action without much thought. It is only through reflection that he arrives at the language to describe such complex problems and situations. Reflection is only found if he allows it to exist—it's a conscious choice to insert the time and force the associations. A different example of think time captured my attention as I watched an online video of renowned violinist Joshua Bell performing a famous piece of music by Vivaldi. While he was playing, he consulted no sheet music and, to my untrained ear, he made few, if any, mistakes. His eyes are closed and his upper body glides from side to side as his mind directs the thousands of impulses that allow him to play the violin. When he is playing, his mind is in another place. I wondered how he was able to remain focused for so long when my mind wandered several times just listening to the same song. Bell explained, "Doing what I do requires the ability to focus and filter out everything that is going on around you; not just on the stage, but also in the practice room. I really think it's harder to focus today." Bell believes he learned to focus when he was very young: "When I was a child, my family would joke that when I would get my mind on something, whether it was a puzzle or even chopping tomatoes, they could be talking to me or yelling at me or an elephant would walk in the room, and I wouldn't even notice. I am not a multitasker. I am a focuser." Bell thinks the ability to go to the quiet and reflective space allows him to concentrate and play some of the most complicated classical music in the world. He speculates that he got these critical skills from his father, who was an author and psychotherapist and liked to meditate in the morning.[31]

Just as Bell has had to practice playing the great classics, he has also had to practice simply having and valuing down time. Reflection is built into his routines. No matter where he goes around the world, the local stagehands will try to speak with him and help to break the pressure of the pre-performance moment through a joke or comments about the latest movie people are talking about. He doesn't want to be rude, but he doesn't want to engage them either as he is holding on to his mind and doesn't want it to wander. He said, "As they talk to me it is sometimes awkward. I am already getting inside the meditative and focused state. So I try to keep it as boring as possible just before a show. I try to slow everything down because when the adrenaline kicks in everything speeds up. Slowing down beforehand helps me get in control."

Bell travels tens of thousands of miles a year and lives constantly away from his home in New York City. He is on the road over 250 nights a year and has performed before millions of people both in concert and on television. As he mentally prepares for a concert, he has a routine. If the show is at 8:00 p.m., he will seek what he calls his "siesta." It's sacred time: "For me, a nap in the afternoon is almost indispensable. I try to allow an hour and a half to shut down my mind." Bell discovered that if he pushed himself all day he was unable to calm his mind down for the actual performance and go to that place of concentration he discovered as a child. In his home in NYC he has designed a room that allows for complete darkness. "When I wake up I feel completely refreshed, even if it's only ten minutes of sleep. It helps me significantly."[32]

While Bell is on stage inside his own mind, I met another person who also values reflection and the outputs that it brings to his work. Jeb Nadaner is a former deputy assistant secretary of defense and speechwriter to Colin Powell. Now with Lockheed Martin, Nadaner has contributed to the transformation of the Department of Defense and the role it increasingly plays in rebuilding nations post-conflict. He enjoys focusing on problems that many find confounding. In 2008, Secretary of Defense Robert M. Gates awarded Nadaner the Medal for Distinguished Public Service. At the ceremony, Gates declared, "Put simply, Jeb has been one of this department's most consequential leaders and thinkers over the past four years."[33]

Like Joshua Bell, Nadaner values downtime—often in the morning he will read something that is far from what he works on. It can be an article from *Atlantic Monthly* or even a book on the complexities of communicating with and training animals. He believes it is incumbent upon him to amass a kaleidoscope of knowledge—not only having reference points from his previous experience, because they may be faulty. I asked him to describe what's going on inside his brain as he spends time alone, simply thinking. He explained, "I have this image in my head. I see a trap door. I just need to find it, push it open, and prop myself through it. Once on the other side, I'm in a different place, a new ground as it were." He arrives at a fresh area in his mind: "It's as if I'm walking around a new setting with different people. This experience can feel almost like being in a novel, but it's not a dream; it's a conscious reflective space, where I can see clues and possible solutions to big, complicated thorny problems." Though he doesn't always find immediate answers in that reflective space, he often does over time.

Whether in the Pentagon or the private sector, Nadaner has successfully worked in a world of consequences—in which decisions must be made, actions implemented, and results achieved. You can't think in perpetuity. Throughout, an integral part of his daily discipline has been to add time on top of his work—particularly in the very early morning, late evening, and on weekends—to read and ponder. He is committed to generating innovative insights that are ultimately practicable—even if they are slow to emerge over several periods of reflection.[34]

The Bell and Nadaner examples describe, as best as simple words can, what it's like to be inside a mind that is focused and reflecting. The products of their think time benefit many. For Bell his product is music. For Nadaner his product is a new way to attack a problem that has no immediate and obvious solutions. Their examples make you take stock and ask, "When was the last time you held concentration on something that lasted even for 15 minutes?" Or, "When was the last time you pondered a problem that allowed you to emerge through a trap door into a new and even uncomfortable space inside your own mind?"

Balance in All Things—Even Think Time

I do not wish to suggest that being alone and thinking always leads the mind to positive and beneficial outcomes. I have also discovered that we can "over-think" things to the point of inaction. Alone time and reflection when one's mental model of the world is perverse can give rise to the unimaginable. In his book *Solitude*, author Anthony Stoor pointed out that Adolf Hitler was alone and in prison when he thought through and dictated his manifesto, *Mein Kampf.* "Without my imprisonment," Hitler remarked long afterward, "*Mein Kampf* would never have been written. That period gave me the chance of deepening various notions for which I then had only an instinctive feeling."[35]

Being alone with one's mind can give rise to kernels of truth and ideas, but human nature always has a duality. Prolonged think time for Hitler gave rise to a well-crafted and perverse strategy that subsumed millions of people. One man alone came to conclude that he could determine which people were worth more and which ones were worth nothing. While Hitler is an outlier in terms of what he was able to achieve, his intellectual capacity exists in many. In fact, too much time alone and thinking about a problem without ever finding a path to a solution can cripple individuals and organizations. A powerful counter-example to Hitler is found in Nelson Mandela's years of incarceration and isolation; this time for Mandela gave rise to rich concepts for forgiveness and reconciliation that helped heal and transform South Africa.

Edward Watkins is a professor of Experimental and Applied Clinical Psychology and a clinical psychologist at the University of Exeter in England. He has studied the effects of over-thinking problems, including the consequences of entering the state of "rumination." In rumination, negative thinking dominates the mind, leading to inaction due to a constant state of worry. He told me, "There are times when immediate rapid response is good and times when slowing down and reflecting are good—the trick is for an individual to be good at discriminating which approach is most relevant for the current circumstances and then being able to make that switch."[36] The moment we all must watch for is when we repeatedly revisit a problem. Watkins said, "Repeated thinking becomes unhelpful when it has at least two components— a focus on the negative, such as a problem or a loss or a stress (i.e., the content of the thinking is about something difficult, such as an unresolved goal) coupled with a style of thinking that is too abstract, too much focused on asking, 'Why did this happen?' 'What does this mean?' 'What are the implications of this?' which moves away from the specific details and process of the situation." In other words, he suggests we should not home in exclusively on the "why" when problem solving. Such questions must be balanced with "how" questions that suggest a path forward.[37]

Dr. Susan Nolen-Hoeksema is Director of Graduate Studies at the Department of Psychology at Yale University. She, too, is a leading authority on rumination and the impacts of over-thinking. She suggests you should be open to questioning your assumptions and ensure you are making course changes so you don't get bogged down. She told me, "One important distinction is that the negative rumination is characterized by an abstract 'why me?' kind of thinking that leads nowhere. In contrast, more adaptive reflection identifies problems and looks for solutions."[38]

Rediscovering Reflection

Given our technology-enabled interdependence, when organizations fail to think and reflect in a systematic way it can come at a sweeping and decisive cost to all. Prior to the economic meltdown, there was a saying on Wall Street that demonstrates a collective lack of reflection: "A rolling loan, gathers no loss." This became the battle cry strategy of many bankers that nearly led to a global meltdown. Bankers have now discovered that nonmoving loans gather tons of new regulations and ongoing economic losses. As you will see through many examples within this book, a failure to think dispassionately about both the up and down side of a problem can sometimes lead to catastrophic ends?

Wall Street was not alone. We have also seen action bias without careful thought to down side represented in the very consequential decisions regarding war. As several government officials admit, the lack of preparation and think time allocated prior to the Iraq war was reckless. The problems we attempted to solve in Iraq were ever-shifting political targets, ranging from finding weapons of mass destruction to forcing democracy to take root in a Muslim nation. General James Mattis, who led the 1st Marine Division during the successful initial ground invasion of Iraq, and is now in charge of U.S. Central Command, shared this chilling statement with me as he reflected on the rush to war with Iraq and what the United States inherited as it took control over the country. Mattis said, "Eventually, you can answer all your emails, rush hither and fro, attack into a country, pull a statue down, and then say, 'Now what do I do with it?'"[39] As you will discover in chapter 7, reflection played a critical role in finally answering Mattis' question, nearly three years after he asked it on the battlefield.

Problems facing business leaders and organizations are more complex than we've ever faced before. While we enjoy significant technological advances, it is often this same technology that undermines rigorous, thoughtful analysis of today's challenges. Coupled with our culture's bias toward action and exacerbated by constant distraction, it can be nearly impossible for today's leaders to consistently pose and then answer the right questions while employing sound judgment. How many leaders claim they can speed up judgment? Judgment arises through the verbal and written expressions of one's core analysis hatched only in moments of thinking and reflection. It can't be rushed.

What reflection and think time offer are specific and deliberate behaviors that allow for meaning to emerge from the vast supply of data that swirls around us. Even more powerful than the moments spent thinking and reflecting is what comes from the minds of those granted moments to pause and ponder. From dissent and debate to the wild and over-the-top, reflection supplies an arsenal of ideas and solutions to the right problems. For those in our culture of immediacy who see reflection and think time as luxuries, such thinking will foreshadow the fall of that leader and the organization. We have entered a time when codifying think time and reflection back into our habits and routines is a mandate we simply can't afford to ignore.

2

Forcing Think Time

Of Presidential Commutes, Personal Battle Rhythms, and Making Time to Wonder

The immediacy afforded by technology, and the increasing responsibilities implied within any one job, fill up our time and hurt our ability to be reflective. All of the "busyness" often makes us feel out of control and scattered in our thinking and our approach, forcing us to make decisions in the moment, sometimes at the risk of the future. Control for our actions and our ideas will remerge if we consciously force, even short moments, to step back and think before we act. In order to examine how individuals can force this time into their routines, I have discovered some historical examples worth emulating; from a balanced way to adopt new technologies to getting the most out of a meeting. All the examples demonstrate the role self-control plays in managing the constant flow and in finding ways to better derive meaning.

We begin with a closer look at two less-understood but relevant sides of Abraham Lincoln: how he embraced technology, and how he fought for separation between his home life and work life so he could ponder big problems.

Managing the Beggars' Opera

Few people could imagine a modern-day president commuting to the office every day. The White House is where all presidents live and conduct many affairs of state. Yet, for nearly 25 percent of his presidency,

Abraham Lincoln commuted back and forth between the White House and a cottage at the Soldiers' Home that he inhabited with his family. Between 1862 and 1864, the Lincolns lived there "usually...from early summer to late autumn," as Lincoln scholar Matthew Pinsker reveals. The modest cottage still stands proudly on the hundreds of acres now called the Armed Forces Retirement Home. To this day, veterans of war come to spend their retirement there. The first national cemetery, predecessor to Arlington, is adjacent, serving as a constant reminder of the horrific human costs of war.

It surprises many to discover that one of our most celebrated presidents kept a second home that had a profound influence on his personal think time. With the sometimes-brutal heat of Washington, DC, and the constant distraction, noise, and pace of the Civil War–time capital, Pinsker notes that the Soldiers' Home and grounds, "offered an attractive alternative to the White House, especially in hot weather, because they were well situated on cool, shaded hills. They also offered the advantage of being outside the city center (located in the northwest corner of D.C.), while not too far from the presidential office. It took an ordinary carriage driver about half an hour to navigate the three mile journey across the District of Columbia."[1]

The Soldiers' Home was nowhere near the retreat that modern presidents have enjoyed with Camp David. Yet, for Lincoln it represented a sanctuary. It buffered him from the harried, and sometimes chaotic, world of being president before modern-day structures redefined access and time spent with the commander-in-chief. Indeed, Lincoln's life in the White House was filled with profound moments of reflection as he wrote some of his greatest wartime speeches within; yet it's also the place where supporters and critics would incessantly line up to seek even only a few moments with the president. The information conveyed to him through countless meetings was substantial. He had a small staff and little to no organizational structures to buffer him from the constant requests and meeting invitations that accompany the presidency. While few of us will ever be president, the pace and flow of Lincoln's day match the elongated days we now live and work. We must prioritize our own meetings and constantly evolve our schedules, respond to constant requests for our attention to matters deemed priority by others, structure how we approach the next discussion and deal with the immediate concerns of day-to-day problem solving. Like Lincoln, we must do all of this with little to no help.

Lincoln's top aide, John Hay, recalled the flow of visitors, commenting that "the House remained full of people nearly all day." During lunchtime, Lincoln "had literally to run the gauntlet through the crowds who filled the corridors." The images such scenes evoke of untamed access to the president remind us that distraction and information overload are not new issues for leaders to contend with. Busyness does not belong only to the twenty-first century. Scholar John Waugh writes: "Lincoln compared himself to a man who was so busy renting out rooms at one end of the house that he couldn't stop to put out the fire that was burning at the other end. On some days he ordered the doors flung open to all who were waiting, and they swarmed into the room all together...he called it "the Beggars' Opera."[2]

By making the choice with his wife to live at the Soldiers' Home for many months at a time, Lincoln purposely created a physical separation between his work and his home life. In the mornings, he made time for his private thoughts and for allowing new ideas to enter his mind. Pinsker describes it: "Like many modern-day commuters, Lincoln scrambled in the mornings to avoid traffic and get a head start on his daily work." "He rose early," recalled John Hay. "When he lived in the country at Soldiers' Home, he would be up and dressed, eat breakfast...and ride into Washington all before 8 o'clock." Some visitors there to see Lincoln would discover that on some mornings he was awake by 6:30 a.m., "reading the Bible or some work on the art of war." Other visitors to the house recall Lincoln's love of reading Shakespeare aloud, sometimes for hours, with just one person sitting in the room with him.[3]

It's important to note that while Lincoln had fewer visitors while living at the cottage near Soldiers' Home, he wasn't isolated there. With a cemetery and hospital in close proximity, he saw daily burials of war dead and was constantly reminded of the true costs of war. While there, he didn't hide from the sadness. Rather, he found ways to detach from the pressures of his job, while directly confronting the sometimes disturbing consequences of his decisions. Erin Mast, the director at President Lincoln's Cottage, explained to me that his commute brought Lincoln into contact with wounded soldiers coming back from the front as well as with contrabands—people impacted by his decisions as commander-in-chief, yet unlikely to be seen in the White House. Mast summarized: "For Lincoln coming to the cottage gave him contact with people who experienced the full weight of his decisions. While it was a place that gave him time to think, it also gave him a reality check."[4]

Lincoln's short bursts of think time spent at the Soldiers' Home and on his commute to and from the White House, bookended the days he spent addressing complex issues, such as his reelection and the creation and eventual announcement of the Emancipation Proclamation. Pinsker described that "Lincoln's model was to be deliberate. He spent an extraordinary amount of time thinking through problems from all angles and multiple perspectives." Mast explained to me: "Lincoln was known to write notes on scraps of paper. There are accounts from servants at Soldiers' Home that they saw snippets of papers with early kernels of ideas from the Emancipation Proclamation." She continued: "Lincoln was the type of person who would jot ideas down as you might do on a napkin today. He was the type of writer who would draft and revise, over and over until he perfected something."

There is no account of Lincoln's personal recollections of the Soldiers' Home. What we do know however, is that simply having the location created a break in routine for the president, even if it was still a site of occasional interruptions. As we discovered with the work-and home-life routines of Brooksley Born (chapter 6), the detachment from one's primary workplace brings a new perspective and helps refocus the mind. It would take a lot of down time for the president to simply digest and assimilate the many points of view and data presented each day. Pinsker summarizes the value of this separation and what it teaches us about Lincoln's think time habits. He told me: "The Soldiers' Home offered Lincoln an escape from the White House, what he called the 'iron cage.' The movement back and forth between White House and Soldiers' Home, and the time spent strolling and reading on the hilltop where President Lincoln's Cottage is located, offered Lincoln a much-needed break in his usual rhythm and perspective. In effect, Lincoln recognized something that many people overlook. Thinking is an activity that requires its own space to be most effective. Creating this space helped make him a more effective leader."[5]

Lincoln's Lessons in Technology

Bill Clinton was the first president to send an email, while President Obama was the first to have a Blackberry. Yet, for all the technological savvy of modern presidents, Lincoln again offers lessons to consider.

He was very comfortable with technology and often enjoyed interacting with inventors, who like so many others, would wait for hours to see him at the White House. He was known to marvel at inventions and had technologies to be used for the war demonstrated before him on the lawn of the White House. He also holds the distinction for being the only president ever granted a patent (a device to lift riverboats over shoals so they would not get stuck). It comes as little surprise, then, that the face of a young Abraham Lincoln is portrayed on the body of an engineer, painted on the beautiful domed ceiling of the Main Reading Room within the Library of Congress. There we find the engineer deep in thought while seated on a large stone bearing the word "SCIENCE," signifying America's contribution to knowledge and learning.

The way Lincoln engaged with the telegraph presents a glimpse into how he may have handled the email and Blackberry culture that so often intrudes on any structure we bring to our modern moments of reflection. The telegraph offered him unprecedented immediacy, yet he was judicious and deliberate in its use. He showed restraint and judgment and thought long and hard before transmitting any message. This was especially important, as the recipients of his direction were often the generals under his command in the middle of the Civil War. While we are all accustomed to email and see ourselves as the first to benefit from its power, Tom Wheeler, author and telecommunications pioneer, suggests that what Lincoln wrote, sent, and read for years of his presidency was actually "T-mail." (Telegraph mail).[6] Wheeler has spent years helping business better contend with the constant changes ushered in through modern digital communications. He also assisted President Obama and the new administration in technology-policy matters during the presidential transition.

Lincoln's use of T-mail, and the immediacy of its response capability, demonstrated the restraint he had. He was not puzzled by the new technology; rather he focused first on whatever message he wanted to convey and the consequences of sending it. Many accounts of Lincoln's life suggest that he crafted the final language of the Emancipation Proclamation while sitting in the telegraph office. Regardless of where he officially wrote the draft, it's the description of his behavior in contemplation that captures the attention. Major Thomas E. Eckert ran the War Department's telegraph office during Lincoln's presidency. The department was adjacent to the White House, where the Old Executive

Office Building stands today. Given how much time Lincoln spent there, especially during a critical battle, or even just to escape from those who sought meetings with him, low-level staff got hours of exposure to the president's demeanor and reflective work habits. Eckert described the pace at which the president would think and write. He said Lincoln, "would look out the window a while and then put his pen to paper, but he did not write much at once. Lincoln would study between times and when he had made up his mind he would put down a line or two, and then sit quiet for a few minutes."[7]

While Lincoln was deliberate in his relationship with technology and placed it as the lowest rung in terms of communication, Sherry Turkle, director of MIT's Institute for Technology and the Self, suggests that things today have changed dramatically. "We are learning a communication style in which we are accustomed to receiving a hasty message to which we are expected to give a rapid response. Our experience raises the question: are we leaving enough time to take out time?" Turkle has written extensively about the reordering of human communication in the many ways we express ourselves through technology. She describes the relationships we have to technology in terms of "tethering," and suggests the opportunity costs of such tethering include the consumption of our attention. She explains: "Tethering takes time from other activities (particularity those that demand undivided attention), it adds new tasks that take up time (keeping up with email and messages), and adds a new kind of time today, the time of attention sharing, sometimes referred to as 'continuous partial attention.' In all of this, we make our attention into our rarest resource; creating increasingly stiff competition for its deployment, but we undervalue it as well. We deny the importance of giving it to one thing and one thing only."[8]

Lincoln was much more deliberate with how he focused and what he gave his attention to in terms of communications, even in the midst of near-constant interruption. Wheeler explained in his groundbreaking book, *Mr. Lincoln's T-mails*, that if Lincoln could not convey his message to you in person, he would next seek to convey it in a speech or by writing a letter compiled only through multiple iterations where the president refined the ideas within. Only as a last resort, if he had to do something quickly, would Lincoln send an electronic message. In the early days of the telegraph, the president would draft his intended message onto paper, then edit it, and eventually give it to the clerk for

transmission. Wheeler explains: "Lincoln's one thousand or so tele-
grams are the closest thing we have to his top of mind thinking. We
have them for history written in his hand with the scratch outs and
the cross outs. You begin to see his mind at work. But the most important lesson is that he had a hierarchy of communications and electronic
messaging was always at the bottom of the totem pole."[9]

As we all do today, Lincoln spent hours immersed in simply gathering and responding to new data pushed at him. His T-mail habits
are revealing not just in how he transmitted messages, but also in how
he received and thought about them. He read nearly every message
received by the telegraph office, even those not intended for him. It
gave him perspective on what was actually happening in the conduct
of war, which allowed him to conceptualize problems and be skeptical
of all that he was being told. He never relied on the aides around him
or on just one account of an incident to form his opinion. Rather, he
read and thought—then read again, until he created a mental model of
what he believed to be truth. From his reading of messages and communications with generals, he would occasionally follow up with a visit
to the battlefield to verify for himself. When reality on the ground did
not match with his stated intentions, he would then correct his course.
Wheeler explains: "It was how Lincoln used the traffic coming from
the other direction—the in-bound reports...that broke new ground.
By reviewing the contents of the telegraph clerk's drawers 'down to the
raisins,' the president turned the telegraph into a window on activities
spread over a vast geographic area and an insight into the thinking at
his general's headquarters."[10]

When Lincoln did write a T-mail it had distinct characteristics. It
was succinct and clear. He was deliberate with every word he used.
The step of writing them out himself, before their actual transmission,
also made the exercise more cerebral. Upon rereading what he had put
down on paper, he sometimes would direct a clerk not to send the message. Wheeler explains that "the instantaneous nature of the telegraph
made self control even more important. An electronic message dashed
off in a pique contains the great potential to escalate the tension at both
ends of the line. Thus, when the president drafted his 'it makes me
doubt whether I am awake or dreaming' telegram to General Burnside
for failing to assist General Rosecrans at Chattanooga, he immediately
though the better of it. Writing, 'Not sent' on the back of it.... Lincoln
has the technical capability to instantaneously dispatch his emotions,

yet he recognized that just because the capability exists, it is not always necessary or wise to exercise it."[11]

Looking back at history and the cases cited above, we realize that for as busy and data-driven as we have become today, we are not the first generation to contend with creating meaningful distinctions between home and work, or in our relationships to new technology. What stands out about Lincoln is that he fought to create, and even force, think time and moments of reflection amidst a persistent barrage of endless requests. He never lost human contact with those who received an electronic communication. Quite the contrary, he put the technology into a hierarchy. For all the speed, immediacy, and fragmentation offered by technology today, it's hard to imagine that Lincoln would have allowed himself to hide behind the context-poor email transmissions that dominate modern communications. While he would act quickly if the situation required, he developed ways to force time to think (if even only for a few minutes) before acting; he would then follow up with face-to-face interaction, where more meaningful context is often conveyed.

"Action-forcing Mechanisms" and Battle Rhythms

General David Petraeus is well known for thinking, action, and impatience. From his role as the U.S. commander in Iraq during its turnaround in 2007 to his current assignment as Commander of U.S. Forces in Afghanistan, he sits within a flow of data that dwarfs anything faced by Lincoln. On a daily basis, the man who is currently responsible for U.S. military efforts in Afghanistan, and recently over Pakistan and Iraq while in Central Command, immerses himself for nearly an hour and a half in his "daily brief." The binders that sit on his desk contain reams of analysis, often compiled overnight, which he must consider. The situations within the troubled region he has military authority over generate an incessant flow of reports, statistics, and intelligence briefings he must consume. Petraeus told me that, "The consequences of all the data and connectivity are that you have to spend a lot of time simply assimilating it. You have to immerse yourself in it and constantly work your way through it."

No matter where he is in the world, or even in transit, he has access and connectivity to those under his command and those to whom he must answer. There is no down time. Within a period of less than ten minutes of discussion as we sat alone in his office inside the Pentagon, he turned his attention back to one of two secure computer systems seated on his desk. He already had fifteen new messages on an electronic dashboard related to developments just in Iraq. He scanned them quickly and told me, "It's a very quiet day out there, exceedingly quiet."

As with those in the commercial world, within the military responsiveness has crept into an accelerated cycle. He says, "If you are a combatant commander, you don't have the luxury of ignoring what your subordinate commanders or what your bosses are asking for. They have an expectation of responsiveness." The decisions made by Petraeus and other senior military leaders involve complex national security situations and often have life-and-death consequences. Such expectations have evaporated prolonged periods of think time, which is why warfighters like Petraeus advise that you must force it back into your routines. He said, "You have to put downtime in. When I was in command in Iraq, I typically fenced an hour a day in the mornings. You'd use it in different ways; sometimes you would catch up what you hadn't assimilated the previous day. Other times you would use it to think through something coming just over the horizon."

Through an exchange we had via email while he was in Kabul in the midst of his current assignment as U.S. Commander in Afghanistan, Petraeus explained that he consistently maintains the hour in the morning to read the overnight intelligence brief and go through his secure and nonsecure email. He shared that he periodically designates specific days to think through problems. In addition, there tends to be a drop-off in inbound email and video teleconferencing on weekends (which the military don't take off) and that allows him some additional "thinking time."[12]

U.S. Army General (ret.) Jack Keane has been a longtime mentor to Petraeus. He described how Petraeus engages with an outside set of "thinkers" as a forcing mechanism. They are charged with a nonstop range of assignments on topics Petraeus knows he must think through but has little time to take on in terms of primary research. Keane explained, "Petraeus is extraordinary at creating space for thinking. He has a slug of Rhodes scholars and Fulbright scholars around him. He uses that mechanism because he's open minded and he wants the contribution of others. He doesn't think he has all the answers—he uses those around him to debate and decipher—forcing him to truly do some thinking and analysis that he probably would not do by just going from one meeting to another and one decision to another."[13] Petraeus shared with me that over the years he has refined a practice that allows him to force some think time into a schedule that would otherwise never allow for it. He uses forward-looking events and meetings, including speeches, conferences, and Congressional testimony, to serve as "action forcing mechanisms" within his personal "battle rhythm." By embracing people with knowledge and training outside traditional military knowledge and training, he allows new ideas to surface. Petraeus said, "We think that we are very open minded in the military, and we think we have big debates, but they are in a relatively narrow band, frankly. We live a bit of a cloistered existence and we don't look up as often as we might like."

Petraeus described that at any one time he has an ongoing set of asynchronous dialogues, often triggered through email exchanges, usually between himself and four or five scholars. They are often PhDs, and many have backgrounds outside of military training; something that Petraeus shares in common, as he received a PhD from Princeton. These thinkers may be anywhere in the world and are often not in a combat zone. Their assignments are tied to thinking Petraeus knows must be done before something, the date of which is already set in stone. They take on initial drafts and put some context and intellectual definition around a problem. These thinkers send drafts of new ideas, and throughout the day Petraeus forces time to read, reflect, and then ask new questions related to the analysis. He told me, "I am someone who has a few intellectual projects going all the time. It might be the twenty-seventh draft of the army's counterinsurgency guidance or it might be to refine thinking about the army's 'Engine of Change' and how we must evolve as a learning organization. You have got to keep the plates spinning and carve time out to think."

Petraeus asserts that leaders must first determine how to structure their days, weeks, and months so they get done what they need to accomplish. This must be explicit. Leaders can't afford to miss opportunities to think through new concepts and constantly learn—even when the immediacy subsumes reflective thought. He says "the first job of a leader is to ensure that you get the 'big ideas' right.'" Petraeus explained that "big ideas—the overarching concepts that guide an organization—don't hit you on the head like Newton's apple, fully formed. Rather, they accumulate over time and develop through continued study, reflection, and discussion with others."

While Petraeus has his personal battle rhythm, leaders like Bill Gates have established their own ways of attacking big ideas. The Gates approach demonstrates that there is no set formula for forcing think time over matters that must rise above cursory, and surface, responses.

Forcing a Week to Read, Learn, and Think

How many CEOs of companies today would consider taking up to two weeks away from their families and day-to-day operations and be alone in a cabin in the woods? Imagine how it would sound if a CEO candidate being interviewed by the directors of a publicly traded company insisted that, for up to ten days a year, he or she will be "out of touch" with the company and unplugged from the office. Let's add one more element to this very atypical situation and imagine hearing the CEO candidate say that they plan to "read a lot" while they are alone. You could imagine the chairman of the board, once the laughter dies down, thanking the candidate for their time and then asking them to leave the room so the search can continue.

Now, take my hypothetical situation and consider that since the 1980s, Bill Gates, the former CEO of Microsoft and current head of the Bill and Melinda Gates Foundation, does just that. In the months before he would force the time into his calendar, Gates solicits ideas, papers, and concepts from leaders around the company. He would then go off in the woods to read them, vet them, and then take action on the ones he saw as having the highest potential.

Wall Street Journal reporter Rob Guth has covered Bill Gates for many years, and he received an unprecedented invitation to observe him during an actual think week. The only condition of the visit was that the location be kept secret. Guth explained to me that he spent time with Gates, just as he was unwinding as CEO of the company he had built from just two employees. Within a modest cabin, Guth saw stacks of papers and magazines scattered throughout several rooms. With no one around to engage Gates in dialogue, this was a time he had carved out to consume information and formulate opinions over what he believed he was observing. Guth told me, "Gates plays a kind of intellectual game with himself. I guess you would call it: the more you read, the more you learn."

Observing Gates's think week, Guth noted the founder of Microsoft was already handing off more day-to-day responsibilities to the current

CEO, Steve Ballmer. Guth recalled, "At the time, Gates was running a company that exceeded some sixty thousand people. After the anti-trust trial in the late 1990s, it became clear that he was somewhat over-whelmed. He couldn't handle it all, so he started offloading it to Balmer and others." It was clear to Gates that the job had outgrown him. Guth said, "He admits that he managed the company beyond the point that he should have."

Guth wrote: The week typically starts with Mr. Gates, 49 years old, taking a helicopter or seaplane to the two-story clapboard cot-tage on a quiet waterfront. It's a tidy, relatively modest place with a small bedroom for Mr. Gates. During the week he bars all outside visitors—including family and Microsoft staff—except for a caretaker who slips him two simple meals a day. He starts the morning in bed poring through papers mostly by Microsoft engineers, executives and product managers and scribbling notes on the covers. Skipping break-fast, he patters upstairs in his stocking feet to read more papers. Noon and dinnertime bring him back downstairs to read papers over meals at the kitchen table, where he has a view of the Olympic Mountains. Thursday's lunch was grilled cheese sandwiches and clam chowder. His main staple for the week, he said, is a steady stream of Diet Orange Crush.[14]

When Gates, as head of Microsoft, executed his think weeks it was not always clear which ideas would result in him taking action. Guth explained to me, "It was almost like a gamble; you throw the paper in the ring and who knows if he reads it and if he doesn't. Then you kind of wait and see if comments come out the other end." While Gates is no longer leading Microsoft, the construct of his think weeks has evolved within the company into a sort of "institution." Now over forty people from across the company simultaneously take part in think weeks so submitted ideas can be vetted across a wide range of experts. Experts are chosen based on their reputation, expertise, and what has been described as, "their openness to new ideas and the ability to get the right ideas to the right people." Tara Prakriya, a general manager within Microsoft's Technical Strategy Group, declared, "It's not really just about Bill—it's our way of making sure grassroots ideas dock with the right place and make the impact that they need to."[15]

It has been years since Guth spent time with Gates in the setting of his think time dedicated to Microsoft, but the two are still in contact.

Guth covers Gates' work now as the most influential philanthropist in the world. In the context of Gates' current work, Guth notes that the scope of what he must consider has changed dramatically. The need for his think weeks are arguably even more important, given the weight of the decisions he must make and the fact that he is not an expert on many of the areas he is forced to consider, including the geopolitics of the underdeveloped world and the spread of, and new treatments for, disease like malaria. Gates reviews ideas from within the foundation and from the many who seek contributions to their cause. "Gates needs to educate himself in a range of topics so he can make smart decisions about where to give money. It's incredibly intense. It's not passive as in 'I'll sit back and I can kind of throw money out the door and wait for something to happen,'" Guth said. The current generation of philanthropists, like Gates, who want to see the impact of their money in their lifetime have set deadlines and structures for how much they will give out. Guth adds, "Gates wants to choose programs and areas where he can have the most impact as quickly as possible."

Pre-reads and Thinking through Questions

While a week of time away may elude some of us given our roles within a company, other leaders are evolving new methods to force short bursts of think time and reflection within the construct of busy days. Meaningful preparation for routine meetings has often evaporated as we move from one meeting to the next, and schedules get packed. With use of PowerPoint technology, those who are doing the briefing simply enter the rooms and present their analysis for a manager's reaction. The presentations can take on a life of their own, as the presenter has often spent much more time thinking through a problem than have those who are about to receive the information. Thus, there is a great deal of asymmetry within discussions that follow, as there has been little time for reflection. But two senior executives are taking a different stance on carving out time to think and reflect—before they enter a meeting.

Steve Ballmer is CEO of Microsoft. His company created the PowerPoint software tool that defines the model for how many meetings are structured today. The presentation is meant to force people to think about what the presenter wants to convey through slides that are assembled into briefings. Yet, without time built in before the meeting to read, think, and digest the story, Ballmer saw that people inside Microsoft were taking him on long story journeys to where they wanted a meeting to go. In an interview with the *Wall Street Journal*, he admitted that, like so many in meetings these days, "You do look ahead. You know you don't like the answer or you are just confused by the answer. They are winding you through, and it doesn't work very well." Now Ballmer insists people send him briefing materials in advance of the meeting so he can actually read it ahead of time.[16] Robert Gates (no relation to Bill Gates of Microsoft), current U.S. Secretary of Defense, takes Ballmer's prereads and adds another edge. Like Ballmer, Gates must consume massive amounts of content. He insists that briefing materials arrive at his office for an initial read "24 hours," in advance of the session. To underscore the importance of the briefings arriving ahead of time, Gates will cancel meetings when people don't follow his rule.[17]

With the time that is forced into his calendar, Ballmer thinks through questions for the presenter. He admits this approach has been tough on some people at Microsoft, as it's breaking a model in which people want to present content to him. He still allows some people to start the meetings with a quick overview of their presentations (even if he's read it in advance). He then jumps into asking questions. This forced think time and short moment of reflection means that conversations can go in the direction he wants versus what the presenter wants. Even if the presentation has a meandering thought pattern he can still "get the punch line." By reading and thinking in advance, Ballmer breaks the cycle of having to make immediate reactions to new concepts.[18]

There's Always Time in the Morning—It Makes Me Wonder

As we have seen, forcing think time within densely packed schedules is possible through a specific and deliberate set of actions. Choosing to get an adequate night's sleep is an action that fewer people are making today with significant consequences for the quality of their think time. Americans are now suffering from sleep deprivation with over one-third reporting that the recent economic reset has had an impact on their sleeping habits. There have also been numerous studies on the effects of long-term memory and recall tied to denial of proper amounts of sleep. Before we go to bed, many of us are on email and Blackberry, sometimes even checking them during the middle of the night. Yet, molecular biologist John J. Medina advises that sleep loss and deprivation have significant consequences for thinking. He says, "Sleep loss means mind loss. Sleep loss cripples thinking…sleep loss cripples attention, executive (brain) function, immediate memory, working memory, mood, qualitative skills, logical skills, logical reasoning ability, and general math knowledge."[19]

Sleep is relevant to a discussion of think time and reflection in ways that are still little understood. How the mind settles and reconciles all that has entered it within a day, and why the body needs sleep, remain largely unknown. Yet, as Medina points out, we are the only mammal on the planet that denies itself sleep. With no sleep we increasingly miss the value of morning time for structured thinking. Starving ourselves of sleep and filling ourselves with technology first thing in the morning denies us an opportunity to take advantage of a time of day that is slower as the connectivity and immediacy of business is just emerging.

Sam Walton, founder of Walmart, had a tremendous capacity for work and was driven to make the company successful. He was known to carry around a small tape recorder so he could "record ideas that came from associates." He valued ideas from throughout the organization, and he loved to create lists of what he thought needed to be done across the corporation. He also forged time to think in the morning, before the day really got going. It was not unusual for him to be in the office at 4:30 in the morning. During a time of no email communications, Walton would write and think about the entire business that was growing beyond his wildest dreams. He said the morning time was "tremendously valuable: it's uninterrupted time when I think and plan and sort things out."[20]

Andrew Belton is a friend and fellow consultant who has adopted a set of rules for forcing time to think when others push to derail him. The original list came to him from Jeff Bradach, the founder of Bridgespan, the admired consultancy to not-for-profits. Two rules impact the morning and suggest ways to push back against the temptation of filling that time with connectivity. Bradach advises starting the day with one hour dedicated to an important and personally challenging task (i.e., important and something we tend to avoid!). This can include writing, or even setting agendas for future meetings in time for feedback from others. Not only will this ritual get something done, it creates energy for the rest of day. Second, the rules advise not reading email first thing in the morning —and then try to limit its use to just a few times a day.

Belton told me, "I used to have a little icon that showed up on my screen to tell me when I received an email. I turned it off, which helped. Email distracts from the real priorities and sets in motion working on the agendas of others versus your own."[21]

Jeff Hoffman is a self-described "serial entrepreneur" with his own unique early morning think time habits. As one of the founders of the very successful and lasting Internet start up, Priceline.com, Hoffman has been at the forefront of trends and innovations that have transformed businesses through electronic relationships. He and his company, Enable Holding, the parent of the inventory liquidation Web site ubid.com, are always on the hunt for the next big idea and company to invest in. Hoffman speaks around the world on topics that include innovation and what it takes to be an entrepreneur. He shares with his audiences what he has learned through years of trial and error helping to launch new companies. Hoffman revealed to me that his morning ritual has been honed across many years. When he wakes each day, he does not turn to his email or voicemail as his first task. He gives himself thirty minutes uninterrupted time to read and ponder topics and areas that he is not expert in; he calls it his "wonder time," as in, "I wonder if this is true and I wonder about that?" Hoffman helped redefine what excess inventory means to hotels and airlines around the world, yet he manages an evolving inventory of ideas and seemingly detached concepts that he jots down into bullet points on a note pad.

During his wonder time, Hoffman explained to me, he plots data points he amasses across all that he reads each morning. "I do most of my reading online. I read articles about things that have nothing to do with the businesses I am working on. I call it info-sponging." He admits that the upfront process is highly unstructured as he meanders through articles and clicks through stories and topics that catch his eye. When he spots what could be a consumer trend, a new law from Congress, or even something from the sports world, he stops and makes a note. Any single note on its own is rather meaningless. With some frequency he also goes to the Google Trends or Yahoo Top Searches tabs on their Web sites. He wants to see the key terms and words that people are driving into the search engines from around the globe. He wonders what the words can tell him about what is happening, and if the data points can be added together over time and create new meaning. He readily admits that "Britney Spears" as a search term might not matter very much; but then he does wonder why so many people are searching on terms like "iPad," "Big Sur Mountain" or Stephen Hawking (As they were on the day we spoke)?[22] He makes about a dozen bullets in his notebook during any morning session and then starts on his normal business day.

"I have no idea how the items relate as I stare at them for a while. I just let my mind wander. Most days I just shrug at what I have written down, and sometimes I laugh. But then I do the exercise again and again, across many days, and occasionally something happens. I say, 'Hey, wait a minute....I wonder if this might be true.'" He continued, "You try to connect the dots, and you ask yourself what I call the billion-dollar question: What can I do today that I could not do yesterday? It's all about connecting the dots?" Hoffman has had a few recent insights for new businesses and opportunities he was taking action on. He has been part of advising technology companies that saw the useful life of compact disks diminish as the recording business was decimated. There was data available that took time to converge; yet the trends were there to be discovered. Few stepped back to force the connections.

Other examples of morning rituals reveal that being alone to think can happen during one's commute into work, while still far away from the office. While he was commandant of the coast guard, Thad Allen (later the lead federal official charged with responding to the unprecedented oil spill in the Gulf) was responsible for 42,000 personnel whose task was securing thousands of square miles of maritime border. Allen was widely praised for his thoughtful leadership and ability to change and modernize the coast guard. He, too, shares a love of the morning and uses it to structure his think time. In the hours from waking up through his actual commute, Allen prearranged the problem solving facing him each day. He told me, "As long as it wasn't raining, most often I would ride a bicycle to work. It was 45 minutes by myself, just peddling. Believe it or not you can do a lot of thinking on a bicycle. I had to carve time out every morning just to think. Because I couldn't control my life once I got to work. The further a day progresses, the less control you have."

Conclusions and Application

From Lincoln to Steve Ballmer, think time only arises if it is made a priority and if we don't succumb to allowing it to be overridden by the agendas of others. In the current culture of connectedness and imme-diacy, think time must be forced into routines and habits. The exam-ples of forced think time within this chapter raise many questions and issues for leaders and managers to consider within their organizations and related to their own behavior.

1.   Control. While none of us can stop the flow of data and the cre-ation of content that swirls around us, we can control how we structure the moments that arise and our responses. As an email comes in, do we succumb to the immediacy expected by others? Like Lincoln, do we dedicate more time to reading and digesting information instead of generating content for others to consume? As leaders, the control we assert in problem solving sets a tone that will be followed by others. If we are frenetic and fragmented in our interactions and communications, it will follow that others will do the same. Over time, this degrades our ability to understand problems and offer meaningful insights that can emerge as potential solutions.

2.   Attention. We now work in a state of giving our "continuous partial attention"[23] to issues before us. This fragmentation is having an impact on taking an argument through to an in-depth conclusion. While not all matters require deep thought, we find the ones that do are afforded equal footing with ones that don't. Many individuals state that certain things are their priority and will command their highest attention. But if we never make a meaningful distinction in the way we apply our attention to the important matters, then this discounts what our words actually mean. We must come to a conclusion about the con-sequences of giving only partial attention to top initiatives. One simple conclusion might be that we can only think deeply about one matter at a time, and if we shortchange ourselves of that time it implies we are failing to perform our most basic role as a manger.

3.   Hierarchies of communications. When, if ever, have you thought through the hierarchy of communication you follow (in all its forms) and assigned value to them? If email is the default way you interact, then you have already declared where it sits in your hierar-chy. Where does human contact and face-to-face interaction fit rela-tive to the use of all the technology available? Where are texture and empathy conveyed in your communication style? It certainly isn't found in an email or text message. Lincoln offers a powerful model

of someone who was deliberate, capable of rounds of "self-editing" because he understood the power of words. Leaders must ask themselves: What value do I place on language and texture that is only accompanied by its verbal expression versus the use of technology that allows for immediacy?

4. Asynchronous dialogues. In many ways, problem solving has devolved into a series of dialogues that take place across digital transmissions with occasional face-to-face interactions. Failing to think deeply about forward-looking events and big ideas will come at a cost. Yet, Petraeus shows that having many ongoing conversations with people who can do some initial deep thinking for him does not absolve him of owning and mastering new content and ideas. He forces bursts of reflection into his day, where he pauses to read, think, and then moves to the next iteration—recognizing that thoughtful insights are not born through real-time analysis. How many such dialogues are you involved in about things that will take place further than a week away? How can you embrace such a concept to force daily think time into what you know will one day be important? Creating such a mechanism into densely packed schedules means you can work in the immediacy of now and not lose the big picture that only emerges through refined and nuanced thinking achieved over time.

5. A meeting with oneself. With the tethering to technology that happens to us throughout the course of a day, it is clear that we treat time with our thoughts as a low-level priority. Leaders from Bill Gates to Sam Walton recognized this. From holding the morning sacred to coming off the field and unplugging for even just an hour, think time can be forced and found. Mornings are a time when the tempo of the day is often slower in relative terms to the rest of the day. Yet, giving that time away, and having no plan for what to do with it will only contribute to anxiety that comes with the expectations of others. Even if you can't book a week away to think, it isn't hard to book a meeting with yourself, when you are off-limits to everything but your thoughts. As Jeff Hoffman explains, the dots are there to be connected.

6. Reflecting on messages delivered by technology. Lincoln did not have the ability to craft an email and hit save or delete as he crafted messages. He wrote his T-mails in longhand through multiple iterations before they were transmitted. While people demanded immediacy from him, because his decisions were final and critical, he tried

never to dash off a message in haste and always considered how people on the other end would receive it. All of us must ask ourselves: When was the last time I used the save function as I drafted an email? Can I add or delete from the messages I will send as I have thought about the ramifications of what I convey? Do I need to send an electronic message at all?

3

Thinking Out Loud

Of Terminal Niceness, Intellectual Awkwardness, and Real Dialogues

In our harried work cultures today, could you imagine walking into a meeting in total silence? You sit at the table reviewing notes you made the day before, when you spent time alone reflecting on the problem. You have read the background materials for hours and forced new connections in your mind that didn't exist before. It's a big problem the CEO wants to vet for the first time with no set time line for final decision making. No decision will be made until every idea has been considered. Your colleagues, all unplugged from technology, are equally prepared for the discussion. In fact, the CEO invited a few atypical people to the room, so their voices will be heard, because they tend not to look at problems the same way as do the senior leaders. In your mind, you ask yourself a question before you say your first words at the meeting: "What is it that I am about to say and will it enhance or derail the creativity and output of this group?" Your peers all ask themselves the same thing before they speak. At the top of the discussion, the CEO reinforces that there are "no (zero) consequences for dissent and debate," and every one knows she means it.

What's described above is rare, but possible, to have happen. It involves an organization making the conscious choice not to allow fragmentation of its ability to sustain thinking on topics of the utmost import. For, as fleeting and fractured as they are today, businesses still progress or rapidly decline through the thousands of daily dialogues in which they engage. Joe Raelin, chair of the Center for Work and Learning at Northeastern University in Boston, notes that in true reflective dialogue (where people are actually paying attention to one another, Blackberries are turned off, laptops are down, and self-awareness is up) learning and ideas emerge through what he describes as a "critical consciousness." He says such dialogues are rare and "ensure that multiple points of view are heard, leading to new ways of thinking and ultimately of acting. Learners enter the conversation knowing it will produce something totally new to each one of them." He explains that, "It's the act of subjecting our assumptions, be they personal or professional, to the review of others. We do this not only before or after an event, but learn to inquire even in the heat of the moment."[1]

Today, we often enter meetings unprepared. Not because we want to but because our time is fragmented and we don't force moments to reflect before we get into the room. This has (at least) four consequences. First, lack of preparation and of reading beforehand means that when we are called upon to speak, we only have cursory conclusions with few meaningful alternatives. Second, we are often overly polite in discussions, as we are empathetic to other attendees who also have had very little time to think; the culture of the firm may not value debate and discussion. Third, those who present content during a meeting leave very little space between their thoughts, as they feel the pressure of the moment and need to "dump" ideas onto the table. Fourth, surface-level discussions rarely probe the assumptions that underlie the discussion. Layer in open laptops and pulsating Blackberries as multitasking is naively attempted, and few meetings ever forge big ideas representing the true sum of the many minds in the room.

The Wisdom of Reflective Crowds

For nearly 40 years, Van Wishard has advised CEOs, U.S. presidents, cabinet secretaries, and members of the U.S. Congress on the context of informed decision making. Wishard is an author and a thought leader with a sweeping view of history. He told me that when we devalue reflection it tends to minimize our own source of inner inspiration. He explained "that it is the unexpected realm from which Einstein said his major discoveries came." In Wishard's view, when we devalue reflection we also hurt our ability to judge a situation and ensure that we have balance in our thinking. Wishard powerfully describes reflection to me as, "Both a conscious and subconscious activity. It is the laying aside of the "known" and reaching for the "unknown." He continued, "It is putting aside the 'rational' capacities for the moment, and reaching inward for the 'irrational' to offer up what we call inspiration."[2]

The dialogues we enter into today are more consequential given the complexity of problems and the need to publicly question and continuously revisit our assumptions. When we show up ill-prepared and fail to allow ourselves the time to explore the intellectual boundaries of the problem, we are devaluing reflection and all the benefits Wishard describes above. As we will see in later chapters, failure to consider the downside risks of investments impacted all of us. During a time when firms have been labeled "Too Big to Fail," the state of discussion and attempts at engaging in real dialogue within those institutions matters to all of us.

In moments of thinking out loud together in an effort to have a "generative dialogue" (where new and powerful ideas emerge instead of repackaged concepts), you see a lot of things happening simultaneously. First, ideas are passed between participants with care and feeding. Second, you hear dissent and debate allowed to flourish, not in a state of ego clashing, but with the hope of uncovering poorly considered arguments and questioning of basic assumptions. Finally, when a group reflects together you will observe something that is generative in the sense that the sum of the participants thinking together exceeds that of the individuals. Within a reflective dialogue we see evidence of a culture capable of not just learning from past mistakes, but one that hopes new mistakes are not embedded in its most recent decisions. Such dialogues only happen when all at the table understand the rules of engagement, and the leader never balks when things get uncomfortable. Textbook "public dialogue" remains an aspiration compared to what most of us engage in; yet in a culture of immediacy, we must find ways to rediscover how we structure each conversation we enter so that complexity is never shortchanged because immediacy, distraction, and egos abound.

Fred Collopy is Professor of Information Systems at the Weatherhead School of Management, Case Western Reserve University. He is a thought leader in the discipline of design management. Collopy suggests that through our social acceptance of interruption and distraction we degrade our ability to find meaning through conversation and thinking out loud. Collopy also believes we all have within us too many preprogrammed responses and templates that limit what a conversation can be. He continues, "We expect others to attend to even our most novel ideas, not just the ones that fit into their preconceived expectations. And responding to that expectation is both a responsibility and a privilege." He concludes, "It's a social responsibility and brings with it the human privilege of surprise."[3]

A Meeting to Remember

Earlham College is a small liberal arts college located in Richmond, Indiana. Not all those who work there believe in the methods and religious principles that founded the school—based on the Quaker way of "consensus." Without delving too deeply into the Quaker methods for meetings, the rules followed by the many who guide the school are countercultural. The president of the school, Douglas Bennett, explained to me that behind all the efforts at seeking "consensus" sits a method of engaging in true dialogue, where groups can become more than the sum of their parts. There are tenets that hold the key to the social contract at Earlham, including: transparency (make relevant information available to everyone in the discussion); speaking constructively and not in opposition to one another; "good clerking" (their term for facilitator) who must have the trust of the group and ensures each person is allowed to speak. The final element of the approach involves listening. Bennett explained that at Earlham people work constantly at listening "unusually carefully" to what the other is saying and to the intent behind their words. He continued, "We also leave moments of silence between spoken messages to allow each contribution to be fully comprehended."[4]

Bennett shared an example of seeking consensus with the entire board of the college, which needed to approve a major investment that would alter the future of the school. The culture of the institution allowed this dialogue to happen. An outsider might have looked at the sessions as a waste of time given all the other decisions to be made, but this was a multi-million-dollar, multi-year decision. After two days of group dialogue with a single facilitator, one of the 24 members of the board still dissented from the group's "consensus." The board member suggested the decision should go forward without his name attached. Rather than move forward with near-perfect consent, Bennett asked the board to sleep on the member's concerns and see if the next

morning they could break the two-day impasse. With side conversations at dinner, and respectful listening throughout the evening, all
board members retired for the night. In the morning, the clerk of the
meeting posed the critical question before them, and all 24 members
reached consensus. Twenty-four people were aligned around a critical
decision that involved nearly 16 hours of reflective dialogue.

While the Earlham example is atypical in terms of the ability of
any organization to achieve complete alignment, it demonstrates that
patience and group dialogue can move toward powerful outcomes.
When we enter a room and allow ourselves to be distracted by the
supposed immediacy of another call, email, or interruption, we are in
effect devaluating the possibilities that can only come from reflection.
It's like a party that never really starts because the guests keep heading
back to their cars. More detrimental to hurting dialogues is when we
push our own agendas into the conversation and listen less than we
talk. The Earlham board example may remain an aspiration for many
organizations, but as you will see in this chapter there are ways to
evolve beyond the meandering meetings and poorly conducted interactions that make up so much of our daily work. Thinking together,
perhaps for the first time, is a critical capability that no organization
can simply leave to whimsy.

Given the interdependence demanded through globalization, and
the speed with which markets can consume ill-prepared participants,
the depth of real and generative dialogue is what will define the short-
and long-term success of an organization. Some decisions can and
should be made in the blink of an eye; but complex problems involving some level of consensus simply can't be rushed and must feature
respectful debate and dissent in which all those in the room are prepared, and conscious of what they are bringing or taking away from the
interaction. We begin by taking a closer look at the habits of dialogue
employed in the first year of Barack Obama's presidency—you may not
agree with his politics or final decisions, but consider what he is doing
to generate meaningful discussions against a workload and expectations of immediacy unlike any other job in the world.

Dithering or Dialogue: You Decide

History always matters; it's the reference point from which we define
the context of the moment. Dialogues between presidents and their

most senior advisors define the direction of a country. These moments of "public reflection" are shielded from immediate view, yet they emerge through the lens of history as the participants tell their sides of the story. What follows next is a look at some recent history involving the Iraq and Afghanistan wars and then back to the Vietnam War. I include these examples because they demonstrate how to prepare for, and participate in, consequential dialogue. Most of us will never brief a president or have to make the decision to send a nation to war; but all of us are in meetings that lead to small and big decisions. Deep within the strain and complexity of presidential decision making, we are given a powerful lens for how to successfully drive, or utterly fail, within the art of dialogue. History's lessons are applicable to all of us. Yet, reflection again plays the critical role in informing consequential decision making.

In 2009, President Obama engaged in three months of structured discussions across numerous meetings over a future strategy for dealing with the nine-year-old Afghanistan War. Assembled in the room was his full national security team, including his closest advisors as well as Secretary of State Hillary Clinton, Secretary of Defense Robert Gates, Chairman of the Joint Chiefs of Staff Mike Mullen, Vice President Joe Biden, and General David Petraeus. While criticized as "dithering"[5] by some political foes, it was viewed by those involved as "a virtual seminar in Afghanistan and Pakistan" given the comprehensive topics discussed. One news account said the president's behavior in the strategy sessions was something "between a college professor and a gentle cross-examiner." While, the Afghanistan sessions may never have arisen to the pure definition of dialogue as noted above, they offer many techniques that can be applied to challenging problem solving.

It will be years before the true context of President Obama's decision-making process is understood. Or, how his own behavior in a meeting may have hurt or helped him make better decisions. Yet, far above the fray of politics, Obama's attempts at driving a reflective dialogue about the Afghanistan War strategy demonstrate he is learning from history. The specific language and techniques he employed during the nearly 25 hours of discussions with his core national security team before making his final strategy decision for escalating troop levels in Afghanistan reveal an iterative process and deliberate approach grounded in some historic lessons learned. The subject may be Afghanistan, but we can all emulate the techniques he employed.

Obama had campaigned on Afghanistan as a war that he initially agreed with when it began in 2001, in the immediate aftermath of 9/11. Yet, once Obama became president, it was clear Afghanistan had unwound from its initial mission as the country spiraled toward chaos with the reemergence of the Taliban as a political and military force. The president faced the consequential decision of winding down troop deployments and removing the U.S. from the war, or determining a new method for turning around a situation that was far from achieving any military victory. The repercussions of this decision would be watched around the world by countries like Iran, North Korea, and in neighboring Iraq.

In accounts that have emerged of Obama's overall meeting style and approach beyond just Afghanistan matters, it's been said that he will question the "dominant proposal" under consideration and its underlying assumptions. He often asks to be briefed on proposals that are not intuitive to his thinking or even to his political views. One news report noted that Obama asked the treasury secretary, Timothy Geithner, "to make a pitch for reinstating the Glass-Steagall Act, which split apart commercial banks and investment banks in 1933 and kept them separate until its repeal in 1999. Aides say Obama didn't support reinstatement but wanted to hear the merits of the idea. During his briefings, he is known for routinely asking staff to argue against themselves and what they just publicly advocated as their positions.

Obama's conduct in many private meetings suggests he is interested in creating atmospheres that generate new thinking, even as he recognizes the limitations inherent in the conclusions drawn by the small groups of advisors serving him. He wants to avoid people critiquing the meeting after it happens. Of the sessions she participated in with the president on Afghanistan, Secretary of State Clinton said he "welcomed a full range of opinions and invited contrary points of view." She continued: "And I thought it was a very healthy experience because people took him up on it. And one thing we didn't want—to have a decision made and then have somebody say, 'Oh, by the way.' No, come forward now or forever hold your peace."[6] This means Obama takes capable minds like Hillary Clinton and David Petraeus and asks them to openly counter their own arguments in an effort to dig at new insights.

He forces them to intellectually counter their own intellectual instincts while perhaps unveiling new mental constructs and biases they didn't know they had.

Secretary of Defense Robert Gates recalled the strategy sessions in detail in an interview with *Foreign Policy* magazine. He, along with everyone else in the sessions, learned through the hours of discussion and tough questions and then thought about risks in entirely new ways. Gates said, "First of all, the meetings weren't interminable. The meetings were generally an hour, hour and a half, occasionally two hours. They were very focused—lots of hard questions being asked. And I think everybody in the room learned as we went along. I mean, as you might suspect, the July 2011 deadline was a hard hurdle for me to get over because I'd fought against deadlines with respect to Iraq consistently. But I became persuaded that something like that was needed to get the attention of the Afghan government, that they had to take ownership of this thing.... And I recognized the risks. And there are risks associated with that. There's risks associated with everything in war.[7]

President Obama doesn't rely solely on his advisors and the analyses they bring into the room. He maintains some window into divergent thinking via how he employs the Internet and the dialogues he engages in via email with those outside his administration. While logs of what he spends his time reading online are not yet available, he is the first president to use Internet technology in the mainstream ways we all do as a personal research tool. Obama has Internet access at his desk in the Oval Office and uses it often. One advisor noted that, "This fingertip access sends him constantly online."[8] Thus, Obama is purposely bringing new insights into meetings such that the ideas presented to him in the heat of discussion don't become an echo chamber of unchallenged assertions.

Based on reports of many techniques he employs, Obama does not allow his personal opinion to emerge early during conversations as he knows it would sway the arguments before him. Within all of these techniques he is trying to avoid what is known as "groupthink." In *Fortune* magazine in 1952, William H. Whyte, Jr., coined this term, saying of groupthink, "we are not talking about mere instinctive conformity—it is, after all, a perennial failing of mankind. What we are talking about is a rationalized conformity—an open, articulate philosophy which holds that group values are not only expedient but right and good as well."[9]

In the end, Obama concluded that he would increase the level of troops in Afghanistan and set dates for an expected initial U.S. troop drawdown as the Afghan military took on increasing responsibilities. While the Afghanistan sessions weren't a pure dialogue with complete consensus as at Earlham College, Obama demonstrates that a leader can drive a team of people to think together across many hours—while not prejudicing the outcome or allowing people to get by with cursory insights. Not every organizational decision rises to the level that we see above; but organizations that don't elevate some critical decisions into new public-reflection dialogues may be promoting a strategy that will never generate the outcomes they want. In fact, these organizations may be lulled into reinforcing an incomplete analysis that never vetted the full spectrum of possible inputs and outcomes, including the blind spots they never wanted to acknowledge as being possible.

Fertility or Lack of Imagination

The decision-making dialogue and approach employed by Obama in the Afghanistan strategy sessions were influenced by his reading of a book on the Vietnam War: *Lessons in Disaster*, by Gordon M. Goldstein. The gripping narrative is based around a well-known academic and presidential advisor, McGeorge Bundy who served as the equivalent of the modern national security advisor to both John F. Kennedy and Lyndon B. Johnson from 1960 through 1966. At this time, America was embroiled in the early years of the Vietnam conflict. For years after he stepped down from public service, Bundy was silent on his role as a key advisor to the two presidents, who relied on his insights as they reached their consequential decisions about strategy in Vietnam.

In our age of sophisticated algorithms and data-driven decision making, why should we go back to Vietnam for any insights? In short, the Vietnam War is a perfect example of the challenge of sustaining breakthrough thinking across many years of problem solving. For over a decade, America fought a war based on a key set of assumptions and tactics. Today, we see examples in companies like Toyota and BP, where years of tackling a problem become ingrained in orthodoxy that is fed like candy to each successive generation of management. The problem is that evidence is out there that counters the orthodoxy and even "best practice," but the evidence is not given a platform for consideration in the dialogues and habits of the company. Then the problems mount until they manifest themselves in environmental disaster or a product recall that brings a CEO to tears in public.

Cultures that learn to bring the unknowns to the surface and constantly question the dominant position will prove capable of managing continuous change and the uncertain markets of today. Lives are on the line at companies like Toyota and BP—safety and risk must be constantly revisited without the dominant narratives being fear of cost cutting, or clinging to expediency. Take a close look below at what, at the end of his life, Bundy realized with regard to his role in the Vietnam War, and ask yourself: What is it I am not reading and reflecting on that could harm the very strategy I so proudly defend? What haven't I read and considered as a set of possibilities that I can bring to the surface for review by others in moments of dialogue and thinking out loud?

While in office, Bundy consistently advocated for the escalation of the war, which was going very poorly and would further deteriorate based partly on his inputs and advice. Goldstein, the author and scholar, worked side-by-side with Bundy as they were coauthoring a history of his involvement in the war; these would be his final recollections, captured for history as his body was rapidly failing him. Through their interactions, Goldstein was astounded as Bundy reexamined and even lamented the fundamental assumptions that drove the war's escalation as a result of some of his advocacy in meetings with the two presidents. The year 1964, was a critical period in the Vietnam War. Revisiting that particular year revealed surprising insights to Bundy about the many inputs, widely available for his consideration, that he chose to ignore and never brought to any meeting for vetting and debate.

It's important to note that 1964 was an election year, and no politician is immune from making policy decisions without considering election consequences—especially decisions regarding the escalation of a growing war. Such a deeply political atmosphere, Goldstein writes, "created multiple disincentives to challenge the status quo and analyze rigorously the limited options and difficult choices in Vietnam." President Johnson wanted to maintain the status quo during this time. Bundy went on to describe the atmosphere and framework of these key meetings by saying, "Johnson wasn't ordering that much action, nor was there much fertility of imagination as to what additional kinds of action were needed, just more and better of the same." Goldstein adds balance to Bundy's recollections and notes, "Although Bundy did not explicitly draw the conclusion himself, the historical record suggests that as national strategy advisor, he largely acquiesced to political constraints and was disengaged from the vital task of evaluating limited military and diplomatic choices."

Three narratives permeated Bundy's analysis and his recommendations to the presidents he served. In hindsight, Bundy admitted he did not engage in rigorous analysis of the complexities involved in each narrative. Quite the contrary, they drove him to approach meetings with a mindset informed by incomplete information and options that he then presented to the president. The first narrative involved making comparisons between the Korean and Vietnam conflicts, even though the Korean conflict had ended in a military stalemate and partition of that country. Second, many discussions revolved around the so-called "domino theory," first proposed by President Eisenhower in 1954. It suggested should Vietnam fall to the Communists, this would lead to the further spread of communism into Laos, Malaysia, and far beyond. A third proposition entailed withdrawing diplomatic engagement that Bundy and many others were loath to even consider.

Had Bundy taken the time to look deeper, he would have discovered evidence that could have been brought into dialogues with the president and the war cabinet. Reports and scenarios had been produced within the Department of State and Department of Defense with data and conclusions differing from Bundy's entrenched narratives. For example, Goldstein writes that in 1964 the "domino theory" was actually challenged by the CIA in a major study that concluded that the fall of Vietnam would not lead to "rapid successive communization of other states." Bundy was aware of all these reports but chose to disregard them or ignore them completely. Goldstein states that Bundy consistently lost opportunities "to test the assumptions underlying the potential American military escalation in Vietnam." By never allowing his core narratives to be challenged, Bundy concluded that, for the president, "the only option left was escalation." Bundy's lack of time for reflection meant he was nothing more than a cheerleader for a single view of the problem that he was attempting to solve through ineffective means.

Through reexamination of data, reports, and information that were readily available to him as national strategy advisor, Bundy faced many unsettling realizations about the impact that a lack of personal think time and reflection played in what he brought for analysis into his meetings with Johnson. In the weeks before his death, Bundy lamented, "I had a part in a great failure. I made mistakes of perception, recommendation and execution." He said, "There are a lot of errors in the path of understanding." Bundy's painful epiphany happened nearly 30 years after he had been in office. He never drove a counter argument in the room, and the president rarely pushed back.

Fostering "Intellectual Awkwardness"

One of the sources of data ignored by Bundy in the Vietnam escalation strategy had emanated from the State Department's Office of Policy Planning. Its functions within State have differed from administration to administration, but its mission is to offer deep analysis on the forward-looking strategies our country should employ in foreign policy. Thus, this office acts as a think tank within the State Department and is often pondering problems—long before they become problems. While the team working on strategy and planning is small, the impact of its work can be significant.

Since 9/11, the mission of the Office of Policy Planning evolved to study the Bush administration's policy choices and their consequences. For the first four years of the administration, Colin Powell was Secretary of State, and he chose an academic and strategist, Mitchell B. Reiss, to head this key function. Powell was often at odds with other senior officials over key strategic assumptions and policies for the wars in Afghanistan and Iraq. He was keenly aware of what it meant to be in rooms presenting alternatives and analysis to a president in need of balanced arguments. Thus, to be the head of his policy-planning unit during this time was very demanding. The data reviewed and the inputs sought for analysis by the policy-planning team would comprise a major source for Powell's think time as he prepared to engage in briefings with the president, vice president, cabinet members, and allies.

Powell had known Reiss from the early 1990s. Reiss was a young lawyer still solidifying his understanding of national security issues as Powell's White House Fellow when Powell was President Reagan's National Security Advisor. Powell and Reiss would interact with each other through smaller projects over many years, but it would be nearly a decade before Powell called on Reiss to serve as head of policy inside the State Department. In this role, Reiss would be a conduit for the compilation and synthesis of geopolitical events, emerging national security trends, and historic context into rich products of reflection that would then be read by Powell for his input and eventual recommendations to the president. From Iraq and Iran to China and North Korea, no country and no context were off the table for Reiss and his team's daily analysis and thinking.

If Reiss and his team failed to think something through and offer a balanced analysis, it would then impact Powell's ability to give his best analysis to the president. A failure to think horizontally, systematically, and dispassionately while offering both pros and cons for a policy position could have dramatic impacts on national security and international relations. While Reiss was not always in the room with the president, his boss was. A failure to consider all alternatives would mean that Reiss was sending Powell into discussions ill-prepared to offer multiple ways to look at a problem. Reiss worried constantly about things that could disrupt America's preeminence in the world, including the consequences of a nuclear bomb going off in a U.S. city or what would happen if the U.S. dollar were no longer the de facto currency of choice driving global transactions.[10]

During his first several weeks at State, Reiss produced a memo in which he and his team questioned two existing policies related to security issues in Asia. Reiss had concluded that the secretary needed a counterview to what had already been decided. He presented Powell with two memos. Uncertain of how his new boss would react, he set a time to meet with Powell and answer the secretary's questions. Reiss recalled that, as he entered the secretary's office, he found Powell was irate, not with the actual analysis, but with the fact that it was related to an issue already decided upon by the president. Powell was keenly aware that his role was to present the president with the pros and cons of any decision. The particular issues raised by Reiss during his first few weeks on the job for Powell were not ones the secretary was willing to resurrect. In this instance, he was offering Reiss a glimpse into how he thought through the difficult dialogues and intellectual battles he had to grapple with and prioritize within. Yet, on the way of out of the office, Reiss recalled that Powell was more subdued and no less interested in hearing balanced and equally weighted arguments in the future. With an apparent smile, he told his new top strategic thinker, "Whatever you do, Mitch, don't stop sending me these types of memos."[11]

Reiss is now the President of Washington College in Chestertown, Maryland, and recalls the data and volume of information afforded to him within his first days at the State Department. He quickly learned to emulate his new boss, who had a habit of carving out downtime to soak in all the information around him. Reiss recalled, "One of the very first things I learned from Secretary Powell is that very few things need to be decided immediately. He would often say, 'Mitch, take your time. You will gather more information with the passage of time.' I think what surprised me about Powell's schedule was how much down time he had built into it every day." Reiss continued, "There would be hours when Powell would sit in his office alone, reading and thinking. That wasn't what I imagined a Secretary of State did. Yet, it's a habit I quickly adopted within my role as his head of policy planning."[12]

In our harried work cultures today, how often do you hear of executives building reading time into their daily routines as part of their personal think time habits? Meaning and insight can't be manufactured on the go. When the issue is systemic and central to the organization, leaders must find the time to force private consideration of their core beliefs—as evidence is usually out there proving their beliefs may have their limits. Reiss noted that, as smart as many senior leaders are today, it's absurd for them to believe they can flip through massive briefing books en route to a significant meeting that requires deep thinking in advance. He said, "Powell understood that absurdity and built in the down time in his schedule for reading just to force the connections that had to be made."[13]

Reiss made a habit of giving Powell memos on issues he thought the secretary had not had time to properly think through or had forgotten in the crush of other business. He saw it as his job to direct Powell to read and consider things that might be unintuitive to the secretary. These were more educational, and they recast issues and factual misconceptions around topics, such as the "real amount of financial assistance the United States gives to the Palestinians" (more than any other country in the world). Reiss said, "When you reach a certain point in government, you are embarrassed to ask certain questions. This is true for all of us. This is a huge problem. The CEO of a big multinational corporation isn't going to admit in front of people that he doesn't know how a division works. The groupthink mentality exists. People don't like to be socially awkward by asking questions about what people think they should already know." Reiss saw his job as presenting ideas that were socially, politically, and bureaucratically awkward—especially to his boss. He remembers, "We had to be willing to say that something people assumed was true was actually not true, maybe even ridiculous. We were willing to say, "The Emperor has no clothes" when he clearly didn't."[14]

As Reiss matured into the role, he was able to question more assumptions and push on how the secretary might better operationalize and even tactically interpret the policy-planning team's work products. Powell later advised him after one meeting where the secretary was dismayed by what had been presented by other officials: "Be a bastard if you have to, Mitchell. Don't worry if you upset people."[15]

Rethinking and Reframing Dialogues

Authors and organizational design experts, Lee Bolman and Terry Deal, believe action without reflection—or without 'reframing,' as they call it—can be fatal to corporate success.[16] They cite examples such as Sears, and even General Motors, who failed to systematically question fundamental assumptions of their businesses in order to "generate sufficiently creative responses to cope with the treacherous environment characterizing the industry." While it's early, and evidence is still being released, it's possible that Toyota Motor Corporation failed to reframe itself and the problems with quality control that emerged across years of complaints. Given the global nature of Toyota, this may just reveal that dialogues and communications translated throughout multiple time zones (Japan headquarters to U.S. local leadership) must feature new mechanisms and rules that force profound questioning of existing mindsets and habits, even if done in the name of cost-consciousness.

The current CEO of Xerox, Ursula Burns, is an example of a leader attempting to reframe the nature of dialogue within the 130,000-person company. While Xerox has many challenges, including a debt structure that is a drag on its overall performance, it suffers from what Burns describes as "terminal niceness." In other words, coworkers enter dialogues during which they are not likely to push back, as there is no incentive to speak up and challenge what is on the table. Given the many market missteps of the once-dominant company, Burns is trying to get at the root of what may have led to weak dissent and poor dialogue that generate few new ideas that impact the bottom line. She told a meeting of her top sales people, "We are really, really, really nice. Maybe the

'Xerox family' should act a bit more like a 'real' family. When we're in the family, you don't have to be as nice as when you're outside of the family." She said, "I want us to stay civil and kind, but we have to be frank—and the reason we can be frank is because we are all in the same family." Burns went on to describe behaviors at Xerox meetings, where people listen without dissent. She says, "We know it. We know what we do. And then the meeting ends, and we leave and go, 'Man, that wasn't true.' I'm like, 'Why didn't you say that in the meeting?'"[17]

Most interesting about Burns is how many times she spoke up to senior executives in the awkward way alluded to earlier. In fact, her ability to challenge thinking in public settings was perhaps one of the reasons she rose so high and so quickly within the company. In 1991, she recalled her own moments of pushing back and questioning assumptions during a monthly meeting with the company's top managers in the presence of then-CEO, Paul Allaire. One account of the meeting said, "Ms. Burns noticed a pattern. Mr. Allaire would announce, 'We have to stop hiring.' But then the company would hire 1,000 people. The next month, same thing. So she raised her hand. 'I'm a little confused, Mr. Allaire,' she said. 'If you keep saying, "No hiring," and we hire 1,000 people every month, who can say "No hiring." and make it actually happen?' She remembers that he stared at her with a 'Why did you ask that question?' look and then the meeting moved on."[18]

Connecting Content, Listeners, and Speakers

Yet, inside many meetings where reflective dialogues can emerge, there is another trend that must be considered and overcome. All too often meetings devolve into "content dumping" by those who are presenting. Sandy Linver, an author and renowned expert in communications, works with senior-level executives of major global companies, including Accenture, the Coca-Cola Company, and Schlumberger. She believes people often race through presentations and just dump content. She explained they do this because—rather than conveying only the essential information necessary to achieve the desired result—they unconsciously want people to know how much they know. She continued, "The speed at which we operate and the availability of content has accelerated content dumping."[19]

Linver, whose education and early work was in communication, education, and television, used her background to found a company called

Speakeasy in 1973. While the focus was on executive presentations, she was most interested in helping leaders develop the self-awareness she believes is crucial to great communication. She sold the company in 2004 and now focuses on leadership/communications coaching. As Linver works with her clients, she reminds them that as leaders and communicators "they are there to make connections, to bring the worlds of the listener and the speaker together. If all that matters is content then the leader can just direct someone to a link on a web site." She continued, "Leaders are there to touch people intellectually and emotionally. To do that when they speak they must be aware of more than their content. But most speakers focus only on the content and don't think enough about the you and the me, in other words the total reality. To do this well demands taking time to be aware."[20]

Generally, communicators don't pause enough in between the many points they are making. While pausing is a useful tool for any communicator, Linver told me that pausing demonstrates to your listeners that you are not afraid to be thoughtful. "When you have the courage to pause in your communications it shows that you don't look at yourself as a machine regurgitating facts. More importantly pausing is crucial to be aware of the reality and be fully in the moment with yourself and your listeners." She continued, "The courage to pause, think and reflect within our communications comes from the courage first of all to have real awareness of yourself and awareness of your listener…to be fully in the moment."[21]

Linver recalled observing Bill Green, the CEO of Accenture, during a difficult set of all-day discussions he was having with his senior leadership team. The CEO was announcing a decision regarding major changes in the company's overall approach and strategy. Toward the end of the morning session, he got some feedback that people weren't one hundred percent on board and were questioning the overall decision. Green reflected, thought about the feedback, and readdressed the decision at the start of the afternoon session. Linver explained, "Bill stood up, created the context for what he had just been told. He then paused, looked out at the audience, and said: "You know the next guy might do it differently, but at this moment, I'm the guy." She said it was one of the most real moments of connection she had ever observed. She told me, "It's rare for someone to have the courage to do something like that in front of two thousand people. It doesn't matter if it was the right thing to say or whether everyone liked it. As the leader, he thought it was right, and it came out totally authentic. Because he was being thoughtful, he was sharing not just his ideas but where he was, which included his feelings in an open way. I will never forget it."[22]

Assumption-breaking Cultures

All the many stories and insights within this chapter describe the atypical, and sometimes courageous, behaviors that can accompany and contribute to the attempt to achieve reflective dialogue. There are many barriers to overcome in efforts to create such dialogues, yet the results and rewards can be significant. Joe Raelin of Northeastern University suggests that reflective dialogues often live within cultures that break commonly held views and assumptions. These are cultures where people are thinking and acting against the herd-like mentality and group synchronization that permeate organizations, and result in weak and inconsistent results. He said, "An assumption-breaking culture is one that deliberately keeps itself off-center." Managers can contribute to this kind of culture by trying to make reflection and learning contagious within their organization.[23] A reflective culture is one that makes it possible for people to constantly challenge things without fear of retaliation.

Raelin suggests there are five levels within true "public reflection." If all are on display, the culture is capable of questioning without alienating, and assumptions will routinely come up for reconsideration in the natural course. If such moments happen, powerful dialogues and new ideas can consistently emerge. The levels impact all the participants, and practicing them demonstrates tremendous self-awareness about how we behave in discussions, about our biases and preconceived narratives, and simply about the power of our words and thinking to move groups to meaningful outcomes. To get at such a moment involves a clearly defined social contract among all those involved—everyone enters into the moment with a common construct. As you read this list, ask yourself when and where you have observed one, if any, of them in practices within your organization.

Level I. Being: Refers to a deep awareness of who we are and our mental models and biases as we enter a dialogue. It creates a climate for reflection within the group and asks that we experience or describe situations, often without our own involvement in them, without imputing meaning. People come to a conversation and ask themselves: What can I learn here? How am I acting to constrain what is possible within this discussion?

Level II. Speaking: With a collective voice and collective meaning within the group. It attempts to characterize the state of the group at a given time. People in this mode will be observed asking: What can I say to help the group understand itself? What social practices is the group engaging in right now? What is emerging in our collective consciousness that I can articulate?

Level III. Testing: An open-ended query directed toward the group as a whole that attempts to uncover new ways of thinking and behaving. In using Testing, one may ask the group to consider its own process, or one may attempt to explore underlying assumptions previously taken for granted. In Testing, the contributor is trying to promote a process of collective inquiry. Questions people ask within this level of dialogue include: Are we helping each other right now? What can I ask to help us all focus on our process?

Level IV. Probing: People within the group make a direct inquiry, typically to one member at a time, to point out the facts, reasons, assumptions, inferences, and possible consequences of a given suggestion or action. Probing might attempt to point out inconsistencies in members' reasoning patterns, perhaps helping them to uncover the assumptions. Far from an interrogation, probing seeks to have a person's entire view and context presented back for their reconsideration. Questions people ask within this level of dialogue include: What is the basis for another's point of view and feelings? Can I explore with others, even though their position may be different from my own?

Level V. Disclosing: Here, people stay within themselves, and at the same time, share their doubts or voice their passions. By disclosing, participants unveil their feelings at a given moment based on what has just transpired, or they may present a story to reveal the depth of their experience. The idea is to help the group learn more about its membership. Questions people ask within this level of dialogue include: What am I holding back that needs to be aired? What might I say to help the group know me better?[24]

The above levels represent a theoretical framework. Yet, the basic construct gives a powerful lens through which one can examine the nature and structure of "public reflection" that lives or has died within our organizations. The stakes get higher with each open laptop, inbound email, and mindless nod as matters of simple and profound consequence enter into and out of our consciousness. Given the complexity of problem solving today, can such thoughtful "counterparts" to distracted and uninspired dialogues continue to be ignored?

Applying the Lessons of "Thinking Out Loud"

Think time and reflection don't just happen when we are alone. Organizations within hierarchical structures will inevitably engage in discourse and dialogue through meetings. When meetings become meaningless and you walk away saying, "that was a waste of time," you can now do something about it. The opportunity cost of poorly structured meetings where no one is listening and group think dominates means you are already inside an echo chamber that will inevitably become unhinged. A leader has responsibility for not only finding time to think and forge connections while alone but to ensure that the organization embraces proven methods to allow dialogue to generate new ideas and explore the downside of a given strategy. There are many lessons to consider:

1. When was the last time you participated in a moment of true "public reflection?" As the workload increases and distraction abounds, the rare moments of public reflection hold significant meaning. If you are working inside an organization, or on a team that never gets to a generative moment, you must ask why and then take action. The action can entail educating peers about the concept that when the group assembles it is subject to the power of groupthink and has within it the potential to develop a consciousness as a team. As we constantly hear about tapping into the so-called "wisdom of crowds," much closer to the daily workload is the wisdom of a small team with significant workloads. At minimum, teams must define a set of rules to govern discussion and understand the art of dialogue—perhaps for the first time. At the other end of expression is applying the frameworks within this chapter to arrive at the real potential for problem solving that can emerge in public.

2. What is the supply chain of analysis feeding into the dialogues you and your team are attempting to have? There is so much data available to teams as they sit in group settings for problem solving. If you are an advisor to a client or to the leadership of your company, can you honestly say you are consistently digesting the contrarian point of view to the proposals you will make in public? As you read and learn are you simply snacking on content that you scan on the Internet or in a magazine? Or are you forcing time into your schedule to digest more exhaustive arguments and contrarian opinions. Like Powell and Reiss, are you building in down time to simply digest all that is coming at you so that you can argue the intuitive and counterintuitive with equal energy?

3. Iterative and deliberate discussions can create the atmosphere for divergent opinions and new ideas to emerge. As a leader within many discussions on any given week, are you aware of what your role is with respect to encouraging the emergence of arguments counter to the dominant opinions on the table? When was the last time you asked someone with a strong point of view who reports to you to argue against their own recommendations in order to become aware of their blind spots? Setting the ground rule that meetings are safe spaces in which to freely dissent will mean your team can become more than sum of its individual parts. You may never get to the purest form of dialogue as described in this chapter, but you are likely uncovering new insights that the group can consider in the context of critical discussions.

4. The existence of "terminal niceness" within your organization is a likely sign that debate and dissent are long gone and groupthink is accepted. At the root of this behavior is a culture that can easily miss an innovation or a market opportunity. As you assess a company you are about to join, ask them to share examples of when they have watched people push back against a dominant proposal? Have them describe to you the career progression of people who ask why something is getting done the way it is. Uncovering evidence that people have an incentive to push back may indicate you are joining a company that will not miss a major market change and will prove itself lasting.

4

Promoting Think Time

Of Intellectual Freedom, Digital Books, and Manly Refrigerators

The late Jim Henson transformed the world of puppetry through his work on "Sesame Street" and the lasting legacy of the Muppets. He represents a powerful example of a "chief thinker," who understood the implicit rules inherent in nurturing creativity. Creativity and idea generation are at the core of what so many organizations try for, yet often stifle and fail to actualize. Karen Falk, the archivist for Henson's legendary company, now run by Henson's two children in California, compiled some fascinating insights for me into how he approached, and then thought through, new concepts. Like many, Henson could not quite describe where his ideas came from. He believed ideas and information were "waiting to be heard" by him. He had unspoken rules about the people and situations that surrounded an idea. To him, it was just a matter of figuring out how to receive the ideas that were waiting to be discovered.[1]

Henson is often referred to as a genius for the ways in which he redefined childhood learning through unforgettable characters and contexts. He grew up as an artist and often looked to nature for inspiration during his alone time. When he needed to recharge, which he had the self-awareness to recognize, you might have discovered him lying on his back underneath a tree simply looking up at the sky. For all the ideas that came to him while alone, Henson never suggested the idea was done or even ready for implementation once he hatched it. Rather, he believed in thinking achieved through dialogue within small groups of people with whom he was comfortable and in whom he deeply trusted. While in groups, he longed for what he described as "absolutely pressure-free situations." For example, working alongside writer Jerry Juhl, his longtime collaborator and the writer behind the Muppet series, Henson felt he was in a "no-risk situation" and that he could say "virtually anything," even if it was silly, stupid, or obscene.[2]

Ideas are what can drive a company to do something better or different. Ideas can and do launch entirely new industries. Establishing trust between two idea generators matters as much as does the atmosphere surrounding their dialogue. What does it mean to create "pressure-free" thinking environments where anything can be said by anyone? How do you create a culture where there are no negative repercussions for taking an idea to another level and seeing if it makes sense or money? Given the day-to-day needs of the company, how do you structure the time inside your organization to promote think time and reflection? With focus on lean—and cost-conscious—operations, isn't it simply a waste of money to invest in new ideas when older ideas are what enabled you to even get to this moment?

Decision Rights and Time to Think

In many ways, think time and reflection live at the core of what enables a business to thrive. Based on the mission and on the outcomes desired, groups of people are organized and presented with problems to think through and then solve. Once it's declared, "We're in business!" a decision-making structure soon emerges—even if it's never explicitly described. The basic problem-solving steps followed within organizations, regardless of their structure, are (1) interpret a problem and assign it an owner; (2) problem owner(s) thinks through potential solution; (3) leaders with authority decide on a course of action(s) based on some analysis, and (4) organizations interpret and react to the consequences of their decisions. This simple process reveals itself thousands of times a day for as long as the entity exists. You can conceive of an organization, then, as a collection of people structured to make decisions based on data, assumptions, and incentives that motivate their behavior. Today, the amount of time given to steps (1) and (2) are sometimes ignored, as the perceived immediacy of decision making trumps the time spent in structured reflection.

Economists broadly refer to the "allocation of decision rights" to best describe the authority managers have to decide on the best way to solve problems. Some organizations are centralized in terms of their construct. In such businesses a few senior-level people closely hold on to decision-making authority, and ideas get funneled to them for vetting. In decentralized decision-making organizations, more decision rights are pushed down into the organization such that lower-level employees are empowered to act on data without having to ask for multiple rounds of permission. Depending on the mission of the organization, the allocation of decision rights will be different, but once an organization's culture matures, "who gets to decide" becomes ingrained thinking that is difficult to change.

Decision making becomes correlated to rank and the perceived power to "make things happen." Ideas that are never vetted simply get passed by, as the tempo of daily operations means that people must "move on" and deal with what is before them. There is a risk-and-reward analysis done within the mind of decision makers, and most decisions are not actually made by the heads of organizations. Economist Ron Schmidt of the University of Rochester's Simon School of Business summarizes the "properties" of decision making and says, "First, they typically involve risk. Business decisions are essentially bets and making them requires a willingness to take risks. Second, they are typically not solitary decisions. Certainly the head of a large corporation and even those who lead smaller ventures cannot possibly make all decisions alone. Even a small collection of top executives can make only a limited number of the important decisions needed for superior performance."[3]

Economists Mike Jenson and William Meckling suggest that looking at the allocation of decision rights alone does not answer core questions about how an organization should be structured to generate, and then capitalize on, new ideas. Looking at the value of giving employees time to think about, and work on, solving the problems they chose in isolation is not a comprehensive way to think through the problem. They say that in addition to decision rights, there are two other "legs of the stool" that should be considered, including: the methods of rewarding individuals, and the structure of systems to evaluate the performance of both individuals and business units. Thus, there is some structure of accountability that must live within organizations to determine what gets done. Without accountability, time spent working on and thinking through problems may or may not yield any value to a company.[4]

When organizations "move on" and ideas are abandoned we see the powerful bias toward action overcoming the alternatives of further analysis and even taking no action and delaying a decision. Unless there is a coherent architecture behind the generation of ideas, they will likely never be revisited or looked at in a broader context. Ideas may surface only to be forgotten. Managers interpret feedback they pick up in the market or environment in order to determine the efficacy of their decisions. Questions and solutions generate lots of data that must be interpreted. Did we enter the right market? Do we have the right skills to compete? Is the product we make sufficiently different? Have we priced this correctly? Are we achieving our stated mission? For publicly traded companies, feedback to track answers to such profound questions is sometimes measured within seconds. Yet, for many organizations, the effects of their decisions take longer to detect and the results are often open to interpretation.

Two different companies, Google and Whirlpool Corporation,[5] illustrate powerful differences in how new ideas are hatched and then treated—across a period of time. These companies offer a nice juxtaposition, as one is synonymous with technology and speed, while the other is a hundred years old and operates in the razor-thin-margin business of consumer home products. Both companies actively promote and then allocate significant amounts of think time and reflection in ways that run counter to the short-term and immediate behaviors of many companies. Both proclaim themselves as "innovative." Yet, within these two powerful examples we see that promoting think time and reflection without a defined context and lens can lead to very different outcomes, including unintended consequences. So, can you promote think time without it becoming a fad? Can you allow precious time for deep reflection upon early and very unproven ideas such that it ultimately has measurable impact on the business? Let's take a closer look.

Nurturing Ideas at Google

It was exciting to read and discover many of the quirky habits and differentiators of Google as it sprang from an obscure academic project into one of the most valuable companies in the world. From Google's free on-site lunches and massages for their employees, to the capability for its users to see their childhood homes at a "street view," the company commands powerful positioning in the minds of billions of people around the world. As we all use Google's search products daily, it was easy to be subsumed in the hyperbolic descriptions of this company, which is still very young. One celebrated technique employed within Google is the allocation of so-called 20-percent time to its engineers. The company encourages its engineers to spend 20 percent of their work time on "whatever they want." This benefit has been widely discussed as a core component of Google's innovation agenda.

The origin of the 20-percent time concept sprang from the founders of the company, who came from Stanford University, where they hatched and nurtured the core technologies that became one of the most powerful companies in the world. What Google founders, Larry Page and Sergey Brin, did at Stanford would influence many of the ideas for how they wanted to run the company. In academia, time is often allocated for people to work with colleagues outside of their domains in hope that it will generate new knowledge. In fact, this freedom is part of what Google's founders used to help forge the early components of the technology that would one day become the choice for 80 percent of the way searching is done on the Internet.

Giving 20-percent time to employees is a powerful example of decentralized decision making. Engineers are trusted with making the decisions surrounding their involvement with maturing ideas that may have little, to nothing, to do with why Google hired them in the first place. Prospective employees are told of this unique benefit before they even apply for a job. In fact, Google's website promoting available jobs states: "We work in small teams to promote spontaneity, creativity, and speed. We listen to every idea, on the theory that any Googler can come up with the next breakthrough. We provide the resources to turn great ideas into reality. We offer our engineers '20-percent time' so that they're free to work on what they're really passionate about."[6]

As new engineers join Google, after what is a very difficult hiring process, they then see the 20-percent time manifest itself in a number of ways. Google has a powerful intranet where employees share ideas and projects they are working on. At Google, you must attract other people to work on your ideas. In essence, you are selling your ideas to an audience that has no direct incentive to make you or your idea successful. They join you because they want to. It's a symbol of intellectual freedom and has become a philosophic guidepost. Garry Hamel notes in his award-winning book, *The Future of Management*, that 20-percent time brings many consequences for Google. He says, "It ensures that short-term pressures don't consume 100% of the company's energies. It makes clear that innovation is everyone's responsibility. It also means

that at any one time, a certain number of people are 'out of control.'"
So be it, says Google's CEO Eric Schmidt: "If you want complete order,
join the Marines."[7]

Google does not release data to the market about the potentially thousands of projects that have been hatched through the 20-percent time
benefit. No quantitative study has been conducted or released publicly
to determine its efficacy in the eyes of shareholders. From a marketing
perspective, Google has noted in numerous publications that the 20-
percent time structure has given rise to many innovations, including
the creation of Google email, a.k.a. Gmail, Google News, which allows
users to simultaneously access nearly 8,000 news publications around
the world, and Google Adsense, which allows bloggers and well-visited
websites to benefit from payments for Google-placed advertising on
their websites tied to the interests of their readers. During a lecture
at Stanford, Google VP Melissa Mayer claimed that 50 percent of the
product and feature launches that Google brought to the market in 2005
came from their 20-percent time program. She said, "When I think
about 20-percent time, the key isn't that it is 20-percent or one day a
week. The key is that our engineers and product developers see that it's
a company that really trusts them and wants them to be creative and to
really explore whatever it is that they want to explore."[8]

Granting employees the time to think and act on what they want
doesn't in and of itself automatically bring about innovation. It must
live within a context as described by economist Jim Brickley from the
University of Rochester's William E. Simon School of Business. Brickley
told me, "Presumably, Google wants the employee to create or develop
an idea that will create value for the company. Whether a person will
do this with 'free time' depends on his incentives. Does he personally
gain something if he is successful in creating value for the company
(increased bonus, promotions, salary raise, or some form of nonmon-
etary recognition that the employee values)? If not, there is little reason
to expect that the employee will spend the time productively from the
company's standpoint."[9]

Google has a prolific number of employees who blog about their
work or have been interviewed about the way they use their 20-percent
time. This is how Bharat Mediratta, a software engineer at Google,
described things: "If your 20-percent idea is a new product, it's usually pretty easy to just find a few like-minded people and start coding
away. But when the thing you really want to work on is to make a broad

change across the whole organization, you need something new—you need a 'grouplet.' These grouplets have practically no budget, and they have no decision-making authority. What they have is a bunch of people who are committed to an idea and willing to work to convince the rest of the company to adopt it."[10] Paul Buchheit is the Google employee who helped invented Gmail (with his 20-percent time) and suggested Google's corporate motto, "Do no Evil." He has since left the company, but thought back to his time at Google and said in a blog post, "If you want innovation, it's critical that people are able to work on ideas that are unapproved and generally thought to be stupid. The real value of '20-percent' is not the time, but rather the 'license' it gives to work on things that 'aren't important.' "[11]

Let's Digitize Everything

Google Books is a powerful example of the types of bold innovation that have catapulted the company to be so dominant in the search business. Google's co-founder and a small team set a bold vision to digitize every book in circulation in the world (both new, and even those long since out of print). Google has described digitizing all books in existence as its "moon shot." Author Ken Auletta chronicled the day that the Google Books project was hatched and the CEO of the company, Eric Schmidt, first learned of the project. He writes, "Schmidt remembers the day in 2002 he walked into Larry Page's (Google co-founder) office and Page surprised him by showing off a book scanner he had built. It had been inspired by the great Library of Alexandria, erected around 300 B.C. to house all the world's scrolls. Page had used the equivalent of his 20-percent time to construct a machine that cut off the bindings of books and digitized the pages. "What are you going to do with that, Larry?" Schmidt asked. "We are going to scan all the books in the world," Page said. For search to be truly comprehensive, he explained, it must include every book in the world."[12]

Such ambitious thinking within Google and companies like Amazon.com has shaken up the publishing industry as it awoke to seeing old models of the production of physical books transformed into user-friendly online content. With the maturity of e-book readers, including Apple's new iPad, many changes are still unfolding for publishers, authors, and readers. The speed with which Google has moved on Google Books gave rise to many lawsuits over ownership, access, and revenue sharing for the digitized content. Google's idea was never seen through a lens on which it was qualified as a project and having its risks vetted and then mitigated. From a moment of reflection realized through the 20-percent time benefit, Google went into action mode and has never looked back. They saw the project through the lens of their vision in terms of creating and evolving the most comprehensive search engine in the world. The costly legal battles that have arisen would have ruined a smaller company but for Google, flush with cash, that has not been a problem.

Auletta further revealed that in Google's bias toward action they failed to engage with the very business partners who would be critical to the long-term success of the initiative. He writes, "In their rush to fulfill their mission, Google did not first pause to extensively consult with American publishers and authors who owned the copyrights to many of these books." "If we had done that," Brin said, "We might not have done the project." Later, Auletta writes, "Looking back, many of Google's non-engineers admit, when asked, that Google made a mistake by not more closely consulting and coordinating their efforts with publishers and authors." "I think that's true," said Megan Smith, Google's vice president of business development, who explained that "we moved too fast" and "involved the Author's Guild much later" than the company should have. "We're a technology company," agreed David Eun, vice president of strategic partnerships. "We thought people would understand that we had good intentions."[13]

The Google Books project is a powerful example of decentralized decision rights that give rise to very big ideas. Yet, there is no evidence that the project was linked inside Google to the methods of rewards and the systems that evaluate performance. In addition, there was no lens through which the concept was vetted so that it could be seen in different contexts (including return on investment). While, bold and aggressive, Google Books is also an unresolved and lingering story for the search giant. With the emergence of lawsuits now lasting several years, other companies would have shut down the project with less tolerance for such risk taking; but not Google. Nearly eight years into the project, with millions of books scanned and countless hours of employee time spent maturing the business, Google has not revealed the costs nor the revenues generated by the project. Their "moon shot" continues and it's unclear when and if they will meet their final destination with the digital space capsule intact.

20-Percent Time Matures

Google has had a string of high-profile departures from the company that raises some questions about the underlying structures that support the 20-percent time. Senior executives in advertising sales and engineers tied to core search products have moved on to other startups—sometimes taking their 20-percent time ideas with them. The *Wall Street Journal* reported, "Current and former Googlers said the company is losing talent because some employees feel they can't make the same impact as the company matures. Several said Google provides little formal career planning, and some found the company's human-resources programs too impersonal."[14] Google is fertile ground for studying the limitations of decentralized decision making and what percentage of 20-percent time projects have been brought to life by those who left the firm. What is the value of those ideas? Why did the employees leave? Could a different structure for accountability have altered the outcome? Who owns the ideas one hatches during their 20-percent time?

Economist Brickley says the practice of allocating 20-percent time gives rise to the issues of property rights. The problem of ownership of an idea can come back to haunt a company and its relationships with former employees. He explained to me, "If an employee develops a good idea, does it belong to the company or him? It probably belongs to the company if developed on company time. However, the employee might claim he developed the idea during some other time period (such as after he quit). This is less of a problem if the idea can only be developed within the company (it is firm-specific). There should be evidence that would clearly link the idea to the time on the job."[15]

Google has matured some of the structure around the allocation of the 20-percent time, even though they don't have employees formally track the way they spend their time. For example, the *WSJ* uncovered several tests the company uses internally to determine if an idea warrants further incubation. These tests include measuring whether: (1) the concepts were popular with customers: (2) other Googlers were attracted to developing them: (3) they solved "big enough problems," and (4) they achieved internal performance targets known as "objectives and key results."[16] In addition, some vetting structures have emerged within the company that try to remove duplicate projects. Engineer Bharat Mediratta noted that "the grouplets need guidance to make sure they are aligned with the company interest. Having a lot of people who are self-organizing can be powerfully positive or negative, and not every idea is a good one. To help deal with that, a number of grouplet organizers meet once a week to make sure they are not at cross-purposes."[17]

Google also has two practices that enable it to vet ideas and take on risks. The first is that applications under development go through a robust internal-use process—if that passes muster they will take it out to actual end-users and engage in an ongoing dialogue. Unlike most companies that wait for the final application to be complete, Google is more than willing to take ideas that are somewhat baked and get them out for feedback. As the saying goes, they don't let "the perfect get in the way of the good." Google's willingness to take risks offers a lesson to other companies. Jeff Jarvis, author of *What Would Google Do?*, recently said, "Perfection closes off the process. It makes you deaf. Google purposefully puts out imperfect and unfinished products and says, 'Help us finish them. What do you think of them?' "[18]

It's intuitive to think that Google will simply adapt its 20-percent time policy when and if it is proven to be less than what they believe it to be. We are all watching as this young company engages in a real-time hardening of their cultural identity and of a core narrative behind their early success: that 20-percent time is innovation time. Twenty-percent time is more of what Googlers describe as a philosophy as much as it is an allocation of time to think about what the engineers wants. As the policy becomes further ingrained, it will likely be harder to change. The former head of IBM, Lou Gerstner, shared this sage advice in his biography: "Successful institutions almost always develop strong cultures that reinforce those elements that make institutions great. They reflect the environment from which they emerged. When that environment shifts, it is very hard for the culture to change. In fact, it becomes an enormous impediment to the institution's ability to adapt."[19] In other words, is it possible that Google's 20-percent time, as a symbol of their innovative culture, may be the exact function that they must transform, when and if they realize that its utility is actually lower than the public relations perceptions and incremental successes that it has generated?

Google has just lived through its first recession. As with all firms that are publicly traded, the company had to assess what it would continue to bring to the market given greater scrutiny, increasing competition, and economic uncertainty. Google is maturing its processes and how it thinks about innovation in new ways. In a 2009 interview, CEO

Schmidt admitted the company was concerned that some of the biggest ideas were "getting squashed," and that senior executives would be more engaged in vetting the many innovations that have been hatched in the company through the 20-percent time policy. Prominent blogs that cover Google have suggested the company's commitment to 20-percent time may be waning. In addition, Google's revenue stream remains tied almost exclusively to the search business.[20]

While 20-percent time has clearly had an impact on making Google better at the core search business, it has not hatched an innovation that has dramatically changed the makeup of Google's revenues. Google is in a market position that will allow it years of investments in order to refine the structure and outcomes that can be delivered through the engineers' 20-percent time. With billions in cash, Google will inevitably mature, and will determine ways to develop the freedom and autonomy of its celebrated perk into an idea funnel that can generate predictable, significant, and diversified revenue.

A decade from now, will we look back to see that Google has matured the 20-percent time allocation in order to better harnesses the potential of all the ideas that surface within? If they want a company to model against in terms of harnessing innovation through a proven framework, Google's leaders may want to head out to Benton, Michigan. They can visit and benchmark what they are doing against a hundred-year-old company known for making basic products, including washing machines.

Embedded Think Time at Whirlpool

With annual sales of over $17 billion in 2009, approximately 70,000 employees, and more than 65 manufacturing and technology research centers, Whirlpool is the world's leading manufacturer and marketer of major home appliances. The company markets dozens of household brands, including Whirlpool, Maytag, KitchenAid, Jenn-Air, and Amana. Whirlpool makes the products millions of consumers around the world use every day—washers, refrigerators, dishwashers, cooking products, and small appliances. Yet, in 1999, the company saw that there was a staleness to its performance that had to be addressed. Growth was anemic, and competition was exploding as the Internet revealed new products and companies for consumers to consider. The current CEO of Whirlpool, Jeff Fettig, reflected back upon the context of that time and said, "It was clear to us that there was something critical missing in our strategy. Growth rates were flat, average selling prices were going down, and margins had become a cost game. We somewhat reluctantly concluded after deep soul searching that the 'something' was innovation. In 1999, we were not an innovative company; we were only an 'operating company.' "[21]

Whirlpool is a century-old company that made a clear decision to allocate think time in a quest to be more innovative. Defining innovation on such a grand scale required interpretation, translation, and execution. Fettig chose Nancy Tennant to own this critical initiative. While Tennant had spent years helping teams develop new products at Whirlpool, she had never studied innovation before getting the assignment and knew she had a lot to learn—as did the whole company. A decade into the transformation of Whirlpool, Tennant still reports directly to the CEO, but the innovation program is far from her responsibility—it also belongs to thousands of employees on what she estimates are tens of thousands of subteams across the world. And while Tennant is pleased with the progress Whirlpool has made to date, she and the company remain "constantly dissatisfied"[22] with where they should be. Today, hundreds of thousands of hours a year are dedicated within Whirlpool to thinking through, and then executing, on a range of new products and enhancements. Think time in Whirlpool has structure, quality gates, definitions, and a track record that proves the change has been worth it.

It took Tennant many years to get to a steady state where innovation became a core capability of the company. She partially faults herself for an inability to quickly make a critical distinction between embedding innovation as a core capability of Whirlpool and actually doing innovation projects or one-off initiatives under the banner of innovation. Tennant summarized the core findings about the culture and issues at Whirlpool that initially prevented them from embracing innovation. They included: anyone can say no; the company was overly process-oriented and internally focused; the company had grown risk-averse; there was a lack of incentive to be creative; and there was no structure or forum for creativity. In her powerful and detailed book, *Unleashing Innovation*, Tennant wrote, "We favored analysis over action; people felt frozen; and we had no follow through when people presented interesting ideas." One person described the company in a survey as "Ready, aim, aim, aim, aim."[23]

The upfront experience is exciting and sometimes overwhelming for employees. Tennant told me, "When you first bring an innovation team together there is this period of great excitement and then there is a period of, 'Oh my gosh, what are we doing? Why are we here?' Things can get chaotic." Within the framework used by Whirlpool, they ensure the exploration and initial think time results in progress because overly expansive assignments can arrest the team's progress to the point where its members don't know where to start. Teams apply "lenses" as they swarm a problem, including a review of the competitive landscape and ensuring the voice of the customer is heard and understood. One key process promoted by innovation author and consultant Gary Hamel has had a profound effect on Whirlpool. It's given rise to differentiated products that would never have been born inside normal business operations. It involves a team challenging what are called the "orthodoxies" within the company. Tennant explained that orthodoxies are "the strongly held beliefs that Whirlpool has about itself. If they can overturn them or smash them then we could see a new insight." She continued, "Teams do a deep, reflective and sobering look at what Whirlpool thinks we are really good at. And then ask, 'What if that were not the truth and we could turn it upside down?'"

Common language and checkpoints allow ideas to move from concept into coordinated and group-facilitated thinking. For example, a project will only enter the company's innovation "pipeline" if it is screened against this very specific definition: the project must meet a consumer need and solve a problem; there must be nothing like it in the marketplace or sit (be positioned to get to the next stage) on the "migration path" that creates a competitive advantage over time for Whirlpool; the last one (and the one people didn't always like to talk about) is that the idea has to make money for Whirlpool. Tennant advises, "You don't bring people to innovation. You take innovation to people. While it's nice for people to have things to work on outside of their regular jobs, the real power is in bringing innovation to every job." Innovation teams are triggered to go into action if there is new data that reveals a gap in the business or that a product line is flattening in terms of growth. Managers are constantly on the hunt for a moment to establish a team with a clear mandate to think differently. Teams can be as small as two to three people. They also can swell at times and involve up to a hundred people participating in what Whirlpool terms "ideation workshops" for up to two days. The average team size ranges between 5 and 15 people.

Even though the innovation agenda has been around for over a decade, Tennant shared that it is not a given that people will be freed up from daily routines to think through a problem. When an innovation team comes together, for example, she will advise the innovation leader that team members assemble every Monday and Tuesday afternoon for a period of six months in order to think through ways to close a gap or extend a brand. This upfront time allows people to expand their thinking inside a safe environment where ideas are welcomed and then built upon. "That whole four-to-six-month process is just about thinking. Teams don't build products at all. Teams look at data and just think about connections and intersections that may be there," she explained to me.

Innovation teams draw talent from throughout the organization. Tennant still hears people push back, given all the day-to-day demands, but innovation more often prevails. "Even today at Whirlpool, people will ask me, 'Are you kidding me?' But you sit down and walk through the process and the outcome and then leaders buy in." Then that person has to go out and negotiate for the people who are not already working on his or her team. "It's an easier sell than it was ten years ago, but it's not an easy sell." Tennant explained, "There was never a set goal in terms of the amount of time an individual would spend working on an innovation project. Coincidentally, it averages to be about 20-percent of an employee's time."

Of Men and Their Garages

A powerful example of how this entire process works is to consider what the think time methods of Whirlpool did for attracting men to their products. One deeply ingrained orthodoxy that has not been challenged for nearly 90 years at Whirlpool was their identification of the key customer group: women. Inside the innovation rooms now, Whirlpool employees are encouraged to speak up and revisit these fundamental assumptions—without fear of being considered difficult or obtuse. In the months of think time teams dedicate to fleshing out new ideas, commonly held beliefs are often tossed out. Innovation teams create "safe space" to put out ideas that are divergent and even wild. When one idea sticks, the group then conceives of new products that can meet the need. Analysis is done, concepts are born, and prototypes convey the ideas up and down the management chain.

During one innovation session in 2002, a team member wondered out loud, "What are we doing for men? Where do men spend time in the house, and is there a market for our products targeted just at men?" It turns out that men in North America spend a lot of time in their garages. Tennant explained that the team wondered if they could better organize the garage for men; if they could develop appliances with "diamond plating" on prominent display inside garages. Before this team sat down to think through this possibility, Whirlpool had little-to-no market share for garage-related innovations. Yet after the team was done, Whirlpool then launched its Gladiator GarageWorks product line. It's now a business generating tens of millions of dollars in revenue, and it continues to grow. The team conceived of organizing units that attach to the walls of a garage, appliances like tread-covered refrigerators that would appeal much more to men. This innovation team conceived of an entirely new line of business directed at a household room traditionally ignored by home-appliance businesses like theirs. Tennant remarked, "It's a phenomenal business and keeps growing and growing. There is no way that it would have happened without the innovation process or asking that question: 'Who is our customer?'"

Upon its initial launch, Gladiator brand had a very minor physical presence on the shelves of just a small number of Sears and Lowe's stores. Over the past several years, the explosive growth of Gladiator GarageWorks at these retailers has led to its presence in every Sears and Lowe's store nationwide. In 2008, Whirlpool further innovated around how to connect with men (and women) inside a retail environment, which led to changes in how the products are displayed in-store and through its advertising and messaging. This has led to additional sales. Further, what started out as an innovation directed at men in the United States, has expanded Gladiator product lines into Canada, Australia, and Europe. The whole thing began with a company that created the space for employees to step away from the day-to-day and question what was long-held to be truth—in this instance that women were the only target customer. It all began with dedicated time for thinking and an atmosphere with no consequences for employees asking difficult and awkward questions that went to heart of what the company held onto as its product line identity.

The Future of Innovation at Whirlpool

The results of Whirlpool's efforts at directing ideas through an "innovation pipeline" have paid off for its shareholders. The company walks the walk with its innovation agenda, and it's not a slogan or one-time initiative—it's embedded in behaviors and practices across every team and on every continent in which it does business. Whirlpool reports that $4 billion of the more than $19 billion in annual revenue reported in 2008 came directly from the innovation agenda established inside the company. In other words, nearly 20 percent of their revenue comes from ideas harvested within a structured process for thinking through entirely new approaches.

Tennant believes that innovation does not care where the idea comes from; it's the great equalizer. Teams care more about the collective, and best, idea—not just what an individual brings. When they are thinking through a problem, innovation teams are unconcerned with the members' levels and titles inside the company. With one facilitator helping to guide the dialogue inside the room, teams search for "the most unusual thought and the biggest 'ah ha' that we can have," Tennant says. While the atmosphere is safe, Tennant admits that she worries about individual self-reflection, shyness, and how some employees might hold back in a group setting. The individual is not the unit of analysis in terms of their innovation program. Rather, the team and its output matters, and that likely helps all in the room to make a wide contribution to key discussions and structured think time. Tennant said, "There is no way an individual innovator could be successful at Whirlpool. They can't. You just need too many people to make a washing machine."

As noted earlier by economist Jim Brickley, there should be some reward tied to innovation and think time and such is the case at Whirlpool. Tennant noted to Bloomberg's *businessweek* magazine that "A third of your pay, if you're a senior leader, is tied directly to what comes out of the innovation pipeline." It was more difficult to tie the economic incentive down to the individual level below senior leadership. She then explained, "When we started this (embedded innovation agenda), we were still in the Internet bubble. The conventional wisdom was people who come up with ideas should be millionaires. We were really hesitant to go down that path, being the conservative company we are. There's a downside: If it's going to be a team of people, how are you going to determine who should be rewarded? We asked other companies, 'How do you do this?' And the answer was over and over: 'The reward is recognition by your peers."[24]

The recent recession hit Whirlpool and other appliance manufacturers hard as those products are tied to consumer spending and are related to the housing market that was severely shaken during the financial crisis. Yet, they remained profitable during the lowest points of 2008 and 2009 and are growing once again. Tennant told me, "Given that we are in a consumer product/durable goods industry, the innovation pipeline that we have developed carried us through the recession." They could have cut the program and returned to thinking through problems in model they shared for nearly 90 years. They didn't do that; in fact the program continues to grow and further embed itself in the fabric of the company. At Whirlpool, reflection is valued in the context of a fast-moving marketplace. Tennant advises that you must be flexible enough to give teams time to innovate and even to dream. She wrote, "When we dream, we are thinking. The hectic workday most of us experience leaves us little time to 'think.' Innovation especially in the first stages...allows innovators the space for freedom to think."[25]

At one point, Tennant knew of every team and every instance where employees were working on innovation, but now the program is much bigger than she and will outlast her tenure with the company. Tennant remains a very curious leader and seeks out smaller nuggets of wisdom that she can introduce into the innovation agenda. She also sits on a governance board for the innovation program. The goal of the board is to ensure that the Whirlpool innovation agenda continues to evolve and that it never becomes an orthodoxy that another team will one day shatter.

Applying the Lessons of Think Time at Google and Whirlpool

These two diverse cases illustrate that think time and reflection can be powerful motivators for employees and senior leaders within organizations. Some describe such programs as granting "autonomy," such that the individuals have the freedom to explore new ideas. Autonomy has merit but not in and of itself. It is easy to read about immediately trying to emulate the freedom that is afforded through promoting think time and reflection as practiced by Google and what they know of Whirlpool. It is not easy or obvious, however, to promote think time unless you have a structure and framework that underpins the freedom. Think time without some structure is like going to school to learn neat stuff without ever having to take a test; how would you know that anything is sticking and that you are learning?

There are many lessons to learn from these two examples including:

1. Define the sandbox. Both Google and Whirlpool have defined innovation to various degrees. Each company is actually at different levels of maturity and is translating what the notion of innovation means to itself and its mission. While Google is synonymous with innovation because its technology has changed the way we all work and live, there is evidence emerging that they are employing more detailed lenses for understanding what projects to fund or let languish. The lessons of Whirlpool's ten-year journey reveal that early efforts to be innovative without a definition around success and the end-state can lead to wasted time and opportunity. In the end both companies are for-profits. Whirlpool has been more explicit that its innovation agenda must contribute to making money. They believe this is part of the reason they have had such measurable success. If your company or organization heads down the path to "be more innovative" you must take the time to define the edges of the sandbox. This way each project team comes back with new ideas that directly relate to the mission of the organization. The opportunity costs of leaving this space poorly defined can mean employees and ideas leaving and working on things that eat time and resources that could be better directed toward a well-defined goal.

2. Idea architecture versus autonomy. There are costs that both Google and Whirlpool bear in terms of freeing people up to work on new and innovative ideas. The autonomy that comes with allowing people to think about and work on what they want is compelling. Yet self-direction can cause individuals and smaller teams to flounder. The architecture that surrounds an idea and innovation team at Whirlpool supplies employees with a soft guide and tool kit that ensures that projects move forward or die—with transparency and accountability. Risks are taken inside a collaborative and deliberate set of gates, all directed toward the creation of a measurable "pipeline" of projects. While no panacea, their methods buttress innovation teams so there is a beginning, middle, and end to the journey of an idea. Whether you follow

the Whirlpool or Google models, be explicit about the process and common set of tools you will employ. In the earliest days of the initiative ask yourself if you are creating a can of beans or growing a bean plant. Having some structure on top of autonomy helps ensure that there are guideposts and bumpers that gently guide money-making ideas into reality. That's what owners and shareholders expect: What is the return on the investment of the think time?

3. Language matters. The late Admiral Art Cebrowski of the Office of Force Transformation in the Department of Defense once advised me that change agents invent new language. They do so, he said, because "You can't expect old language to carry new ideas."[26] Whirlpool has adopted a unique and company-specific set of language around innovation that ensures they focus on challenging future states (e.g., dream spaces and migration paths), and they don't become mired in the details and everyday language of the business. As you set out to interpret what think time can mean to your organization, ensure that it is described in new ways that convey what it is and is not. Make it distinct from the daily rhythm and language of the business.

4. Challenging orthodoxies. The Strategos model and concept of "smashing orthodoxies" is very powerful. What precedes the act itself is the atmosphere in which people are able to challenge the status quo. There must be "safe space" for people to express and offer ideas that get to the root of ingrained concepts the firm has about itself, its market place, and even its customer. It's only by granting people the time to step outside of the day-to-day that such a notion can even come into one's mind. The orthodoxy exercise can lead to some uncomfortable and even destabilizing realizations for firms to grapple with. While the technique can lead to breakthrough thinking, it must sit inside an architecture that rewards such atypical thinking.

5

Taking a Step Back

From Abusing Email to Exceptional Organizations

Habits and routines rapidly form inside organizations. This hardening can make changing things difficult as people defend what seems to be working. Keeping things "as is" can be comfortable. Maintaining the current state is easy. It discourages doing anything drastic, because with change comes tumult and anxiety. In the midst of the status quo, institutions rarely step back to reexamine the assumptions and behaviors that are inevitably altering the trajectory of the company. As author Nicolas Taleb powerfully reminds us in his book *The Black Swan*, it's what is "unknown" about the future that often has a disproportionate and destabilizing impact on an organization. In other words, it's our blind spots that move in on us quickly, subsume orderly transitions, and reframe the entire future for an organization. When was the last time your organization formally and systematically moved away from the incessant pulse of "now" in order to reexamine critical and fundamental assumptions, routines, and strategic direction? If this occurs only once a year, during the "annual leadership retreat," you are likely missing the larger context that may imply very different strategies and metrics.

To define new ways to behave and operate requires leadership that has the ability to take a big step away from what we are living as "the status quo." Leaders don't just define the "new" for the sake of it. They do it as the marketplace and the speed of business demands that the organization never fall into a lull in which urgency is replaced by complacency. Sometimes, it takes a leader to realize the organization may appear to be moving fast but in fact is standing in place. Freeing up time for people to think about the right problem or codifying reflection into a radical reconsideration of the status quo can prove the organization capable of reinventing itself.

Two diverse cases illuminate the actions that can be taken in order to step back from a problem and reconsider your desired outcomes. First, we will meet Scott Dockter, CEO of a small storage and transport company based in Atlanta. Scott shared with me how he reevaluated the company's use and reliance on email communication and determined it had redefined the company's interactions—and not necessarily positively. Email had become the center of every worker's time and routine. For years, few have taken a step back in order to look at the costs and benefits of the world's most popular collaboration tool. Through a simple policy shift Dockter helped the company reestablish human connection and free up time to think about what mattered the most to them—their clients.

In the Midwest, we meet up with Sister Mary Jean Ryan, Chair/CEO of SSM Health Care based in St. Louis. In the course of running a multimillion-dollar business impacting the lives of millions, she sought to redefine patient outcomes by utilizing the nation's highest award for quality achievement. Dissatisfied with performance metrics that never seemed to get better, she asked that the entire organization take part in the assessment and application process, an arduous endeavor that challenged many assumptions, systems, and processes. Even if it was awkward and uncomfortable, she would not back away from using the wisdom of outsiders to push the leadership group to listen to, and then act on, feedback. Sister Mary Jean and several from her leadership team told me they not only used moments of reflection to question the organization's very mission, but they now celebrate moments of pause, when employees question even routine procedures. With key metrics all pointing toward higher quality, reflection is not a fleeting concept—it's demanded in the course of managing the incessant flow of work related to those in need of care.

These examples demonstrate that it's only when the most senior leaders of an organization insert reflection into the status quo that it becomes the valuable tool it is. Otherwise, we can all fall back to the fast-paced way things are currently done and hope that somehow we work better and more efficiently. The examples also demonstrate that the cost of systematically rethinking a problem is much lower than allowing broken systems to produce average and below average results. Our first story begins with a moment we all find ourselves in sometimes, yet rarely if ever do anything about.

One Day without Email

Can you imagine even one day at the office without email? The CEO of PBD, a small inventory management and shipping company, did just that. In 2006, Scott Dockter finally had enough of the barrage of email that had built up inside his 30-year-old family-owned business. He stepped away from his desk one afternoon and laughed aloud, because he had just emailed his assistant for the third time on a routine matter; yet she was sitting only 20 feet away from him. About the same time, Dockter was shocked to discover that one of his colleagues had nearly 200 emails awaiting him after spending a full day interacting with clients. He thought about time and how he allocated it and what role email played in taking him away from the people side of the business. When the weekly email load of divisional reports clogged his inbox on Friday, as it always did, he knew he needed to do something. He told me, "Some people would hit a 'reply all' on a comment they might have about something within that report and it was just generating a tremendous amount of follow up emails."

Dockter mentioned his concern to the head of human resources, and she told him jokingly about a "national no email day in August" that had been proposed in a news article. PBD had a culture where Fridays were more casual; Dockter thought that such a program could "lighten the mood a little" and tackle the email deluge. Such a simple policy shift could force people to stop and rethink their relationship with the technology and one another. He thought to himself that, at least for one day a week, staff could get to know each other again and talk face-to-face when possible, or connect via phone if they were in different cities. He told me, "We were not going to fire anybody or anything drastic. We were just going to say, 'No Emails on Fridays. Period.'" The only exception to the rule was for external email: if a client emailed someone inside the company on that Friday, then a PBD employee could respond. All other email traffic generated from within the company was strictly forbidden.

On the first PBD "no-email Friday" it appeared as if the experiment was going to be a great success. Traffic was down and people seemed to speak to one another versus relying on email. Yet what actually happened was that employees wrote emails to internal colleagues and then cued them to be sent on Saturday morning at 12:01 a.m. As has been discovered with other organizations attempting this approach, the traffic nearly crashed the servers inside the company. Dockter recalled, "We got an initial laugh out of that, but we were very frustrated that people would see it that way." The implementation of the new policy actually revealed that people were doing a ton of work on weekends, and that email time was eating into people's personal time. For a family-run business that encouraged a separation between home and work, Dockter felt such behavior ran counter to the values of the company. He stuck to the no email Friday idea and over subsequent weeks employees took the challenge more seriously. He was determined to create some boundaries distinguishing between employees' home and work time, as well as to help the company establish a new hierarchy of communications.

He was amazed at the reactions of some people, who resisted the very idea of a day without email. Dockter discovered that employees were deeply coupled with the technology and the connectivity it affords. He recalled, "I had people personally mad at me, because they said they couldn't work without email and that they could not generate what they needed to get done." All employees were encouraged to give it a real try. Over a short period of time something unexpected began to happen. "After about four to five weeks, I all of a sudden was considered a miracle worker. I had basically come up with a way for people to get to know each other, to solve things quicker, to shorten people's workdays, to make them more efficient and productive. I didn't want to take personal responsibility. I was as guilty as anybody in generating email traffic," Dockter said.

The change was underway, as email use on Fridays dramatically dropped. In fact, email traffic on other days of the week began to decline as well. Clients even heard about the initiative, and while they admitted they could not do it themselves, they emailed PBD less and contacted staff directly more. Buoyed by the results, the company rapidly conducted an analysis of what was being emailed internally (on any given workweek) company leadership determined that 80 percent of what was being sent internally was unnecessary and wasting many people's time; 10 percent of the email traffic was really useful and conducive to making decisions, while the other 10 percent was "to be determined" in terms of its usefulness. They calculated that prior to implementing the no-email rule, employees spent over a half of their workday simply reading and responding to email that was of no real value to serving clients.

It's been three years since the no-email policy went into effect, and PBD has dramatically decreased the volume of email traffic without losing any efficiency or productivity. In the last year results have leveled off. Email has been put in its place through an intervention that forced people to step back from they way they were doing things. Dockter believes the policy has actually changed the culture of the company for the better. For example, the service metrics in 2009, including accuracy and volume in shipping, were at their all-time best. In addition, the company was honored as one of the "Best Places to Work in Atlanta," and that, too, has some connection to the policy, as retention and morale have also hit their highest levels in PBD's history. While the value of email is that it enables collaboration, Dockter believes that the experiment proves that its use must be accompanied by doubling-down on human connection. It's through the moments of connection that ideas are hatched, improvements are suggested, and client problems are solved. Unless you step away from the behavior of incessant connectivity, you simply can't break away to think about what matters the most. PBD will never go back to what they had. Dockter concluded, "You will not be a good teammate at PBD if you only use email."

Three years after the policy was implemented, people now step back and ask basic questions before they transmit something electronically: questions such as "is that really good for email or can it be posted to an intranet?" It's an ongoing process in which they question the use of technology. It has freed up time for thinking and reflection. Dockter said, "With less email to contend with, our people are solving things in new ways, which actually gives them the time necessary to be a great manager. To be learning on their own and to be innovating ideas about how PBD is going to continue to be better at what we do." Dockter also believes that the whole examination of the nature of email within the firm has had an impact on the company's bottom line. He says, "In the last three years, we have had our most profitable and highest growth rates in our history. Even with the seasonality of our business we have performed this way with the same or less people. We have a kind of a mantra of 'how are we going to get better' as a company. No-email Fridays and just less email in general has helped make us a better company."

Breaking Our Addictions, and Rethinking
Responsiveness

Growing data around the addictive and all-encompassing nature of email backs Dockter's intuition and forced rethinking of email inside PBD. In 2009, researchers at Basex reported that emails sent by corporate employees are projected to increase to over a hundred a day. Other studies put this number closer to 200. *The Wall Street Journal* recently reported that "one-third of users feel stressed by heavy email volume, according to a study of 177 people by the University of Glasgow and Paisley University in Scotland. Many check email as often as 30 to 40 times an hour, the study showed."[1] Dockter put email addiction into context for me as he shared an analogy he used at the outset of the no-email Friday policy. He told me, "If a postman hand delivered your 'snail mail' eight to ten times a day, would you be so anxious and run down to the mail room? It's amazing, because we don't do that with snail mail. Typically, you come home at night and get your mail and you go through it. You are a lot more relaxed about that than you are email."

Email remains the major technology organizations rely on for collaboration. The benefits and instant reactions one can get to any matter deemed of concern is at times powerful. The low-cost transmission of information is undeniable. In addition, the ability to link teams globally to comment on each other's work with rapid turnaround moves projects forward. Yet, email also creates a significant barrier to think time and reflection, if the most senior leaders of an organization never put it into a context and offer a rule set to live on top of its function.

Jonathan Spira runs Basex. For over fifteen years, he has been studying the impact of information overload on knowledge workers. In an innovative and ongoing study of thousands of workers' habits and routines, Spira and his colleagues uncovered that 28 percent of working hours are spent responding to interruption and distraction by things that are simply not important or relevant. Most often it is incoming email that supplies the distraction that disrupts a thought pattern. In contrast to "productive content-generation" and "attending meetings," their study reveals that we spend no more than 10 to 12 percent of our days "thinking and reflecting." Spira told me, "The problem is that time for both thought and reflection is understood to be important to organizations but it's also something that's frequently overlooked. It is clear that thought and reflection are not only a secondary, but perhaps tertiary, activity. At best, I think people assume that thought and reflection are catch as catch can; something you do on your way to something else if you're lucky and maybe you get a few minutes in."[2]

Author John Freeman has written a sweeping survey of how organizations have arrived at breaking points like those experienced by Dockter. In *The Tyranny of Email*, he powerfully describes what is lost through the way we communicate today. He says, "We need context in order to live, and if the environment of electronic communication has stopped providing it, we shouldn't search online for a solution but turn back to the real world and slow down. To do this, we need to uncouple our idea of progress from speed, separate the idea of speed from efficiency, pause and step back enough to realize that efficiency may be good for business and governments but does not always lead to mindfulness and sustainable, rewarding relationships."[3] As email redefines relationships through the delayed and context-less expression, organizations can chose to ignore such evidence or force the moment of reconsideration, as Dockter did.

How About One Night a Week, When You Are Not "On"

Beyond email, the nonstop workweek is another real concern to some organizations. The boundary between home and work is blurred and rendered meaningless with each connection that intrudes on the personal time of the worker. When you never stop to question it, it becomes part of the narrative that such constant connectivity is just a part of work today. Consultants, lawyers, and bankers (aka service professionals) symbolize the nonstop nature of work today. Few in these professional industries question the costs of connectivity as PBD did. In these environments, the 24-hour-a-day and 7-day-a-week nature of the work implies that hours logged is often correlated to productivity and even promotion. Yet, there is evidence that even within such action-oriented cultures, basic separations through forcing mechanisms and policies can have a dramatic and positive effect.

Boston Consulting Group (BCG) was the source for a recent study by Harvard professor Leslie Perlow and research associate Jessica Porter. They wanted to experiment with establishing forced boundaries between home and work through what they termed "predictable time off." In a series of experiments done with the highest level of buy-in from BCG's partners, some small teams of consultants were "forced" to take a day off, often in the middle of the week, thus working 80 percent of a normal schedule. In other experiments, team members would take one night off during the course of a workweek, where they would detach from the office at 6:00 p.m. In all experiments, employees would have no contact with the office via email or voicemail until the next day. The logistics to accommodating these experiments included clients being made aware of the study, and teams ensuring that the right amount of consultants were allocated to the project to balance workload and high-quality delivery. The clients and projects chosen for the experiments were demanding in nature, involving complex analysis and high client expectations. They were not easy engagements.[4]

After getting past the early guilt participants felt through being part of the study, evidence came in that showed the new ways of working were having a positive impact on some separation of work and home life. Within the first month of the study, a survey asked employees to score how well they agreed with the question, "I feel respected for setting boundaries." People gave the ranking an average score of 3.7 on a scale that ranged from 1 (strongly disagree) to 7 (strongly agree). Yet, five months into the study, participants rated it a 5.2, demonstrating their "slowly rising levels of faith in the concept." The study noted that "compared with those not participating in the experiments, people on time-off teams reported higher job satisfaction, greater likelihood that they could imagine a long-term career at the firm, and higher satisfaction with work/life balance." The forced down time also allowed BCG to experiment with new ways of collaborating across the company, as the absence of team members because of the experiments fostered new methods to connect with one another.[5]

The introduction of these experiments forced those involved to reconsider their entire relationship with work, home, and the lack of separation that is now ingrained in today's work environments. It's important to note that the experiments were conducted during the economic downturn, as BCG's leadership did not waiver from uncovering some potentially new ways to rethink the lost separation. Given that such "always-on" work narratives are rarely if ever questioned in such professional firms, employees wondered if their careers might suffer if they were part of the study. Harvard revealed that 94 percent of consultants reported working 50-plus hours a week, and that does not include the dozens of hours they estimate that employees check email after established work hours.[6]

The Harvard study reveals long-held narratives that the frenzied pace of work for professionals simply "comes with the territory." Professionals enjoy being in the middle of projects with the buzz and adrenaline it engenders, but there exist what the study calls "bad intensity" elements of work and home life that they don't value. This includes having no control over their own work and lives, being afraid to ask questions that could help them better prioritize their work, and generally operating in ways they know are inefficient. BCG has taken the findings of the study and is now at the forefront of asking entirely new questions about the way they work. The study concludes with what so many organizations today can learn. It said, "When people are 'always on,' responsiveness becomes ingrained in the way they work, expected by clients and partners, and even institutionalized in performance metrics. There is no impetus to explore whether the work actually requires 24/7 responsiveness; to the contrary, people just work harder and longer, without considering how they could work better."[7]

Back in Atlanta, Scott Dockter and his colleagues at PBD are also experimenting in new ways beyond the no-email policy. PBD has developed a culture where employees are encouraged to control themselves through the habits ingrained in the responsiveness narrative. Dockter summarized: "You know that moment when someone has their Blackberry vibrate in their pocket and you can hear it go off? You know that little tap dance they do with their feet, because they want to see what just came in? At our company you just don't bring your Blackberry to meetings or to lunch. Those times are off-limits. This is particularly the case with any interactions with our customers." He concluded, "We tell people to leave it in their car or brief case and bring their minds to the meeting. Let's get something accomplished and move on."

Aren't We All Exceptional?

Dockter used the incessant nature of email and its connectivity to redefine relationships within his company. Our next story goes well beyond technology in order to find new ways to save lives. Could you imagine annually asking your company to pause for a moment of reflection? Could you then imagine investing hundreds of hours thinking through and then filling in an exhaustive application that caused you to openly discuss every facet of your business? If you can get past that, think whether you would voluntarily pay outsiders to come into your company and spend even more time with people, at every level of your organization, questioning its overall coherence and effectiveness. SSM Health Care's use of a nearly 30-year-old government award process and program demonstrates the power of taking time to think and reflect at institutional levels. It all begins with a powerful mission statement that was to resonate with every one of SSM Health Care's employees: "Through our exceptional health care services, we reveal the healing presence of God."

SSM began with five religious sisters who in 1872 journeyed from Germany to St. Louis. Their goal was "to be of service to people in need." Now, 139 years later, those five sisters would marvel at how their early efforts have evolved into a system of hospitals and nursing homes sponsored by the Franciscan Sisters of Mary. With more than 23,000 employees, 5,400 physicians, and 3,000 volunteers, SSM owns and manages facilities in Wisconsin, Illinois, Missouri, and Oklahoma and serves more than 1.4 million people a year, whether or not they have the financial means to pay for their care.[8]

Sister Mary Jean runs the SSM Health Care system. In the mid-1990s, SSM had been focused on process improvements tied to patient care. Yet process improvements and pursuit of the then buzz phrase "total quality management" were not enough. Projects were not linked and results were not examined systematically. Sister Mary Jean learned about the nationwide, government-sponsored, Malcolm Baldrige National Quality Award Program. "To us it has always been about how do we operate better and provide better patient care," she said. She was unimpressed with the results that SSM was getting, both clinically and financially. Each year, metrics stayed flat or never seemed to improve, including malpractice claims, clinical errors, and patient satisfaction. Sister Mary Jean thought that seeking an outside entity to engage them in a reassessment of quality would help improve results. She said, "I don't know that you can talk about the pursuit of quality without reflecting."[9] The current president of SSM, Bill Thompson, told me, "The process of writing the Baldrige application was a significant reflective activity. We didn't call it reflection at the time, but in essence that's exactly what it was."[10]

An Award Based on Reflection and Agility

The Malcolm Baldrige National Quality Award program came into existence during another time of economic crisis and uncertainty in

America. In the early to mid-1980s, America was living through very difficult economic times as the stresses of globalization were forcing a competitive reconsideration of the manufacturing sector. American companies were losing to foreign competitors, especially Japan, often based on product quality. While many still think of Baldrige as a government-driven initiative, it's actually a public/private partnership. In fact, 90 percent of the support for the program comes from hundreds of volunteer "examiners" from every sector of the U.S. economy. These examiners come face-to-face with the hundreds of organizations that apply for Baldrige; the program allows atypical people to examine companies with a fresh perspective.

The program is run by the Department of Commerce through the National Institute of Standards and Technology (NIST) and is led by Dr. Harry Hertz, who sees Baldrige and the framework that it supplies as giving forward-thinking organizations a tool through which they can look at themselves and the context of their work as one system. Hertz says, "Baldrige is really an awareness and thinking tool. It provides a systems-level perspective to thinking and managing an enterprise and more importantly all of its inter-relationships."[11] Given the low probability of receiving the award and the lengthy application process, the value of the Baldrige program remains in the process of reflection it facilitates. Baldrige forces applicants to take a big step back in order to see themselves in a different context that day-to-day operations never allow.

Today, strategy is often created within organizations only to rapidly see it proven irrelevant through unseen market changes or short-term thinking. Hertz explains, "Almost all of our award recipients have a codified 'retreat in the woods' kind of think time built into their strategic planning process. There is a period where they will go off and develop white papers beforehand or designate individuals who were charged with thinking about and then presenting new ideas." Part of what separates recipients from nonrecipients (referred to within the program as "learners") in the Baldrige process is how that strategy translates across the organization. Hertz continued: "most organizations do their strategic thinking upfront and then put it on a shelf. They don't take the time to think through the deployment and measurement system to see if they are achieving their strategy." Hertz speculates that this is likely because organizations are so action-oriented. He says, "We are focused on the action of the moment rather than the action that is important. What we need today in strategy is more agility. The question is how do you reflect on your strategy on an ongoing basis? We now ask questions such as: Does the organization have a process for looking at its 'blind spots' on an ongoing basis to see that they are actually considering all their options and the changing environment?"

Within the program sits a framework that continues to evolve. Applicants are assigned examiners representing theirs and other sectors of the economy. Over time, Hertz has discovered that some of the most powerful feedback given to Baldrige applicants comes from those outside their sectors. He said, "It's the learning that matters as organizations are forced to open their minds to how others think. Applicants learn from nontraditional sources about where their blinders may put them." The basic Baldrige framework, below, along with pages of criteria explanations as to its use is free and was downloaded over two million times in 2009.

Baldrige Criteria for Performance Excellence Framework: A System Perspective

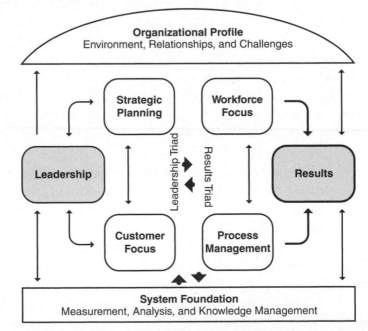

Source: 2009-2010 Baldrige National Quality Program | Criteria for Performance Excellence

The Baldrige process reveals evidence that an organization is reflective. Hertz told me, "Most organizations in the United States measure what is easy rather than what is important. Then they ignore their measurements because they don't mean anything." Hertz notes that category (2), Strategic Planning, and category (4), Measurement, Analysis, and Knowledge Management, are also areas that reveal evidence that an organization is more reflective. What matters is the flow within category (4), which is foundational, as depicted within the diagram. Hertz says it asks, "What do you measure? How do you determine that it's important? How do you analyze the results? And how do you then turn that into knowledge? That implies a lot of reflection and deep thinking."

Four Times Is a Charm

A year before SSM applied for the Baldrige award for the first time, a careful look at the Baldrige criteria prompted the organization to recast its mission through a reflective process that involved nearly 3,000 employees at all levels of the organization and across all four states. Having so many employees involved in recasting the mission statement made it more of their own and not just a top-down exercise. SSM's culture united around the mission statement exercise; leadership never counted what it cost to take busy health care professionals out of their routines to put the new statement together. From 1999 through 2002, SSM applied for the Baldrige National Quality Award Program within the Health Care category. Every year, except for 2000, their application resulted in a site visit from a Baldrige team comprised of commercial executives from outside the health care industry and a government liaison.

The Baldrige process pushed SSM to consider many issues that get lost in the day-to-day operations. What does quality mean? How does the organization's strategy translate into actual implementation? Does the lowest level employee in the organization understand how what they do in their everyday job relates to the mission of the organization? In today's work environments, where action and activity often trump reflection, the Baldrige process supplied SSM with a sustained period of introspection, where receiving the award was not the goal—getting better and saving lives was. In a very countercultural way, Sister Mary Jean never sought the award as the end-state through the years she pushed SSM to apply. The treasure was the feedback report that brought light to opportunities for improvement. A photo opportunity with the vice president of the United States (as happens often during the award ceremony) might be nice for some organizations; what mattered to Sister Mary Jean was the care of the people served by SSM Health Care. She told me, "We always felt Baldrige was such a worthwhile exercise because the feedback helped us get better and better. It helped us focus on the things that really mattered to our patients. Every time we applied, we used the feedback to improve."

Leadership across SSM saw the Baldrige process as a chance to get better, and each round of feedback gave Sister Mary Jean and her team dozens of ways to improve processes so that patient care improved and people worked smarter and toward better outcomes. Early on some executives pushed back on Sister Mary Jean because they already had a huge amount of work before them. For example, Ron Levy, then president and CEO of SSM Health Care–St. Louis, felt he didn't have time for Baldrige because he was already involved in a huge financial turnaround of his part of the business. Sister Mary Jean listened to him but let him know that she would not accept anything but full participation from her entire team and that he had to get involved in their Baldrige efforts. Levy gave in and joined in the process as he embraced the questions and elements of the framework to help design a $50 million financial turnaround. As the results came in across two years of assessments and applications, he turned from Baldrige-skeptic to Baldrige-believer.

During their first site visit, SSM discovered they were still a long way from living what they were saying in their mission statement. The Baldrige team held meetings with the corporate headquarters office in St. Louis and 17 facilities in four states involving over 800 employees and physicians from throughout the system. At the direction of Sister Mary Jean, SSM made its application as a system; the organization did not want Baldrige to look at one site or one region, as some applicants for the award prefer. Rather, she wanted to consider how they could improve systemically. There would be hundreds of questions around all aspects of their organization, from ethical behavior to financial transparency, including questions such as: "What's in your finances that you would least like to talk about?"

The questions examiners asked went to the heart of the core assumptions SSM had made about itself. Each new question allowed the examiners to see how much thought had gone into the thousands of processes that existed across their complex health enterprise. Then one question made them really take a step back. Sister Mary Jean told me, "When we got the feedback from the first site visit, the examiners said, 'It's a really wonderful mission statement, but what do you mean by exceptional and how do you measure it? Because if you can't measure it, then you can't improve it." SSM president Bill Thompson said that applying the Baldrige criteria was a way to evaluate and improve the overall organization. He remembers the feedback as well and said, "Our mission calls on us to deliver 'exceptional care.' We had to ask ourselves are we even organized to deliver 'exceptional care?'" The inability to answer such a key question was a contributing factor to their not receiving the award the first year they applied. By challenging SSM to question their most basic mission, Sister Mary Jean was inserting the reflection that would allow them to improve as an organization. SSM was learning as an organization.

Even if you are not selected as a recipient, the Baldrige program supplies organizations with a detailed analysis of their findings and many opportunities for improvement. At SSM the opportunities were handed off to subteams that would reflect upon the critique and then take action to improve across the next year of operations. On the feedback around their use of the term "exceptional," SSM knew they had to take action lest it remain words without measures. They concluded that there would be three characteristics they would identify as meaningful distinctions for assessing "exceptional." First, they would measure "exceptional satisfaction" for patients, employees, and physicians; second, they would measure "exceptional clinical outcomes," including safety; and third, they would measure "exceptional financial results."

As year after year the notifications came in from the Baldrige program that they were not selected, Sister Mary Jean sat down with her leadership team and reinforced what the whole exercise was about. She helped them see the bigger picture. Sister Mary Jean congratulated people on the good work they were doing and on the improvements made from one year to the next. To this day, she makes the time to thank and motivate people as quality and consistency improve. In 2001, a team reviewed the feedback from the third Baldrige application and site visit and unanimously agreed that SSM should not apply in 2002 so they could focus on addressing the "Opportunities for Improvement" emanating from the earlier applications and rounds of feedback. The team then went to see Sister Mary Jean. She told me, "I thanked them for their efforts, and immediately decided to move forward with an application that next year. My reasoning was that to take a year off would interrupt the momentum we were building, and would demonstrate a lack of faith, not only in the process, but in the system." She reminded them that this was not about winning an award and to get that off their minds.

In a session with an examiner during another site visit, Thompson recalled another challenging question that prompted SSM to take another step back from business as usual. He told me, "The examiner said that 'We are a little bit confused: You have this mission statement that calls for you to be exceptional, yet you measure yourself, your results and your comparisons against averages.' It was one of those palm of the hand to the forehead moments." He continued, "We recognized that we were inconsistent between what we said and what we did. We took that feedback to heart as well and asked ourselves, 'How do we know that we are driving toward being exceptional and not just average?'" Since 1999, the quality of available data has improved dramatically, and SSM now has access to proprietary and publicly available data on clinical and other performance outcomes, which they use in setting goals. SSM now uses top decile or quartile comparisons versus averages. They have also purchased data sets and use a number of websites, such as whynotthebest.org, featuring information on the relative effectiveness of thousands of hospitals.

Stop the Line If You Need To

SSM uses another moment of reflection as part of their routine business processes. Part of why SSM ultimately was a Baldrige award recipient in 2002 ties to the results they have achieved with regard to the life-and-death decisions they make for millions of patients. Since they received their first Baldrige award, they continue rolling out new methods for quick transitional meetings at the beginning of shifts so that nothing gets lost in a transition moment, where distraction can cost a life. Employees at all levels are given authority for a moment of pause to reconsider what is about to happen for a patient or course of treatment. Thompson explained to me, "We try to heighten everyone's awareness that what we do in any moment has impact on clinical quality and patient safety. We encourage and expect our staff, including physicians, nurses, and other clinicians to 'stop the line.' They are expected to step up and prevent things from happening if they don't feel that the care that we are about to deliver is absolutely safe."

Sister Mary Jean said, "At all times we must be able to ask ourselves, have we done the right thing?" She noted that stopping the line wasn't always SSM's policy and they have had breakdowns in the past. She explained, "The person who stops the line is actually congratulated. If, in fact, either a manager or an administrative person does not support the person who stops the line, the manager or the administrative person will be fired. It's something that we feel very strongly about. In the past, when a nurse and doctor were involved in an error, the chances were that the nurse would get fired and nothing would happen to the doctor. I take responsibility for that. That is unconscionable and it will not happen again." "Stop the line" also extends to SSM's corporate responsibility process, including their billing and administrative procedures.

SSM is not the only medical facility to empower employees and require moments of pause that change outcomes. It's becoming a standard practice tied to documented procedures and even basic checklists tied to dozens of medical practices. Author and journalist Dr. Atul Gawande writes extensively about the processes followed by medical professionals in order to save lives. Gawande wrote about a critical-care specialist Peter Pronovost, at John's Hopkins Hospital in Baltimore, Maryland, who employed "stop the line procedures" coupled with a simple five-step checklist relating to the insertion of a "central line" into a patient's blood stream. Such routine procedures, when done incorrectly, lead to infection and death for thousands of patients each year.[12]

He describes the steps in the process as essentially "no brainers" to critical-care specialists. They range from washing one's hands to putting a sterile dressing over the catheter site once the line is in. Gawande writes, "Pronovost asked the nurses in his I.C.U. to observe the doctors for a month as they put lines in the patients, and record how often they completed each step. In more than a third of patients, they skipped at least one. The next month, he and his team persuaded the hospital administration to authorize nurses to stop doctors if they saw them skipping a step in the checklist. This was revolutionary." In the first year, the clinical results achieved at one hospital were outstanding; the average ten-day line infection rate went from 11 percent to 0 percent. With the combination of process and forced moments of reflection, the new methods prevented 43 deaths, and saved two million dollars in costs.

SSM has taken the "stop-the-line" procedures and pushed them down into the fabric of their culture. A well-known and studied case within SSM involved a young nurse, with less than two years of professional experience, working in cardiac care. She received an order to take a patient down for a cardiac catheterization, but she was certain that the order was for a different patient. She voiced her concern to the lead in the cardiology unit and she was assured it was the right procedure for the right person. She did not accept the answer and escalated her concern to the director of cardiology and the patient's actual physician. Finally, when the cardiologist came to the floor and, after a small conference to clarify the patient's identity, they discovered the nurse was right to question the procedure. It was actually the patient in a nearby bed who required the procedure. The young nurse not only stopped the line, but was also given a monthly "good catch" award for preventing the error from happening.

As do so many organizations, SSM increasingly relies on technology to lower the costs of operations and assist its efforts at reducing patient errors. For the last several years, it has been implementing the electronic health record (EHR) in all its hospitals, an investment of more than $391 million. The EHR will allow caregivers within the system access to patient information at any time, from anywhere, in all its hospitals. This investment implies that new measurements for quality can be achieved. Yet, the availability of the data within the EHR will likely give rise to new processes that ensure its existence does not consume the thoughtful, reflective, people-driven processes that have made SSM such a standout organization.

Over a decade has passed since SSM applied for their first Malcolm Baldrige award. Over time metrics have improved around mortality rates and errors in treatment tied to pneumonia, acute myocardial infarction (heart attacks), heart failure, and general surgical care. People took pride in this, as the moments of reflection were giving rise to exactly what is at the core of their mission: exceptional care. The biggest frustration Sister Mary Jean has is not the lack of improvement, but the lack of magnitude of improvement. Accelerating the rate of improvement is now a focus.

In a system-wide announcement in early 2010, Sister Mary Jean relayed that even though SSM had already received the award, they would apply yet again for Baldrige. She wrote to all employees: "I made the decision that, as a system, we will apply for the Malcolm Baldrige

National Quality Award in 2011. (We'll prepare in 2010 by identifying the things we do well and addressing the areas where we don't do well.) The Baldrige process was critical to our improvements a decade ago, and I have every confidence that it will be invaluable to us now as well.... I am absolutely convinced that you are exceptional at what you do. And I am committed to ensure that you have the very best processes to provide the best care humanly possible to our patients. Our Mission calls us to be exceptional, and I know we can do it."

Applying the Think Time Lessons of PBD and SSM Health Care

The stories in this chapter reveal that organizations can take both big and small steps to freeing up time to reflect about the core mission of an organization. "No-email Fridays" and applying for the Baldrige quality award come about when leaders are dissatisfied with the current state of things. Such efforts will not happen organically unless leaders are willing to ensure that it happens. For all the costs that can be incurred by having people step back from their assumptions and habits, we see many benefits. Taking a step back as an organization can mean reconnecting with clients or reaffirming the contract between patients and caregivers. Otherwise, the immediate needs of the moment become the habit and posture—sometimes signaling an organization that may not stand the test of time.

The bias toward action and activity, combined with unprecedented amounts of data to process, means that organizations must find mechanisms to force think time and reflection. Time for thinking will not arise unless leaders and managers take deliberate actions to drive new outcomes and models for working. Key areas for dialogue to apply the lessons from this chapter include:

1. Questioning email and putting it into context. What is your organization's relationship to email? When, if ever, have you structured an analysis of what it is really doing to productivity? Does your company even employ a basic set of policies for use (creation and dissemination of email) so that useless and distracting messages don't destroy time that could be spent on new ideas and innovation? Does your organization have an explicit hierarchy for communications? If not, the default is usually instantaneous

email response. Email remains the default choice for collaboration, but its overuse and the addictive nature as practiced by senior executives and then aped across the company remains the largest killer of think time and reflection. Organizations that rethink email and direct its judicious use recapture think time they can direct toward more important purposes.

2. Discuss what responsiveness is and what it does to your organization. When was the last time you questioned the "responsiveness cycle" in your organization? It's the time it takes from when a request comes in (via email, voice mail, or even face-to-face) from customers or other employees to when an employee gives a response. While maintaining high levels of customer service, is it possible to imagine some rule set around response? Failure to ever question this, or just assume it's always immediate, creates the need for more and more responsiveness. Thoughtful and deliberate action is taken without stepping back to consider the cascading consequences. Habitually automatic responsiveness carries with it expectations that quickly overstress workers and burn people out.

3. Openness to outside scrutiny that comes with forced moments of reflection. The Baldrige program is like the Olympics; most applicants don't actually expect to receive the award. When was the last time you willingly opened up a function, let alone your whole business, to any level of outside scrutiny? Doing so may yield unexpected insights from people outside your industry. If taken seriously, such scrutiny can serve to break patterns; and it can help to stand up new methods to address "blind spots." What matters more is what you do with the feedback that comes to you through such a process. Will you put it on a shelf, or let it take root throughout the organization? Vulnerability to outside scrutiny may just show the humility this allows for your organization to prepare for the unexpected.

4. Encourage system-wide thinking. Process for the sake of process can drain an organization and potentially codify broken methods. The complexity of relationships and the translation of strategy to implementation require thinking holistically about the problem before drilling down to the details. What is the system-level view of your organization? Could you describe it coherently to those inside and outside? What are the checks and balances that help

ensure that as much time is spent pushing a strategy down and through an organization as is spent creating the strategy? Given how fast markets change, what if any evidence exists in your organization that some moments of reflection take place on an ongoing basis—thereby demonstrating agility and adaptability?

5. It's okay to "stop the line." SSM's model presents a powerful example of decentralized decision making that can be applied outside the medical facility. When was the last time an employee was rewarded for "flagging" something they saw as likely to harm a desired outcome? With the ethical lapses that have been so widely observed in many industries, what is your organization's response to "stopping the line" and protecting, even celebrating, those with the courage to compel a moment of reflection?

6

Too Big to Think?

Of Cassandras and Cognitive Dissonance

Cassandra, from ancient Greek mythology, was the daughter of King Priam and Queen Hecuba of the fabled city of Troy. She was said to have spent a night "resting" in the god Apollo's temple. During the night, temple snakes licked her ears clean so that she was able to hear the future and make predictions. Cassandra never returned the love expressed to her by Apollo. He placed a curse on her so that no one would believe her predictions. She has come to symbolize the type of people who can foresee what others can't but are rarely, if ever, believed by the masses.

In the dizzying run-up to the financial collapse, reflection was seldom to be found. Without dissecting the many causes of economic bubbles, what becomes clear is that there was a collective failure on behalf of thousands of very smart people, government regulators and millions of homeowners, to step away from the lure, temptations and consequences of too good-to-be-true real estate investing. One of the most powerful barriers to think time is not just the lack of time spent thinking amidst all the busyness and immediacy of modern life; but the rationalizing away of downside risks and unknowns presented in a globalized marketplace. Systematic failure to encourage debate, dissent, and push back against poorly thought-out investment strategies nearly led to the catastrophic collapse of banks—along with everyone they do business with.

Two atypical thinkers pondered the financial markets with all their increasing complexity and arrived at far different conclusions from the masses and Wall Street market makers. Both rarely give interviews, but they agreed to sit down with me to discuss how they frame problems in their minds and how their mental models evolve. First, attorney Brooksley Born wondered about the emerging over-the-counter (OTC) derivatives market in the late 1990s and concluded that the unknown risks associated with their compounding use might one day have debilitating impacts on Wall Street and average taxpayers. The more she learned, the more she questioned what she was seeing, and she issued warnings that no one wanted to hear. Global investor Kyle Bass and his hedge fund team at Hayman Capital in Dallas immersed themselves in much of the same data as Wall Street's smartest people and reached very different conclusions about the downside risks of subprime mortgages. He concluded that the assumptions underlying the meteoric rise of these assets were deeply flawed. His structured analysis involved stepping away from the herd mentality, through debate and dissent; this played a key role in making his investors hundreds of millions of dollars.

Within the last decade, people took part in a buying frenzy of real estate assets in which there seemed little downside risk. Banks attempted to outsource risk through complex investment instruments like Collateralized Debt Obligations (CDOs). We learned that lessons of economic bubbles are not easily digested, and that changing a business-as-usual mindset inside long-standing institutions is very hard. We learned that even the smartest people among us have their limits when it comes to understanding the complexity inherent in financial innovations coupled with the velocity of global markets. But there were a select few who looked at the data, trends, and assumptions and came to very different conclusions from the mainstream. Their habits of think time and reflection offer a glimpse into the sometimes lonely world of skeptical thinking tied to taking thoughtful actions. Their examples demonstrate that mental models born with a view to seeing a larger context and holding competing ideas in one's mind are now prerequisites for today's decision making. They also prove it takes a lot of courage to finally act on what one has thought through.

The speed of today's global financial markets and attendant decision making means bankers must quickly think and act—thousands of times a day. The cultures of Wall Street firms demonstrate the powerful bias toward action, as money is made or lost globally every hour of the day and on nearly every continent. The amount of data that pours through a Wall Street firm is simply staggering. Trillions of dollars move through incessant transactions and for workers there is an unforgiving daily pace required given the global marketplace. The recent economic reset has taught us that decisions made within these firms have significant global consequences. Wall Street and Main Street are inseparable partners within a very complex macroeconomy. Thus, the dialogues and debates that happen (or don't happen) within these firms are now of significant concern to everyone. If there is no element of reflection within these dialogues as people "think together," then rationalizing away the downside risks to an investment type or complex transaction can easily take root and become ingrained orthodoxy that no one wants to question. Rationalizing away the downside of a given strategy demonstrates what happens when a firm devalues reflection and rewards short-term immediacy and groupthink. Such rationalizing allowed banks to make assumptions that were ill-founded and rarely questioned. Rationalizing nearly resulted in far more than a protracted recession with millions of jobs lost and lives affected. The global marketplace neared collapse.

Kyle Bass bet against every assumption that drove banks in the real estate buying and financing frenzy from 2001 to 2007. He believed banks were holding on to assets in the form of bundled subprime mortgages that would one day prove worthless. His hedge fund capitalized on the downfall, turning millions of dollars in profit for a select set of investors. Ten years before the economic reset, during a time of exuberance in the late 1990s, Brooksley Born warned fellow regulators and Congress about the dangers of OTC derivatives. Her warnings included pointing out how little was known about the transactions behind the scenes of global deal making. She saw a future where a lack of basic transparency and understanding would give way to firms making unprecedented bets that appeared to hedge risk, thereby increasing more risk taking. These unregulated bets—interconnected as each bank has some risk exposure to the next—could one day implode in cascading defaults, thus exposing unwitting taxpayers to trillions of dollars of exposure through bailout scenarios. Born was dismissed, and even rebuked, as few, if any, wanted to consider the downside of what might be wrought.

The permutations of risk in a connected world are infinite and can't be diversified away. However, institutions and leaders must find the time to restructure problem solving through more deliberative, analytical, and reflective business processes. The Bass and Born examples are powerful, as both envisioned a possible future that so few wanted to acknowledge. What made Bass and Born think the way they did? What, if anything, do they have in common? As we strive to make our organizations places of action grounded in thoughtful reflection, can their skills be found and replicated? We have just witnessed the consequences of weak organizational architectures that discounted debate, dissent, and questioning of basic assumptions. If Bass and Born worked in your company, it's unlikely they would stand on the sidelines and rationalize away poor decision making based on faulty assumptions. Would you hire them or fire them? The answer depends on how much you can handle dissent or push-back through dialogue and discourse. With either of them in the room, think time is never quite the same.

A Derivative Is Born

Brooksley Born is a lawyer who came to Washington, D.C., in 1964 and spent most of her career at a major D.C.–based law firm, Arnold and Porter. Her legal expertise includes a deep understanding of financial derivatives she was exposed to years before they would become a ubiquitous financial tool and infamous household term. While derivatives have been around since there were markets, they have exploded in use and sophistication in the last three decades. In many ways, derivatives are an insurance policy that helps mitigate the risks of transactions in almost anything. Born explained to me that "rather than a true investment instrument like stock or bonds, derivatives are an instrument that serves other purposes. They are used by organizations to hedge or protect against price changes or to gamble and speculate on price changes, rate changes, financial indices, or something else." She continued, "It's an instrument that changes in price based on the price of an underlying product or the rate of an underlying instrument."[1]

In 1996, Born was appointed by President Clinton to head the Commodity Futures Trading Commission (CFTC). At the time, this little-understood agency reported directly to Congress. As the head of the CFTC, Born had a seat inside the President's Working Group on Financial Markets, a powerful committee composed of, among others, then Secretary of Treasury Robert Rubin, and Chairman of the Federal Reserve Bank, Alan Greenspan. The CFTC focused mostly on exchange-traded derivatives associated with energy, metal, and agricultural products. While at the CFTC, Born publicly warned that the agency was not well informed of the nature and construct of the OTC market with its complex contracts and many players. She suggested that such a lack of understanding could come at a cost to the American people and the world. She wanted to better understand the downside risks and was willing to put the topic up for public discussion. Her calls for forcing some thinking about the nature of this opaque market were ignored. She was personally attacked and dismissed by many as an alarmist and a meddler in a marketplace that could regulate itself. After serving her three-year appointment, Born left the CFTC. She watched from outside the government as Congress stripped the agency of the authority to even ask the basic questions and to challenge underlying assumptions about a very complex financial innovation.

After pressure from friends, Born finally spoke out in 2009 about her work nearly a decade earlier inside the CFTC, where she warned of the dangers inherent in a completely "black box market." She said, "I didn't want to speak out until it was an appropriate time and until people would pay attention. When markets are melting down that is the wrong time."[2] Born believes derivatives are good and useful business tools but she also believes that in the absence of regulation, their complexity could do harm. To understand how she came to see this, we must begin by looking at the forces that shaped her thinking and the role that reflection played in her training.

Shedding Emotional Appeals and Contextual Thinking

Born grew up in California, her parents both public servants. After graduating high school at the age of 16, she studied English literature at Stanford and eventually went to Stanford's law school, graduating in 1964 at the top of her class. That first year of law school featured a barrage of new ideas and concepts that challenged Born. No semester tests, progress reports, or even paper grades guided one's sense of how well one was doing. It all came down to a series of tests in the spring semester that would gauge how well students grasped the overall framework of law. She told me: "Going to law school gave me a new mental model for looking at the world. One of the reasons why the first year in law school is difficult is because you are putting aside the way that you have looked at events and issues by learning entirely new ways to analyze problems. You no longer let the emotional appeal of individuals or circumstances affect you as much as the framework of activity within the social charter and the laws that society has set up."[3]

As a woman at Stanford Law School, Born was exposed to the pervasive sexist mentality alive on many campuses. She became the first woman ever chosen to be the president of the prestigious Stanford Law Review. Manuel Roig-Franzia of the *Washington Post* noted that "you would think this would be a moment of triumph for Brooksley Born. Instead, she gets a phone call from one of the deans. And he says, 'Brooksley, I just want to let you know that the faculty stands ready to step in if you're not able to pull this off.' It goes on like that, on and on and on, at each step of Brooksley Born's life and career."[4]

Born learned the value of reflection early in her career as a law clerk for U.S. Court of Appeals Judge Henry W. Edgerton, who wrote seminal case decisions on matters such as desegregation and civil rights. "Judge Edgerton started something with me that I carried forward throughout my career," Born said. "After a case was submitted, we engaged in a free-flowing conversation, looking carefully at the facts and the relevant law. We would sit one-on-one and just talk it through." She continued: "We talked about the context in which the case arose or about the impact of various potential decisions on society or on the parties involved in the case. It was a little like a continuation, to some limited extent, of the Socratic method we used in law school. He was teaching me how to think about the problem before me."[5] While at the CFTC and in her years as a partner at Arnold and Porter, Born maintained this reflective practice. She believed in one facilitator driving the meeting and, as she became a more experienced attorney, learned to speak less and listen more to the arguments being made.

Born's mother was a public school teacher while her father was head of the public welfare department in San Francisco. Their example, and the context of how her dad saw his job, also had an impact on how she thought through problems, especially at the CFTC. "My father taught me to keep an eye on the public interest. Serving individuals who were seeking welfare was very involved but he was always thinking about the tax money he was actually spending. I was very aware that you need to look not merely at the day-in and day-out handling of immediate issues before you, but that you must also keep in mind the bigger picture."[6]

She employed a number of thinking techniques while at the CFTC. For example, she related that "morning is my best time of day to do some thinking. I had back-to-back meetings (at the CFTC). But I kept an open early morning where I could think and go through and prepare for the day." Yet, it was not just the use of early-morning time that she attributed to her ability to step back and problem solve. There was a subconscious process that factored into her approach. In a work culture that values employees engaged for a full workweek, she discovered that time away from the job was valuable and helped her generate new insights and solutions.

Early in her career, when she had young children, Born began working a three-day week (Mondays, Wednesdays, and Fridays). Tuesdays and Thursdays she would be with her children doing the work of a mother versus an attorney. She noticed that she would leave the office on a Monday night with still-unresolved client problems in her mind. The next day, when home with the children, she would purposely avoid conference calls and tried to detach as much as possible from the office so she could focus on her family. Then, as she stepped back into the office she began to see a pattern in her problem-solving skills. She said, "I would arrive back at the office on Wednesday and all kinds of strategy issues surrounding cases would be resolved. At least it would be clear to me how to proceed even though I spent Tuesday playing with my children." Had she been in the office working on the cases, she concluded, it would have taken her hours to "consciously think through solutions." Yet, when she stepped away from her work, even for a day, she concluded that problems were resolved "almost subconsciously."[7]

This realization taught Born that it was a good thing to leave the office and clear one's mind just by thinking about other things. During her time at the CFTC, she used sailing on weekends to create some space for subconscious thinking. She noted, "When you sail, you just don't think about other things. I found that it cleared my head while working on some big issues. Things would be much clearer to me when I arrived back at the agency."[8] What Born discovered through her personal experience has been strengthened through a series of neuroscientific studies involving the subconscious mind. Dutch psychologist Ap Dijksterhuis at the University of Amsterdam recently concluded that we are likely to make better decisions when we are not consciously focused on the actual decision. Dijksterhuis said, "The idea that conscious deliberation before making a decision is always good is simply one of those illusions consciousness creates for us."[9]

Rationalization and Exuberance

Born allows many competing and even conflicting ideas to enter into her mind at the same time. For example, she believes that derivatives are good business tools that should be widely available and is keenly aware of the systemic dangers inherent in their fraudulent misuse. Her ability to hold competing ideas in her mind is a rarity. As humans, we observe, form opinions, and then usually defend what we perceive to be reality. At the time that Born grew skeptical of derivatives, America was experiencing a cold war peace dividend and an accelerating stock market driven by a technology boom that few politicians or business-people wanted to question or, even worse, derail.

Social psychologists Carol Tavris and Elliot Aronson, authors of *Mistakes Were Made (But Not By Me)* teach us that far too often humans are simply unable to allow competing ideas to simultaneously, occupy our minds. Instead, people accept one truth and then dig in to defend the one idea—regardless of how much competing informa-tion and evidence indicates they could be wrong. The discomfort we feel at the prospect of being wrong is called cognitive dissonance. They describe it as "the state of tension that occurs whenever a person holds two cognitions (ideas, attitudes, beliefs, opinions) that are psychologi-cally inconsistent such, as "Smoking is a dumb thing to do because it could kill me," and "I smoke two packs a day." Dissonance produces mental discomfort, ranging from minor pangs to deep anguish; people don't rest easy until they find a way to reduce it."[10] In the mid-1990s, America was resting easy as life was telling us that good times were here—perhaps to stay. There was a lot of consonance that we had entered a new and unprecedented time along with a rewrite of the basic rules of economics.

Tavris explains that when people learn to hold the two competing ideas in their heads, they benefit by being able to assess the support for each side of a problem independently and make better decisions—or correct bad ones after the fact. She concludes: "Dissonance may be uni-versal; but how we live with it, what we do about it, how we understand and learn from mistakes we have made and wrong-headed beliefs we held on to for too long—all that is learned and changeable."[11]

Cognitive dissonance was reduced over and over on Wall Street and Main Street in the run-up to the recent financial crisis. In other words, few were encouraged to take a contrarian view of conventional wisdom that suggested real estate values would go up constantly. With poorly understood and very complex financial instruments, as well as the market's speed and size, bankers were able to easily explain away what they thought was reality. This means that think time within dozens of institutions failed to generate counter arguments and balanced actions and tangible projects that formally challenged the real downside risks involved in trillions of dollars of transactions. Reflecting back on recent lessons learned since the near-global financial meltdown, Goldman Sachs CEO, Lloyd Blankfein told a congressional inquiry commission: "At the top of my list [of lessons learned] are the rationalizations that were made to justify that the downward pricing of risk was justified. While we recognized that credit standards were loosening, we ratio-nalized the reasons with arguments such as: the emerging markets were more powerful, the risk mitigates were better, there was more than enough liquidity in the system." He continued, "We rationalized because a firm's interest in preserving and growing its market share, as a competitor, is sometimes blinding—especially when exuberance is at its peak."[12]

Detecting Fraud and Floating a Concept

Born had more than her share of mental discomfort in 1996 as she dug into the opaque OTC market. She explained to me, "One of things that was most troubling for me was how little information our staff had about the OTC market that we were supposedly overseeing. We knew who the big over the counter dealers were and this was before Enron and AIG joined the market. We didn't know very much about how the contracts were structured, who all the players were or how much lever-age there was. We didn't know how much was speculation and how much was actually hedging."[13]

She recalled cases of fraud that she has seen in her law practice outside government. Digging deep into fraud gave her a more balanced view of what can go wrong when a marketplace has no rules. She explained that the CFTC was seeing real problems in the OTC market. "Before I had arrived we had a major case of an over the counter derivatives dealer, Bankers Trust, dealing in fraud with its customers. The agency had not been able to detect that fraud. While it had the duty to detect fraud, it had no form of investigative powers. The agency didn't require record keeping and reporting."[14]

Prior to Born's arrival at the CFTC, Congress gave the CFTC the ability to exempt certain kinds of derivatives contracts from the exchange trading requirements. In 1993, Born's predecessor acted on that exempted power. Born explained that the CFTC exempted "certain customized swaps (bilateral contracts) between highly sophisticated parties from the exchange trading requirement. They kept the CFTC's anti-fraud and anti-manipulation powers over that market and made it into a regulation. When I came into the CFTC, I came in and wanted to revisit that because that market had grown from virtually nothing to 30 trillion dollars in notional value."[15]

Born calls it "notional value," since such contracts don't necessarily involve posting collateral, and pricing models calculate the costs at day one of an OTC transaction as zero. What is an insurance policy worth that has no money paid in and a very low probability of ever being used? She explained, "By the time I left the CFTC in 1999 the OTC market was valued at ninety trillion dollars in notional amount. Before I took over at the CFTC in 1996 I hadn't realized how large the market had grown. In private practice, I had had only one case that dealt exclusively with OTC derivatives." She continued, "I knew that the CFTC had adopted the exemption when it occurred in 1993 and had been surprised that the banking regulators were allowing banks to act as OTC derivatives dealers. It seemed to me that it was extremely risky for banks with insured deposits to undertake such an activity."[16]

Stepping back from the fraud cases, with a market that was literally growing by trillions of dollars a year, Born commissioned a formal study to be done on what was really happening in the OTC and why her predecessor had granted an exemption so the market would not be regulated. She explained, "I was being told that the CFTC's rationale for exempting this market was that it was a market involving very large and sophisticated institutions trading with one another and that they didn't need any kind of oversight or supervision."[17]

The report came back to her stating that there had been repeated major collapses (over 60 defaults were cited) by big institutions speculating in these markets with borrowed money that they couldn't repay when the market moved again. Born also remembered that California's Orange County had been speculating with the public's funds (tax money) using OTC derivatives, and it actually went bankrupt in 1994, a few years before she took office. The county's debt obligation was over $1.5 billion, and at the time was the country's largest municipal bankruptcy.

After months of time spent alone and reflecting with her team, Born felt compelled to take action. Her team created what the agency called a "concept paper" derived from months of analysis. That paper signaled that the CFTC was seeking feedback on a potential set of rules that could bring some degree of transparency into the OTC market. One memorable section in the concept paper sought public comment on risk management in the context of a clearinghouse the CFTC could facilitate for the OTC derivative marketplace. Such a clearinghouse is now finally under consideration by Congress nearly 13 years after it was suggested. In 1998, Born's CFTC said: "An OTC derivatives clearing facility could choose from among many potential risk management tools. These include capital requirements for participants, reporting requirements, position or exposure limits, collateral requirements, segregation requirements, mark-to-market." It went on to say, "The Commission requests comment on how best to assure that a clearing facility uses appropriate risk management tools without preventing flexibility in the design of such tools or inhibiting the evolution of new risk management technology."[18]

In the wake of the financial collapse, every bank in America has now beefed up and reengineered their risk management functions in order to ask the awkward questions that ensure balanced consideration of downside risk. Over a decade before such actions, the CFTC wanted the banking industry to comment on how it should think about systemic risk for a clearinghouse that would never be built. Larry Summers, Alan Greenspan, and Robert Rubin did not want to allow for regulations or even basic oversight for a marketplace that was booming. From senators to congressman and throughout the executive branch, no one wanted to believe the market was worth regulating as this would risk disrupting the balances supplied within the market itself. In 2009, Born received the John F. Kennedy Profile in Courage Award for having the courage to think through a threat to the country that few wanted to even hear about. In her acceptance speech she issued yet another warning, "If we fail now to take the remedial steps needed to close the regulatory gap, we will be haunted by our failure for years to come."[19]

Chosen by Speaker of the House Nancy Pelosi, Born now sits on the bipartisan Financial Crisis Inquiry Commission (FCIC) that has the authority to subpoena and to make recommendations to Congress for substantive change. With millions of bad decisions to revisit, the panel symbolizes the bodies of reflection that so often are put in place after a major setback. Short-term thinking, perverse incentives, and rationalization gave rise to speculation and risk that nearly catapulted the world into global financial meltdown. The commission's report will be a product of a year's worth of dialogues and reflection. During its second public hearing, Born had her first chance to question and engage a once-unknown banker from Dallas, Kyle Bass.

Of Honeymoons and Hedge Funds

Kyle Bass is a global investor and oversees a large hedge fund. Hedge funds are investment funds open to a limited amount of investors (usually up to 100) and often subject to less-stringent regulation than more widely known mutual funds. Hedge funds often exploit derivatives to execute their strategies. In 2005, as managing partner of Hayman Capital, Bass formed a hypothesis, as the basis of a fund, that said real estate mortgage buying and selling was a gathering storm with a powerful reconciliation yet to come. Bass gathered data from many publicly available sources to inform his view. He remarked to CNBC: "Name me a market that's one trillion dollars and touches a consumer and it's unregulated? There's only one—mortgage origination." But that wasn't the only thing he picked up on as he thought through his strategy; he continued: "Historically, median [personal] income had been parallel to housing prices. All of the sudden the average home price in the United States started to go up, not at one-and-a-half percent per year after inflation, but six to eight percent per year. Either incomes had to double or home prices had to drop 35 percent to make that relationship work again."[20]

The more time Bass and his team spent thinking about and reflecting on what they saw, the more he knew something was not right. To put this in perspective, while thousands of bankers and their customers around the world synchronized in a poor set of assumptions regarding mortgage origination, Hayman Capital acted counter to the herd. By immersing themselves in the same data sets and forcing lengthy discussions in which they stepped back from the behaviors of many—who were arguably smarter than they were—Hayman and its clients profited. They questioned the downside of key investments with equal vigor and analysis to their supposed limitless upside. While the market collapsed around the many banks who ignored the downside risks, Hayman created two funds to execute their strategy, including the

Subprime Credit Strategies Fund, LP, and Subprime Credit Strategies Fund II. Across the life of these funds, an investor would have enjoyed returns of 474 percent and 434 percent respectively for every dollar they invested in a twelve-month period. Most who were briefed by Bass on his strategy, told him he was wrong and was solving a problem that didn't exist. Further, Bass had to convince investors that his fund was about to reap the rewards of poorly thought-out strategies by banks and institutions with far more credibility than him.

As a child, Bass had been encouraged by his parents to study mathematics and science, where there is seemingly an answer for everything. Generate a hypothesis and then find the answer became his reflexive response to problem solving. Yet, his core hypothesis as an investor has been to be very skeptical of what he thinks he is observing. He has learned that many people answer questions with weak and ill-defined answers. In 1995, logic met human behavior when Bass took a job with Bear Stearns in Dallas. At age 25, his work as the head of a small team was to analyze "event-driven" and "special situations" companies all around the world who were involved in spinoffs, arbitrage, and contract negotiations. Bass's team was charged with determining the odds associated with companies performing well or faltering. Based on their analysis, they advised companies on investment policy and decision making.

In 1996, through an independent study he conducted of East German ship builder Bremer Vulkan, Bass learned that skepticism pays off. As he analyzed the company, it seemed the firm could do no wrong. Here's how the UK's *Independent* newspaper described it: "Vulkan was wallowing in what seemed to be an ever-lasting economic miracle. As the dry docks of Britain and other West European competitors were being turned into marinas, the company could not keep up with orders, and expanded into eastern Germany. The rationale for absorbing the derelict slipways of the east appeared to be sound: West German management harnessing cheap skilled workers in the east would see off the Japanese. Throw in large dollops of EU subsidies for the shipyards in the east, and the recipe could not fail."[21]

During the exciting yet uncertain times of German reunification, investment banks like Bear Stearns were finally provided financial views into companies and assets that had been subsidized by the East German government and hidden from global market makers. Bass said, "The more and more I read through their financial statements and did intense balance sheet and income statement analysis, the more I realized that the numbers just simply didn't add up as to where the money was coming from and where it was going to. So we were skeptical of their ability to continue as a going concern."[22] Bass then alerted his team and upper managers. He was about to discover that his ability to step back from data and question what others chose to ignore was a rare skill.

Around the same time as the Bremer hypothesis solidified in his mind, Bass was married. While on his honeymoon on Hayman Island (hence the name of his firm), off the coast of Australia, he awoke one morning to see that news of Bremer Vulkan was on the front cover of a financial paper. Bass told me, "I will never forget that story. The German government was closing the doors of Bremer based on fraud. It turned out that all the subsidies pumped into the company were going to executives to buy homes, yachts, and planes and not into the shareholders' pockets. It was a moving situation for me because I had dug deep into what they were doing wrong and thought I understood it. I offered my advice to other holders of the company's stock." He continued, "In the end, my hypothesis of skepticism rang true and it was a defining moment of my life—of learning to be skeptical of publicly available data. It was the first time in my life I realized that skepticism can really pay off."[23] Over the next decade, Bass would mature his one-man skepticism into a company that valued deep thinking, debate, and dissent—amidst a backdrop of rapid decision making and rationalizations.

As the pace accelerates in business, organizations that overcome the inclination to routinely rationalize away dissonance will be prove lasting, relevant, and distinguished. This involves changing the cultures of firms so that moments of think time and reflection are more valued, and there are incentives to react contrary to what seems like the right way to solve problems. Social psychologist Tavris advises, "Companies must make it possible for employees to speak up, offer suggestions, report flaws and problems, and *disagree with management... all without penalty.* You structure discussions to encourage and reward dissent (yes, that is a behavioral principle) and break out of 'groupthink,' as President Obama reportedly does, and as President Bush famously did not." She continued, "Dissent and debate must become part of the organizational culture, starting from the top down. Managers can ask not only, "What are the reasons we want to go with Plan A?" but "I want to hear from every one of you all the reasons that Plan A might go wrong, what its risks are, why it's a dumb idea."[24]

A Data Point from Dallas

Bear Stearns became the symbol of the financial meltdown as its value eroded to nearly zero before J.P. Morgan acquired it, with government prodding, for just under $250 million in 2008. The 80-year-old investment bank had withstood many recessions and even the stock market crash of 1929. For years, it had many moments when it valued and profited from original thinking as it exploded to a global company with nearly 15,000 employees. Yet, in the 15 years before it would implode, there was already evidence the company did not value critical and skeptical thinking that can only survive within a culture that is reflective. In fact, a decade before "subprime loans" became an infamous term, Bear was speculating in what was then known as the "second tier" real estate financing market. In this case, lenders allowed homebuyers to get 125 percent of the value of their home so that borrowers could package credit card debt into their mortgage payments so they became tax deductible. This risky business practice foreshadowed the larger economic collapse that would come less than a decade later.

Recalling his days at Bear, Bass said, "As a culture, I remember Bear Stearns as actually neutral to original thinking. If you were telling the truth with data and could verify the claims that you were making on the balance sheet and income statement, they had no problem with it." Bass continued: "In 1998, we had companies like FirstPlus Financial, AMES Financial, Citiscape and others who were 125 percent loan-to-value lenders, and Bear Stearns was doing all of their securitization. Bear had 'buy' ratings on all these companies in the equity markets. This is when gain-on-sale accounting was really nouveau."[25] In gain-on-sale accounting, if a company makes a pool of loans to people at 10 percent interest, the bank will securitize the loans and agree to only play out 8 percent. Thus the bank has a supposed 2 percent net interest margin of profit. The bank determines the duration of those loans, and immediately books profits without taking into account the risks inherent in the transaction or whether all parties can actually pay their debts. In other words, banks could recognize whatever revenue and, therefore, profit they wanted regardless of the risks associated with the transaction. Bass explained that the valuation of these firms took off because they were all trading at three to five times supposed earnings.

At that time, gain-on-sales accounting methods were predicated on the fact that the lender knew how many losses they were going to have across all of their loans. Something that is impossible to do. The CEO of FirstPlus Financial, Dan Phillips, once came into Bass's Bear Stearns Dallas office and asked: "Kyle, what can I say to make the short sellers [those betting that his company would not hit his projected numbers] cover their positions in our stock?" Bass informed him that the first thing he needed to do was figure out whether he was going to make or lose money. Bass told him, "If all you're going to make is 2 to 3 percent on interest margins but at the same time you are going to lose 10 percent of the money because you are lending out so much against the house [in a second lien position], then your business has no business." Phillips supposedly responded to Bass that he had 26 PhDs modeling potential loan losses. Bass retorted, "I don't care about your modeling, Dan. What I care about is what are your real losses? Within that year his company went to zero. It went bankrupt."[26]

Atypical of other hedge funds, Bass believes in openly sharing his strategy and the details of his hypothesis (not his actual trading methods) with as many parties as possible. He spends months thinking through his position with the people inside his firm and then looks forward to engaging in "intellectual debates" with practitioners and academics so that if he is making a mistake it can be pointed out and he can adjust the strategy. For the subprime strategy, Bass spoke to hundreds of people he thought smarter than himself. He wanted them to poke holes in his thinking. "We think through a concept like subprime from ten thousand different angles and then game theory the potential outcomes. When we are right about a hypothesis, it can actually accelerate the outcomes that we see envisioned as it accelerates the thinking of others."[27]

Bass recalled working with debt-ratings agency leaders charged with modeling out growth in the housing market during 2006. He told CNBC: "When I sat down with them, I said 'What kind of home price appreciation are you modeling in these things?' And they said, 'Six to eight percent per year.' They were modeling that into perpetuity; like it was going to happen from now on. And it was clear that it wasn't going to happen. No one I met with thought it was even remotely possible that home prices could go down."[28]

Through a series of conversations tied to courting a potential inves-tor, Bass even found himself inside his old firm, Bear Stearns in New York, for one of the strangest moments of open-sourcing Hayman's hypothesis on subprime. He explained, "I went back to Bear Stearns in late 2006 and I met with the head of risk management, Bobby Steinberg. He actually brought in the heads of almost every fixed income group in the firm for me to go through my thesis that the subprime market was about to collapse. After I finished my presentation, I said, 'You realize if I am right what is gong to happen to you guys?' And he said, 'Kyle you worry about your risk management and we will worry about ours.' As we walked out of that room he actually put his arm around me and said, 'It's a very compelling presentation Kyle and, God, we hope you are wrong.'"[29]

Hayman's team even went into the Federal Reserve Bank in Washington, D.C., to float their concept and get feedback. They wanted to find someone who could prove to them that they were wrong and that they had conceptualized a strategy that would never prove relevant or lucrative. He said, "We actually sat in the Federal Open Market Committee's (FOMC) boardroom and I went through the same thoughts we shared with Bear. Now remember that at the time I am a no-name guy. I am just a data point from Dallas. We didn't have any-thing on our company's marquee yet. But I said to the regulators, 'Do you guys realize what's about to happen if I am right?' And they said, 'Jobs growth and income growth are what lead housing prices. Here's a chart for jobs growth and here's one for income growth. Therefore, we don't believe you are going to be proven correct.'"[30]

What the Fed and Bass's former colleagues at Bear Stearns sim-ply could not allow in was any dissonance to their long-held beliefs about what they had confirmed was reality. While Bass was allowed in the room, his ideas never had a chance to be seriously considered. Psychologists Tavris and Aronson conclude that, "Dissonance theory has exploded the self-flattering idea that we humans, Homo sapiens, process information logically. On the contrary: If new information is consonant with our beliefs, we think it is well-founded and useful: 'Just what I always said!' But if the new information is dissonant, then we consider it biased or foolish: 'What a dumb argument!' So powerful is the need for consonance that when people are forced to look at discon-firming evidence, they will find a way to criticize, distort, or dismiss it so that they can maintain or even strengthen their existing belief.

This mental contortion is called the 'confirmation bias.'"[31] In the heady days before the largest erosion of wealth in human history, millions of us, including homeowners, bankers, and government regulators, confirmed beliefs and truisms that were simply not reality. Think time and reflection had devolved into shallow examinations based on flawed and unoriginal thinking.

Pavlovian Response Detection

Bass runs what he calls a "benevolent dictatorship" within his company. He has assembled a team of what he sees as atypical thinkers, including people with understanding of credit markets, geopolitical trends, and even the former assistant treasurer of Countrywide Mortgage Bank, who serves as the head of Hayman's financial group. For the fund that bet against companies with subprime mortgage debt, Bass brought in experts, including one who had spent years modeling out mortgage cash flows, which was critical to the analysis. He didn't hire anyone who supplied the bad assumptions related to subprime mortgages at the traditional banks. "The guys that modeled the cash flows didn't get it wrong. The guys that gave them the inputs to model with, they got it wrong."[32]

It took Bass and his team over five months to think through the strategy for the two funds that bet against the subprime mortgages and won big. Hours of discussion, where Blackberries are not permitted, resulted in the stunning conclusion that the entire market had peaked and that banks were simply avoiding the painful reconciliation that was about to come. Hundreds of iterations later a strategy emerged as the firm's first major product of reflection. It would travel through boardrooms and across email only to be met with objection and rationalizations. Although many people within hedge funds often trade with their own money in other transactions throughout the day, Bass will not allow it. He demands focus on the fund and Hayman's clients. Every employee in the company has part of their annual bonus tied to the fund's performance. Think time is focused inside Hayman, and incentives prove powerful motivators to overcoming distraction.

Debate is encouraged inside Hayman, and employees often openly disagree with Bass. He said, "The last thing that you want is your ego to get involved in a decision involving money. I always say when you mix ego with money you will lose every time. What we try to do is determine when the Pavlovian responses of markets will be broken because sooner or later they will be. To us, it's an exercise in psychology as much as it's an exercise in quantitative analysis." Bass is careful to note that you can't simply think all the time without setting in motion the action that accompanies your analysis. Leaders must act. He said, "In the end, someone has to tie up all of that data and look for an assimilation that counts and ultimately make a decision on how to apply that thought by putting an asymmetric investment into the fund."

Kyle Bass was the fifth person called to testify before Brooksley Born and the FCIC. In his opening statement, he said: "I believe that there is a role for leverage and for aggressive risk taking in the economy, but that role should be played by firms that are open and susceptible to the risk of insolvency and failure. Capitalism requires failure and bankruptcy as a consequence in order to guide behavior. As the old adage goes: 'Capitalism without bankruptcy is like Christianity without hell.' If we cannot allow a firm to go bankrupt, then we should regulate its activities so that it cannot engage in the sort of risky transactions that put it at risk of bankruptcy. To be clear, we should not prevent all firms from taking on leverage or engaging in risky behavior; we must ensure that they are not allowed to become Too Big To Fail."[33]

Applying the Lessons and Examples of Born and Bass

Born and Bass offer insights into the power of think time and reflection in wrestling with complex problems. For all that they both "got right" before the financial collapse, there have been times when Born lost cases she took on for clients and Bass's fund has lost money. Yet, examining their thinking habits and some similarities in approach as related to the near financial meltdown suggests several actions and questions for leaders and managers to consider inside their organizations:

1. Finding and studying cassandras. How would you attract a Kyle Bass or a Brooksley Born to join your company? These methodical thinkers rely on data, discussion, and the ability to question things based on skeptical mindsets. Would you have the ability to detect their unique skills if they existed within your company? One interview question you could ask of candidates is to describe their "mental model" of how the world works. Ask them to give you an example of a high-level strategy they see working inside

firms today and have them argue about what they see as the downside of that strategy. Then see if their answers echo any of what Born and Bass have employed in their careers.

2. Better managing of cognitive dissonance. This means acknowledging that there are viable alternatives to what you see as reality. Given how markets are so complex, and the speed at which they work, how does your company formally question business as usual? What reflective business processes and functions exist to entertain two versions of reality at the same time? Are lower-level employees encouraged to push back with well-structured arguments against a given position? Does the leadership team of the organization routinely take, and argue through, the contrarian position—without consequence or backlash? As Tavris shared with me, "Scientists live with dissonance all the time. And as we say, you don't have to be a scientist by profession to learn to think scientifically: to assess the evidence for a belief (e.g. vaccines cause autism) and let the belief go if it's wrong. We can learn to recognize the uncomfortable feeling of dissonance and instead of trying to suppress it or deny it, realize it is a sign that something is wrong and we'd better fix it."[34]

3. Learning from and detecting fraud. Fraud is a leading indicator of potential concern with an existing model. What does your company know about detecting fraud, both internally and on the outside? Who in the company is skilled at understanding the consequences of fraud? Will the training of managers to see and detect fraud lead to having managers who will speak up if they are skeptical of what they see before them? How much think time is dedicated to understanding where fraud is and what its short- and long-term impacts are for clients, the company, and its employees?

4. Open-sourcing strategy, even in hostile environments. Once an idea has been thought through, you must have the courage to open-source a hypothesis. Seeking feedback with different points of view will ensure you are not rationalizing one direction at the cost of another. In the end, a leader must take action with reputation and money on the line. When was the last time you shared a contrarian view that was born out of healthy and balanced skepticism and backed up by facts? Would you ever consider taking

such thinking and vetting it in meetings with people who are supposedly more expert than you?

5. The power of doing other things. Born's story powerfully demonstrates that when people are not in an office environment and have the opportunity to focus on an alternative task (in Born's case with her children) then subconscious processes are under way that could be beneficial to their company. Our bodies decouple from the office, yet our unconscious minds continue to solve the problems that challenged us the previous day while at our job. How do firms encourage such detachment for improved problem solving? How does your organization support moms who choose to work part time? The ones who are not always in the office may just prove to be the most productive and insightful people of all.

7

Rapid Contemplation

Rethinking War in the Middle of War

Once a war has begun, the military bias toward action and defeating an enemy is relentless. There is little time to think about fundamental concepts and foundational elements of a strategy—except if the strategy is failing. In 2005–06, as the Iraq war was being fought, reflection played a key role in turning the tide against a diffused, adaptive, and entrenched insurgency. Under the leadership of Marine Corps General, James Mattis, and U.S. Army General, David Petraeus, a small and atypical group of war fighters and thinkers rewrote the doctrine of counterinsurgency in less than nine months. Far from the battlefield in Iraq, time was given to think and reflect upon new models for turning the war around and proving the military was adapting. The way the army and marines rethought counterinsurgency presents many lessons for other organizations to consider. First, there was a willingness to recognize a failing strategy and take top leadership off the battlefield to step back and rethink the approach. Second, structure and methods of the sessions for vetting the new ideas offer novel ways for attacking complex problems—even when time is against you. Finally, when reflection becomes habit we see evidence of a learning organization; a critical hallmark that proves an organization can stand the test of time.

In order to discover the essence of these lessons, I interviewed six key people involved in not only creating the new policy for counterinsurgency, but in executing the larger strategy for the conflict in Iraq. Beyond engaging in dialogues with Generals Mattis and Petraeus, I also interviewed retired army general, Jack Keane, who was a lead architect of what became the "surge" of troops and ideas that turned Iraq away from a dangerous edge. I also interviewed: U.S. Army Lt.-Colonel (Ret.), John Nagl; Sarah Sewall, former director of the Carr Center for Human Rights Policy at Harvard University; and General Petraeus's former West Point classmate and friend, Dr. Conrad Crane. What follows are their stories and insights around what exactly happened once Petraeus took on rewriting the military's counterinsurgency doctrine. Beyond these firsthand accounts and recollections, I reviewed video recordings of days of key meetings and facilitated sessions involving this unprecedented undertaking so I could experience the actual flow and techniques employed. As the sessions were all "off the record" when they first happened, I agreed not to quote directly any one participant. Beyond this, I also reviewed key documents, meetings, summaries, and other accounts of the extraordinary moments of rapid contemplation that happened in Washington, D.C., and Fort Leavenworth, Kansas. All good military stories feature acronyms, and this one is no different. In military circles, counterinsurgency goes by the acronym: COIN. Our story starts with the painful realization that amidst all the action and years of work, the United States military was failing to address the insurgency in Iraq.

Understanding the Nature of War

General Jack Keane is a rarity among military men. His influence in Washington was most felt after his time in the army, as he helped think through the strategy of "the surge" employed with great success in Iraq. The surge was much more than an increase of troops in Iraq. General Petraeus, who executed the surge his mentor helped conceive, said, "The surge was not just 30,000 additional troops sent to Iraq. The surge was a surge of ideas, concepts, energy, much more meant to foster reconciliation in Iraq."[1] Where did those ideas come from? How did the situation in Iraq change so drastically in such a short period of time? Why did we fail to get it right from the first day we entered Iraq? How is it possible to structure think time when immediacy and action seem most appropriate? What can others learn from the ways leaders like Petraeus structured the time that allowed them to rethink war in the midst of war?

The Afghanistan and Iraq conflicts have brought America's war fighters to face volatile insurgents in unfamiliar settings that exposed gaps in knowledge and strategy. There is no simple answer for why these gaps existed at the outset of the Iraq war. Gaps emerged after Vietnam and the end of the Cold War, as political and military leaders failed to deeply consider prolonged insurgency warfare in an age of sophisticated U.S. military superiority. Keane takes part of the responsibility for this gap and said, "We were completely ill-suited intellectually to come to grips with irregular warfare and just as much unprepared for it. We were wrong, guys like me and others, we were wrong for not having our officers better prepared for it than what they were. Hopefully, we will not make that mistake again."[2] He then put the problem into a larger context and said, "You need to understand the nature of the war and that it requires analysis, a sense of history, and an understanding of your enemy in terms of who they are, what their intent is." Too often we don't take the time to think it through. Analyze the answers to, "Who is the enemy and what are they trying to do? What are their objectives? Then you can start fashioning a strategy to deal with it."[3]

Keane believes that lack of think time has something to do with the frenetic pace people move at today. He notes that much of a leader's time is spent on matters that don't require deep and strategic thinking, such as annual budgets and what he calls the "habits of routine." As in the civilian world, data and distraction abound for military leaders and their soldiers, as their connectivity has never been more pronounced. Keane sees this connectivity manifesting itself in many ways: "There's a bias for action. There's a bias for activity. And activity is a meeting or a briefing, as opposed to being more concerned with the input and making sure we have it right, before we start thinking about the outputs."[4]

It's important to note that the military is responsible for the questions of "how" a war should be executed and not "whether" it should be undertaken. "Whether questions" belong to the politicians.[5] In the case of Iraq, political leaders claimed overwhelming firepower and an aggressive ground campaign would unseat an ill-prepared and disorganized Iraqi army—even if they had chemical weapons. Initially, they were right. The political bias toward action had, however, subsumed reflective dialogue within the military about how quickly Iraq would stabilize after the initial campaign. Would the people resist or greet us as liberators? If an insurgency did arise, would it last very long? How would the United States respond to an insurgency? As the United States went to war with Iraq in 2003, it did so with outdated counter-insurgency policies still grounded in contradictory conclusions from the last time the United States faced an insurgency, more than 25 years earlier in Vietnam.

General Mattis, now Commander of U.S. Central Command, co-led the ground invasion of Iraq, with 20,000 troops under his immediate command, and oversaw conflict in Iraq's El-Anbar Province, including the controversial "Battle of Fallujah." Mattis would partner with Petraeus as coauthor of the new COIN doctrine for the army and marines. As a war fighter, he agreed with Keane's assessment of the lack of time given to thinking through big problems, saying, "It's the immediacy as much as the quantity of data that comes at us. Everyone has a computer, we are on operations literally around the world, but there's an expectation of an immediate response and perhaps immediate decisions. So if you do not stay on the Net, do not stay engaged, you could spend six months undoing the damage—or worse, because you weren't engaged at the pace of the decision making. We have really gotten to the point where we no longer make the time to reflect. I'll go so far as to say this is the single biggest deficit we face to the value of mature senior leadership. This is it: the lack of time to reflect. This is *the* single biggest problem."[6]

Keane continued, "Even when you have the inclination to be more contemplative, if you genuflect to the process, then your mind is not going to be as open as it should be to the contemplative thought, to the kernels of good ideas, to true intellectual dialogue with the thinkers you've brought around you. You're going to wind up doing the listening because you can't get your brain engaged, and they're going to do the thinking."[7]

By the summer of 2006, the Iraq war was not going well. The political situation within the emerging democracy was unstable, and the country had shown little ability to take on the national security challenges they would eventually own. Images were difficult for Americans to consume, as daily car bombings and killings revealed a complex insurgency. The Iraq Study Group, which eventually made a series of recommendations to President Bush about a potential course forward, somberly catalogued the situation in their final report: "Attacks against U.S., Coalition, and Iraqi security forces are persistent and growing. October 2006 was the deadliest month for U.S. forces since January 2005, with 102 Americans killed. Total attacks in October 2006 averaged 180 per day, up from 70 per day in January 2006. Daily attacks against Iraqi security forces in October were more than double the level in January. Attacks against civilians in October were four times higher than in January. Some 3,000 Iraqi civilians are killed every month."[8]

As the war in Iraq commenced, Keane recalled how far America was from understanding the enemy it was fighting: "What were the factors that we're looking at, in terms of Iraq, a culture that is foreign to us? How little we truly knew about it in 2003 even though we were dealing with Saddam Hussein for 12 years. We knew his army. We knew his limitations. But did we know the people? The culture? The mores? You know, when I look back at it, it's extraordinary how little we knew about the enemy."[9] It would not be until 2004 that a true picture of the enemy started to emerge and further solidified in 2005. That picture was one of a complex insurgency the military was fighting with a conventional approach and thinking. If things continued as they were, it was increasingly clear the war would be lost.

Meta-Dialogues

In addition to Sarah Sewall's former role as director of the Carr Center for Human Rights Policy, she was also a former deputy assistant secretary of defense in the Clinton Administration. As we went to war with Iraq in 2003, sarah could not have guessed she would eventually become a key figure in the rethinking of COIN doctrine. Sewall knew General Petraeus through many years of interactions and long before he would take on responsibility for all of Iraq. In November of 2005, Sewall's Human Rights Center cohosted a conference in Washington with the U.S. Army War College around the U.S.'s COIN posture. It was years of relationship building between civilian and military leaders that enabled such an atypical conference to happen; no outcomes were guaranteed but within such settings trust and generative dialogues often emerge. Attendees were a who's-who among experts in COIN. Sewall said, "The question we asked at this conference was different from what you would have seen at a military only event. Our question was: how do you protect the civilian and how is that relevant to your strategic success?"[10] While the conference was off the record, a later summary highlighted that, "participants identified a broad set of problems that have hindered the creation of unity of effort in Iraq. These pose challenges not only for U.S. COIN efforts in Iraq but also the prosecution of comprehensive campaigns against irregular challenges in the future. The first and most important of these is a lack of a real consensus on approach or 'doctrine' when confronting the complexity of an irregular conflict."[11]

Lt.-Colonel Nagl, who had studied COIN for over a decade and even wrote his PhD thesis on it at Oxford, attended the conference and spoke passionately about what he had learned about irregular conflict. The lunchtime speaker on day one of the conference was Petraeus. The general was about to publish a paper on his conclusions and lessons-learned after two tours of duty to Iraq fighting the insurgency. After his prepared remarks, Petraeus fielded questions from conference participants. One asked what the army would do about the outdated COIN doctrine that seemed to be at the root of the problem. Nagl recalled, "Petraeus said to the questioner, 'You are absolutely right, and that's why John Nagl is going to lead the writing of the new COIN field manual.' And that was the first that I had heard of the assignment."[12] Given Nagl's workload and responsibilities at the time, he and his commander concluded he could not be the lead writer but that he would support this unprecedented effort to rewrite the manual as the second lead. Soon after, Petraeus turned to his former classmate from West Point, Dr. Crane, a military historian from the Army War College, to be the lead writer.

Nagl's dissertation on COIN was based on his study of the U.S. response in Vietnam and the British army's struggle with Malaya's insurgents in the years after the Second World War and contained two core ideas that would stand the test of time. First, in order to defeat an insurgency with a conventional army you have to protect the population and second, that army must show the capacity to learn and adapt. The manual would codify these ideas into a new and official doctrine for the military to employ. In the United States military, the creation and evolution of doctrine is extremely important. Nagl wrote, "Doctrine codifies both how the Army thinks about its role in the world and how it accomplishes that role on the battlefield. Doctrine drives decisions on how the Army should be organized (large heavy divisions or small military transition teams to embed in local security forces), what missions it should train to accomplish (conventional combat or COIN, or some balance between those two kinds of warfare), and what equipment it needs (heavy tanks supported by unarmored trucks for a conventional battle field on the front lines, or light armored vehicles to fight an insurgent enemy."[13] Thus, doctrine is the sheet music employed by a commander and his soldiers—until they riff based on the recognition that what they are playing no longer sounds right as the audience and venue has changed.

Following Sarah Sewall's COIN conference in Washington several army colleagues joined Nagl in sketching the outline for a new counter-insurgency manual on the back of a cocktail napkin at the Front Page restaurant and bar in D.C. A few days later, Crane and Nagl met in the Pentagon to further outline the full vision for the document. Sections were to be written around the principles, imperatives, and even the paradoxes of COIN. In December of 2005, Petraeus, then head of the Combined Arms Center at Fort Leavenworth, Kansas, held an initial meeting at his office there, with Crane and Jan Horvath, who had been instrumental in earlier attempts at updating the manual. Petraeus wanted drafts of all major sections ready for a vetting session within 45 days. The war raged on, and he expected rapid and focused think time to produce actionable doctrine. The enemy showed no inclina-tion to stop the insurgency as the attacks continued, and Petraeus was updated daily.

While the army and marines had been immersed in Iraq's COIN, there was no common and agreed-upon solutions to the many prob-lems presented by the insurgents. Soldiers and marines were learning and sharing insights on a small scale, but application of techniques and lessons learned were not codified and adopted. Therefore, the military needed to catch up to what it had learned and observed through thou-sands of engagements with an enemy who reacted quickly and unpre-dictably. Nagl served as operations officer of Task Force 1–34 Armor of the 1st Infantry Division in Khalidyah, Iraq, from 2003 to 2004. He saw firsthand that COIN theory and practice were two very different things. Upon completion of his last tour, his troops gave him a mug he proudly sips tea from. The mug says in bold letters: "Iraq, 2003–4—We were winning when I left." Nagl said, "But we weren't winning and we knew it."[14]

Possessing overwhelming force did not mean we could easily defeat the insurgents. Quite the contrary, sometimes a soldier's violent actions simply awakened more insurgents to the cause while endangering mil-lions of Iraqi civilians. Each day troops were bringing mental models of fighting a war that, when translated into action, often had the oppo-site results. These paradoxical problems vexed many leaders consumed with the fatigue of war. Soldiers and marines needed to show agility in their approach and not assume that one method of warfare would lead to success against an insurgency. For the first time in over 25 years, the COIN doctrine for the United States Army and the Marine Corps needed to be revised. Failure to do so would have dramatic implications for the Iraq war, as well as for future military confrontations. Soldiers and marines awaited the new guidance and adapted with their leadership in the absence of the formal doctrine. Four of the major players involved in the new manual revision, Sewall, Nagl, Crane, and Petraeus, had all written their final thesis papers on some aspects of the lessons of the Vietnam War; 30-year-old insights would resurface and quickly mesh with the painful reality of the war in Iraq.

Time to Think in Leavenworth

The rebuilding of the U.S. Army/Marine Corps Counterinsurgency Field Manual, published in multiple drafts and final version from 2005 to 2007, stands out as an example of the power of reflection in the midst of unrelenting action and the chaos of war. Its creation presents insights into the thoughtful methods and tools that brought forth a sometimes-radical reconsideration of an immediate and complex problem. For example, while U.S. troops had kept their distance from civilian populations at the start of the war, the new doctrine called for them to live and work in towns and cities. The insurgents in Iraq would not stop in their relentless attacks against the U.S. presence, but the U.S. military could create the space for leaders to think through a new doctrine. Both Petraeus and Mattis agreed that while in theater in Iraq, it would have been impossible to rethink the manual. Taking these top soldiers off the battlefield to think and recast policy and strategy runs counter to what so many institutions would do under the strain and uncertainty of challenging times.

Petraeus thought back to his time as the head of doctrine and training for the army and said, "In Fort Leavenworth, Kansas, we reflected and thought it through as we were fostering intellectual and organizational transformation of the Army—which was already well under way. A lot of this was happening in Iraq. I already had two-and-a-third or two-and-a-half years in Iraq at that point in time." He continued, "What we sought to do at Leavenworth was to capture lessons of COIN over time and then put them in a modern context that captures some of the new dynamics of COIN against religious extremists."[15] General

Mattis recalled, "When Petraeus and I decided to do this, we knew we had to distance ourselves from the daily routine. We could not have done it while we were over in Iraq. We could have made an effort, but it would not have been as good. You need time for reflection."[16] Mattis and Petraeus had a deep relationship built through years of service in Washington and then in the first two years of the Iraqi campaign. Conrad Crane noted that, "The creation of the manual resulted from the fortuitous linkage of two soldier-scholars with similar backgrounds and interests who had been forged in the crucible of Iraq to change their respective services, and were given simultaneous assignments where they could make that happen."[17]

When Petraeus took over as head of army doctrine in Leavenworth, it quickly became clear he was going to use the time wisely. In late November 2005, Crane flew out to get guidance directly from Petraeus on his expectations for the rewrite and Crane's role as lead writer. He knew Petraeus was working on an article that would eventually be published in *Military Review*, titled "Learning COIN: Observations from Soldiering in Iraq." Petraeus wanted Crane's insights incorporated into the new manual. Crane told me, "We also discussed the outline for the volume and the makeup of the writing team. It was very apparent to me that Petraeus was going to be an active participant in the creation of the new doctrine, and we soon established a pattern of weekly, and sometimes daily, communications about the manual."[18]

It's important to note that while the think time was happening in Leavenworth, the war in Iraq went on. The enemy would not wait for these moments of reflection as they adapted their strategies through increasingly sophisticated communications channels. It's only because the army and marines have redundancy in their leadership ranks that two tested warriors like Petraeus and Mattis could come out of theater and embrace the moment of reflection. Without redundancy in leadership, the military would be forced to rely on just a few war fighters to lead the organizations amidst simultaneous conflicts around the world. Military leadership training is such that the required skills are abundant among many individuals, and the transfer of leadership can and does happen with frequency. If only a few generals were capable of leading, they would soon burn out amidst the fatigue of war that goes on seven days a week for years. Constant succession planning creates the space to allow two top generals to step away from the fight to rethink old assumptions.

Petraeus carefully considered whom he wanted in the room to vet the initial drafts of the COIN manual. He was fully conscious of the potential for groupthink. He was keenly aware that anything they were about to publish would soon have a worldwide audience, given the role of the Internet. The manual would demonstrate that the military had learned deep lessons from two-plus years in Iraq, and it would continue changing the way the insurgency was fought until the war was won. Crane, whose work prior to his time on the manual had largely been focused on stability operations, said, "Contemplation needs direction, and Petraeus had developed a very clear idea about where he wanted the project to go. He used the *Military Review* article he was working on to focus all the ideas he had been developing over the years, and in Iraq. John Nagl's initial outline of the manual was also important in providing structure, as was my development of principles and imperatives for the project [all which were developed in a fairly short time]. But the key person was Petraeus."[19]

Crane suggested Petraeus call Sewall to gauge her interest in attending a "vetting conference" in early 2006. In Petraeus's mind this was an opportunity to rebuild trust with the human rights community and get feedback from some of the military's most vocal critics. Sewall saw the opportunity for what it was. While she would not write the final content, given that it was an inherently military undertaking, Petraeus offered her and her hand-picked colleagues a seat at a very atypical table. She wanted to show her commitment to the process and even helped the military underwrite the costs of the conference. She recognized the potential for what could happen, considering who was driving the dialogue and the importance of the topic. Sewell explained: "We all had a sense of alternatives that were historically based. It wasn't as if we were trying to describe a new color that didn't exist. We had different angles on what was important, what was missing, and what the blocks were to getting there." She continued, "We had different constituencies and assumptions that we felt needed to be brought in or challenged. For one person to have thought about this would have been limiting, even if the common shared framework about what needed to be changed was similar. In the case of the creation of the manual, many were driving toward the same objective but coming at it with different sensitivities."[20]

Mattis believed in the manual project because he was convinced the right thinkers were contributing to the creation of the content. Like

Petraeus, he knew it would take people with a sense of history to codify the new policy and get it right. After what he had seen in battles in Iraq, he recognized the manual had to get the inputs right in order to convey new ideas to hundreds of thousands of troops. He said, "The problem would have been if we only had people who know infantry, for example—or only know their cockpit, or only know the bridge of their ship—working on the manual. But if they haven't studied war, then I guarantee that they will actually write the wrong manual. And so you need people who have studied the human condition, and have spent as much time reading Mandela or Marcus Aurelius as they have their tactics books." Petraeus assembled people who understood the "human condition" as the lessons of Iraq, and the human toll it had taken were clear in his mind. The manual required fresh thinking from diverse perspectives. Leavenworth could not become a military echo chamber.

In the end, Petraeus organized an unprecedented collection of people to think through the vexing problem of COIN. At the table in Leavenworth were people from backgrounds that included: military (both American and coalition leaders), human rights, diplomacy, intelligence, congressional affairs, military history, academics, anthropology, and also experienced war veterans (including Vietnam). Petraeus also authorized several prominent journalists to attend the conference for background purposes. He knew he was waging an information campaign as much as a doctrinal revamp. "In such a process as the creation of the COIN manual, you want to build constructive intellectual and personal relationships with all you seek to involve. You want to be as inclusive as possible once you get them all together."[21] On the eve of the February 2006 conference, Conrad Crane noted it was Petraeus's goal "to shake things up."[22] With the people he had assembled that winter in Kansas that would not be difficult to do.

At the Table

On day one of the February 2006 vetting conference, Crane sought to get people out of their comfort zones early. Accounts of the meeting revealed that he began his talk by handing out more than a hundred small, hard pieces of green stone with pretty red veins running through them. It was something called "coprolite." These stones resembled the polished ones you might buy at a New Age store in a shopping mall. In fact, Crane had handed them fossilized dinosaur excrement. Then, linking the stones to the work they were about to do, Crane warned that their final work product shouldn't be simply a new polishing of old crap. He had their attention. This was not an exercise that would waste people's time or simply put a gloss on something of no value.[23]

Petraeus insisted the conference be opened with a sobering honest talk from British Brigadier-General Nigel Aylwin-Foster. Our ally and partner in the Iraq war decried American inflexibility and inability to actually do COIN. Petraeus and Sewell sat at the front of the room and participated actively in the debate, Crane recalled. He saw his role primarily as a ringmaster to keep the sessions lively. He also took a lot of notes for future revisions to the manual, and provided summaries of the sessions. The workshop was a whirlwind of conversations that covered a host of topics tied to the chapters in the new manual. From a synopsis of "Mao Zedong's Theory of Protracted War," to supporting economic development of the host nation, it was a dizzying amount of content to review in just a few days of interactions. No one was watching their Blackberries nor checking email incessantly, because the dialogue mattered more than routine issues and never-ending data flows. All were there to think and rethink their core assumptions so the new manual would finally get it right.

Sewall said Petraeus invested himself personally in the conference and this made a big difference in the tone and outcome. She recalled, "General Petraeus's energy was high and he inserted new ideas continuously. He relished the exercise and he embraced contrary views. He set a tone of excitement and enthusiasm."[24] Prework and thinking had been done before the conference; the lead writers for the eight sections of the manual spoke, and the dialogue followed. The conference was recorded so the thousands of comments and ideas would not be lost. Notetakers were positioned throughout the room.

Conference attendees had a sense they were participating in something very different. For example, while the human rights participants were not guaranteed a vote in the final product, they were given a seat at a table that few thought ever possible. Their expertise in the subject matter was clearly on display. Sewall recalled an instance where one of the human rights experts with a deep expertise in COIN pointed out that a speaker had taken a famous quote by the late French COIN guru, David Galula, out of its true context With excitement, Sewall noted, "My colleague explained to the military folks in the room what Galula was actually trying to say through the quote. It was a beautiful moment. It was not a case of human rights advocates acting as interlopers at the confer-ence. It was a case of people who were truly expert and truly value added and they were problem solving right alongside the war fighters."[25]

The conference featured serious discussions on very controversial topics, including a revised section of the manual, focused on ethics. Crane said, "It included a 'ticking time-bomb' scenario discussing the ethical decision-making process concerning extreme interrogation measures to foil catastrophic terrorism. That section sparked consider-able debate. The strong consensus of that group was to eliminate any discussion that seemed to imply acceptance of torture, especially after the revelations from Abu Ghraib prison and the passing of the Detainee Treatment Act." Petraeus listened closely as these dialogues generated new language and insights that married military necessity with a con-stant reminder of the human toll of war.[26]

While Mattis did not attend the February conference, the Marine Corps was well represented and contributed greatly to the manual through a number of writers, including Colonel Douglas King. Mattis would be briefed on the progress and outcomes of the conference, and he remained deeply engaged through dozens of versions of con-tent. General Mattis insisted the marines take the lead on the chapter titled, "Designing COIN Campaigns and Operations." Crane noted this seminal chapter dealt with the "idea that commanders needed to do a systematic analysis of the problems they faced before developing a campaign plan. This was new to Army doctrine, as was the assertion that plans had to be continually adjusted in an iterative process as the situation changed. For the enemy-centric operations of the Cold War, the enemy and related defeat mechanisms were fairly standard and rel-atively easy to identify, but in the complex and murky world of COIN that is not the case." Since the manual was formally adopted, campaign design has become a standard part of all army operational doctrine.[27]

Each author of a chapter gave a presentation before the whole group, followed by someone who was instructed to "brutally critique the draft." Crane would then open the meeting to a general discussion of the ideas presented, while encouraging constructive criticism. He had a significant impact on the flow of the conference dialogue: "I chose who would ask questions and make comments, and frankly tended to avoid those who I thought would tend to stultify or over-dominate discus-sions in favor of more provocative (and shorter) commentators." The conversation moved and the content vetting flowed.[28]

Paradoxical Thinking

A key innovation unveiled in the conference dialogue and final content of the manual was the inclusion of what Conrad Crane describes as the "Paradoxes of COIN." Macmillan's Dictionary defines a "paradoxical statement" as "consisting of two parts that seem to mean the opposite of one another." Thus, when people engage in paradoxical dialogue it implies that participants are capable of holding two competing, and even opposed, thoughts in their mind at the same time. Such conversations quickly reveal there are no simple answers to complex questions, and that old ideas and language may mask real solutions. Teaching troops to think paradoxically would be a lasting legacy of the manual. It would not be easy to change minds, and such techniques would prove lasting and powerful learning tools.

Crane's scholarly friend, Nagl, commented on the use of paradoxes in the creation of the doctrine by saying, "COIN is a paradoxical sport. To succeed in COIN you have to use jujitsu in some ways. You must make your weaknesses your strengths and your strengths your weaknesses." He continued, "Not to get too zenlike about it, but to succeed in COIN you must change your mindset. The paradoxes Conrad introduced were paradigm-shattering for an enormously powerful but conventional-thinking American military."[29]

The paradoxes were in fact partly derived by Crane from Petraeus's widely read *Military Review* article that contained "14 lessons learned" of his time spent in Iraq. Crane recalled it wasn't until the content made its way to final review that there were major changes made to them. "While the writing team for the manual wholeheartedly endorsed the paradoxes, they became very controversial among reviewers of drafts and the published manuscript." The paradoxes are a combination of insights about the use of force, contending with a bias toward action, organizational decision making and never falling in love with one approach to solving a problem. The final list of paradoxes as featured in the COIN manual:

- Sometimes, the more you protect your force, the less secure you may be.
- Sometimes, the more force is used, the less effective it is.
- The more successful the COIN is, the less force can be used and the more risk must be accepted.

- Sometimes doing nothing is the best reaction.
- Some of the best weapons for counterinsurgents do not shoot.
- The host nation doing something tolerably is normally better than us doing it well.
- If a tactic works this week, it might not work next week; if it works in this province, it might not work in the next.
- Tactical success guarantees nothing.
- Many important decisions are not made by generals.[30]

Crane said, "The paradox section of the manual was heavily edited by senior officers as they added many qualifiers to statements they thought were too dogmatic. Yet the intent of the section had always been to provoke thought."[31] Petraeus saw the paradoxes as valuable and much-needed tools that would help to ensure the army and marines didn't oversimplify the complexities of the problem. He recalled, "I changed the paradoxes quite substantively when I took control of the final content. For example, I changed, "The best weapons in COIN do not shoot," to "Some of the best weapons for counterinsurgents do not shoot." I had to remind writing teams that when you're being shot at, the best weapons actually do shoot. In the end, the paradoxes encourage what we seek to foster throughout the manual—critical thought about the conduct of COIN. I think use of paradoxes can be applied to many other studies as a thinking tool."[32]

In Crane's estimation, the conference structure is worthy of reuse by other organizations for a number of reasons. He said, "I think presentations followed by brutal critiques and frank discussion, is well worth copying. We completed the whole project in less than a year, which is light-speed for military doctrine. This proves long contemplation periods are not essential. Gathering a lot of smart people, giving them clear direction with a lot of freedom to develop new solutions, and then reducing the team to a couple key players to make the final product, is the process I would recommend."[33]

Sewall believes the conference and the manual project unveiled a dialogue that should happen so much more often but does not. Most enduring for her is that it was a moment that stands in contrast to the sometimes limiting ways institutions think through and attempt to solve complex problems. She says, "We are now in a world of increasing specialization, where people get narrower and narrower in their viewpoints in order to become more expert and 'useful.' My view is that people become more myopic in how they can think about problems and solutions. We wind up shuttered in our ability to think about possibilities. Therefore, the only way to counteract that is to take specialists and combine them in unexpected ways. Or we must find those rare people that have crossed into different worlds and rely heavily on them as brokers of important dialogues."[34]

After the conference was over, the work was funneled to a core set of writers responsible for final content. Petraeus and Mattis would eventually lose count of the hundreds of iterations of drafts they reviewed. Following the conference, feedback continued to flow into Crane via email as people had a chance to step away from the conference to think once again about what happened. He sent comments on to the chapter writers, and others he adopted for use in his own sections. He recalled, "I read everything, as did General Petraeus, and we both made a lot of changes throughout the manual. Having the varied inputs provided ideas from sources we never would have tapped into through normal processes."[35]

While the manual was rewritten, the Iraq war went on, and innovative soldiers and marines were already employing new tactics. Petraeus and the writing team sought and received feedback from many who were in Iraq and living the war every day. Crane added that, "much of the material in the manual, despite all the theories and ideas of the authors, reflected best practices developed out in the field. We got literally thousands of comments, and read every one. Any project like this must have a way to incorporate the best ideas from throughout the organization."

Evidence of a Learning Organization

The creation of the revised manual would become evidence of the U.S. Army and Marine Corps as learning organizations. In Nagl's book on COIN based on his PhD thesis, "Learning to eat Soup with a Knife," he states that militaries that are capable of learning and adapting prove best prepared to address COIN: "Even under the pressures for change presented by ongoing military conflict, a strong organizational culture can prohibit learning lessons of the present and can prevent the organization's acknowledging its current policies are anything but completely successful."[36] General Petraeus was not going to let this happen with the creation of the manual, and he said, "I decided we needed a new COIN manual before even taking command at Leavenworth in late 2005; there was no question about that. However, I did seek the thoughts of others on it, without ever indicating that I'd taken the position with that decision in mind."[37]

Petraeus now sees the manual as one piece of a related set of changes he has helped introduce into the army. He said "To enact change in a large organization like the U.S. Army, you first have to get the big ideas right and that's things like the field manual and doctrine. For example, secure the population was a huge idea, because previously we were told to hand off control to the Iraqis. So these things weren't idle thoughts. In the letter that I sent to the troops on my first day in command in Iraq, I applied the COIN manual and conveyed that we were going to secure the people. To do that, we had to live among them. We are going to get off the big bases. In fact, we created 77 additional patrol bases, combat outposts, and joint security stations just in multinational division Baghdad area alone that did not exist before we began the surge. This was in the neighborhoods, with the people."[38]

Yet, once the manual was published Petraeus knew its dissemination to troops would not be enough. He was more convinced than ever of Nagl's ideas from decades before Iraq, that the army had to persistently demonstrate it was learning—lest it fall into old models that would prove it irrelevant against a complex insurgency. He said, "There needs to be feedback mechanisms, lessons learned, capturing best practices, worst practices, and everything else. They help you refine the doctrine, adjust your curriculum, change the training center rotations, and change what you are actually doing down range. All this is enabled by how the organization manages its knowledge. The idea is that you want an organization that is constantly learning and adapting. As we put it, "leaders who get it."[39]

Author Thomas Ricks summarized the groundbreaking nature of the manual in his best selling book, *The Gamble*. He also set the context for what was next for Petraeus, who would soon return to the war front now the period of reflection was behind him. Ricks said: "Published at the end of 2006, just 11 months after the meeting at Leavenworth, the new manual had two striking aspects: it was both a devastating critique of the conduct of the Iraq war and an outline of the approach Petraeus might take there if ever given a chance. In political terms, it amounted to a party platform, the party in this case being the dissidents who thought the Army was on a path to defeat in Iraq if it didn't change its approach."[40]

No document like the COIN manual would be complete without criticism from those outside the military. Where possible, Petraeus engaged vocal critics and invited them to Leavenworth to vet their concerns. At times, it was a painful task requiring significant patience. And while the military has shown evidence it is a learning organization through efforts like the manual and the changes ushered in by leaders like Mattis and Petraeus, the political decision makers and civilian agencies remain unsynchronized around the larger questions posed by the manual. Crane notes, "Even an avid supporter of the new doctrine like Sarah Sewall has described it as a 'moon without a planet,' since the interagency capacity and guidance for the U.S. government to properly conduct COIN are so sadly lacking. The process of developing a national capacity for successful COIN should ideally start with a coherent national security strategy that sets out policies and objectives for such conflicts. Then the government should develop the capabilities and procedures for each part of the interagencies to contribute as part of a unified effort."[41]

Authors Greg Jaffe and David Cloud made observations about the manual in their book *The Fourth Star,* saying it "helped the exhausted Army feel as if it had expertise in the type of warfare it was facing in Iraq, and it positioned Petraeus as the most cogent thinker about the deepest strategic and tactical questions the country was facing. Anybody could see he wanted to get back to the war. In his second-floor office at Leavenworth, he would obsessively log on to the classified computer network used by commanders in the war, tracking operations, movements of units, and causalities as they unfolded four thousand miles away."[42] Within just a few months of the publication of the manual, Petraeus left Kansas for Baghdad to lead the effort in Iraq during a time that many have suggested was its lowest point. He came back to the fight in Iraq with a copy of the manual and the lessons from months of reflection seared in his mind.

The manual has been downloaded from the Web millions of times, and pages have even been found in Taliban-inhabited caves in the remote regions of Pakistan. The military open-sourced its thinking, since its nuanced and strategic actions in actual combat never follow every word of the manual. COIN warfare is slow and involves engaging the local population as much as it does overcoming the paradoxical hurdles presented by insurgents. As Petraeus unexpectedly took over as commanding general in Afghanistan in the summer of 2010, he issued revised COIN guidance on how the campaign could achieve the objectives he helped set in motion through the Afghanistan strategy review (described in chapter 3).

After all the think time and reflection embedded in the manual, it comes down to the actions taken by soldiers and marines. Ridding Iraq and Afghanistan of insurgency remains the goal, and ensuring the army and marines remain adaptive is critical. The manual purposely featured an annotated bibliography that writers like Nagl felt was an important symbol. The bibliography's inclusion was an admission they had not thought through everything, and that soldiers and marines needed to do even more reading and thinking.

John Nagl is now head of a major think tank in Washington and serves on the powerful Defense Policy Board, where he shares his lessons in COIN in the context of the Afghanistan campaign. He said, "It's hard to get people to think differently. You still hear soldiers and marines in theater today who say things like "We are killing more of them than they are killing of us, so we're winning." In 2010, we should be beyond that level of understanding of COIN. We still have a ways to go."[43] Thinking back on the extraordinary months he spent working on the manual, Conrad Crane said, "History will judge whether the ideas and concepts we ended up with in the manual were the right ones or not."[44]

Applying the Lessons of the COIN Manual Think Time

The creation and rollout of the COIN manual demonstrate agility and resourcefulness while rethinking a failing strategy. The ideas within the manual were hatched through a confluence of events driven by people with varied skills. Few of us will be faced with the creation of a set of policies and procedures that will impact the lives of millions of people as demonstrated by this manual. Yet, because the stakes were so high and the results were so evident, the creation of the counterinsurgency manual can inform how we think through strategies in our own organizations where the immediacy of the moment often discourages reflective dialogue that can change outcomes. Several insights are revealed:

1. Recognition of failing strategies that require new thinking and energy. When was the last time you allowed the words "this is clearly not working" to be said of a strategy you helped create? Managers and leaders often perceive admitting to failure as a sign of weakness; yet doing so can give rise to resetting a problem through new dialogues. People will forget the failure if new methods built through reflective dialogue prove successful and adaptive to changes in the environment.

2. Use history as a guide, not as the only reality. Even in situations like the military faces in Iraq and Afghanistan, it's clear there is often very little "new under the sun." COIN had been around since humanity has fought wars. The historical lens gives rise to many strategies and lessons learned that can change outcomes. Who in your company represents the reflective thinker capable of framing the challenges of your organization in a historic lens? Would you listen to such a person if they existed? How do you chronicle the history of your firm so an institutional memory emerges that frames the consequential decisions made over time? Does anyone on the leadership team of your division or company have such a role described in their job description? How can you reward this person when they offer the intangible as their work product?

3. Engaged and dedicated senior executives turn moments of reflection into powerful cases for change. Petraeus and Mattis engaged enthusiastically in the creation of the new manual. Their direct involvement was the difference between making the manual as a "me too" exercise or, what it represents, an innovative moment. What is the last document or strategy you can point to as a "product of reflection" built with all parts of the organization and senior-level involvement? If you can't cite one, it may indicate a culture that values immediacy and the short term over reflective and scalable problem solving. As leaders, we must assess the percentage of our time allocated to structured problem solving versus contending with the day-to-day running of our organizations. It's far too easy to be subsumed by the "habits of routine" over thoughtful discourse that leads to informed action.

4. Meta-dialogues help build trust among problem solvers. The COIN manual came together through a series of conversations among

diverse players. The results of attending any one dialogue unrelated to your immediate business needs may not be clear or "self-evident" as a good use of time. While the content may not be immediately applicable, the relationships you build through years of atypical discussions may prove beneficial when and if you need to engage atypical thinkers. When things go wrong and new thinking is required, how would you engage outsiders as Petraeus did? What formal and informal channels have you created should you need to completely reconsider the future of key strategies and policies?

5. Finding evidence of a "learning organization" capable of adapting. The manual has come to symbolize that the military is modernizing and becoming a "learning organization" in contrast to what happened to it in the Vietnam War. What is the evidence your organization is learning and adapting? If it wasn't learning, how would you even detect it wasn't?

6. Management through paradoxes. The introduction of the paradox method presents a relevant tool for thinking through very complex problems. It forces thinking simultaneously across two conflicting ideas that have no easy reconciliation. People who think like this show agility and the ability to manage amidst ambiguity—which is the hallmark of the many interwoven and global problems leaders are faced with today. Yet, the business world presents us with paradoxes each day, paradoxes we often explain away too simply. Paradoxical problem-solving frames balanced views into difficult problems. It consistently pushes people out of their intellectual comfort zones so think time is rich and yields meaning. It also acknowledges that there are some things that can't be easily answered but must be monitored and revisited over time.

7. Atypical players invited to atypical tables. As leaders you have to be willing to allow voices to the table to overcome the "siloed" thinking that can permeate organizations. In addition, you must recognize when there is an opportunity at least to "be at the table," even if you will not have a deciding vote. In the end, it's who contributes to the moment of think time that matters much more than the amount of time that is given to thinking through a problem. Embracing diverse perspectives during reflective dialogues ensures that strategies are not born inside an echo chamber with few divergent viewpoints represented.

8

Outside the Day-to-Day

From Radical Sabbaticals to Unleashing Reflective Capacity

I often ask people about their vacations. It's an illuminating question in terms of picking up on narratives about how that person relates to both work and home. I once attended a luncheon during the early days of summer where two executives from different companies were engaged in a conversation about work and vacation. The companies they worked for were very large and while both were senior, neither was in the top position. These executives did not work for companies that competed against each other, so I assumed it was an honest and frank exchange between old friends. In between multiple checks of their Blackberries, with little eye contact, the male executive said: "Are you thinking about taking any time off this summer?" The female executive shook her head and said, "No. There's just too much going on. We might take a few days off in August when everyone else is out of town, but there's just a lot happening and I really have to be here. I have been putting in a ton of hours." The man said, "Yeah we have a bunch of deals about to hit and its all hands on deck. I just can't see breaking away. I don't think we're going to take any time off." Topics then turned to other matters. In less than one minute of conversation a lot was actually revealed.

The narrative above probably sounds familiar. The dialogue between these executives never put vacation on an equal level with work. Far from it, actually, as both had quickly dismissed it. As I came away from the lunch I thought more about what was really going on, and two thoughts emerged. First, both executives projected a need to be connected to what was happening, with an underlying fear they "would miss something." Second, both had linked their physical presence at work with "things happening." In other words, if they were not there, things would not get done. This implied a sense of their own self-importance as related to the nature of work before them and their companies. Both worked for companies with hundreds, if not thousands, of employees, where an individual's contribution sits within a much larger context. No one person is the "only human" capable of taking on the work that comes in. Yet, these people were pushing themselves with no break in sight.

Researchers Louis W. Fry and Melanie P. Cohen have studied the effects of—and longer-term remedies for—companies with what are described as "extended work hour cultures." They noted in the *Journal of Business Ethics* that, "a half century ago, social scientists predicted that technology would allow employees to enjoy a 15-hour workweek at full pay by 2030. So far, this prediction appears far from coming true. Today's reality is that workers, worldwide, face increasing demands to work extended hours, and consequently experience considerable work overload—working more hours and more intensely during those hours than they can reasonably cope with." These researchers postulate that the reasons why people are working more can be divided into one of three categories. "One explanation is that the combined effects of technology and globalization are forcing people to work longer and harder because of email, wireless access, and the fact that globalized businesses never close. Another explanation is that people are caught up in consumerism: wanting to buy more goods and services, which requires more income earned through longer work hours. A third reason, called the 'ideal worker norm,' is that professionals expect themselves and others to work longer hours. Toiling away far beyond the normal work week is viewed as a badge of honor—a symbol of their superhuman capacity and superior performance."[1]

As we have seen throughout, think time and reflection can happen within an organization, but only through structure and explicit commitments. Yet the time away from our jobs also feeds our need to think and reflect. In fact, companies allocate time back to employees as a "benefit" in the form of vacation and paid or unpaid leave. This is time people can spend thinking and reflecting about what they choose to and not what they are told to focus on. Yet, in many ways, technology has removed that separation, as "working hours" are never contained in a neat box.

Rather, work presents itself at any time, in any place, provided that data is allowed to reach the employee. We are attached to work, and work is forever attached to us. Rakesh Khurana of Harvard Business School told me, "Sometimes technological choices made by managers have not been made in the interest of efficiency, but in the interest of enhancing managerial control. The decisions are sometimes about the manager keeping power, dominance, and subordinates in place more than they are about improving the effectiveness of the organization. I think that in some ways it's a kind of soft control." He continued, "At one level we can say, 'now you are liberated from the confines of your office,' but now technology penetrates into every aspect of your life. You are always on call 24/7. It has dissolved the boundary between the organization and the person."[2]

Nothing symbolizes the dissolution of the boundary between the organization and the individual as much as email. Use of email provides unprecedented coordination of the flow of data among parties and allows for collaboration. Yet, the never-ending flow of email feeds the need for millions of people to constantly monitor and respond to matters that others perceive as urgent. Anyone at any time can declare urgency. This means that vacations can be expected to be interrupted and time away from the job with one's family, or alone, can be trumped by urgency. With no rules defined for the use of email, the blurring of home and work now sits in a hazy and unspoken nether land. Email is loved and loathed, depending on what you are working on and when you declare that you are off—if in fact you even make that distinction.

Beyond the constancy of technology, economic anxiety because of a floundering economy has forced people to cling to jobs and take on more and more responsibility. We see examples of employees hoarding their vacation time so they would be perceived to be eager to contribute, and companies cutting vacation benefits almost reflexively to manage costs and increase productivity. Over two-plus years of a protracted recession and an anemic recovery, this tempo has had an impact on people. Stress in the workplace is at an all-time high. Psychologist John Medina summarizes the impacts of stress in his powerful book, *Brain Rules*. He says, "Stress attacks the immune system, increasing employees' chances of getting sick. Stress elevates blood pressure, increasing the risk of heart attack, stroke, and autoimmune diseases. That directly affects health care and pension costs. Stress is behind more than half the 550 million working days lost each year because of absenteeism."

He goes on to say that there are two key "malignant" facts that make up occupational stress: "a) a great deal is expected of you and b) you have no control over whether you will perform well." He concludes that it "sounds like a formula for learned helplessness."[3]

There is also the stress that has come with the rounds of layoffs over the last two years. More than seven million people have lost their jobs, and millions more are underemployed, meaning their employer can't afford to hire them on a full-time basis even though they would prefer full-time work. Another factor for employers to consider is what is truly on the minds of their employees as the economy stabilizes and even grows over the next several years. If consistent growth comes, it will be the first opportunity in a long while for many to leave their current jobs. A study by CareerBuilder and Robert Half International concluded that 45 percent of workers reported they planned to seek a new employer, career, or industry when the economy revives. This suggests a complicated time period for managing people, as companies must give employees clear and compelling reasons to stay.[4]

Think time and reflection forced through a firing can be a scary, but even liberating, experience. The Associated Press recently highlighted the story of a global operations consultant, Agatha Melvin, who had been out of work for nearly 18 months. She was looking at the rest of her career through a very different lens based on her experience. She thinks much more about whether the work she takes on for the rest of her career will satisfy her enough to even justify the hours she puts in. In what she calls the "pressurized environment" of finance where she was working 15-hour days, she had little time to think at all and rarely made time to envision her future. Agatha claims to have a different perspective on what is important to her, as she has drained her savings to survive the downturn. She says, "Time is a commodity you can never get back."[5] Such thinking poses many questions for employers to consider, including: how many millions more workers have come to the same conclusion as Agatha? What are the short- and long-term implications of managing people who have such a transformed outlook on life? We will not know for a while how many people used the forced separation from work as a time to rethink their whole careers, but the impacts of this economic reset are likely to be profound.

Beyond the stress and rethinking of careers forced by the economic reset, it's likely there will be even more changes for businesses under way as loyalty is trending downward. The Center for Work-Life Policy, which studies and consults on trends shaping workforce management, noted in a survey that the proportion of employees who pledged loyalty to their employers fell from 95 percent to 39 percent between June 2007 and December 2008. While employees have been asked to hunker down and take on more and more work, a day of reckoning may be ahead as the *Economist* points out: "In the longer term workers can take comfort from the fact that history may long be on their side: in the rich world, low birth rates, an impending surge in retirements and caps on immigration could reduce the number of people of working age by 20 to 40 percent. Today's unhappy workers may one day be able to exercise the ultimate revenge, by taking their services elsewhere."[6]

Given the changes underway in working models, consultants Barbra and Elizabeth Pagano see sabbaticals fitting into new corporate mindsets that don't ignore the larger trends that are happening. As the lines between "work" and "life" are increasingly blurred, they see the use of an employee's time away from the firm as a new type of "currency." In addition, they note that retirement is becoming less of an "event" and more of a "process" that people experience. They conclude: "People are working longer and yet still yearn for a large enough chunk of time to go and do something that's important to them. Sabbaticals fit perfectly in this new mindset. We're a few years behind European countries when it comes to the concept of sabbaticals, but we're well on our way. Companies understand that attracting and retaining top talent now requires a holistic approach."[7]

The Benefits of Some Real Time Off

Sabbaticals are periods of leave from an organization, ranging from weeks to months. They are granted to employees based on policies unique to each company. Sabbaticals have taken many forms since they arose inside academia in the nineteenth century. Harvard University was the first to formally grant sabbaticals to its educators. Today, 19 of *Fortune Magazine*'s "Top 100 Companies to Work for" have some form of sabbaticals offered as a benefit. The sabbatical is often tied to tenure and to one's performance within the organization. Some are paid and some are unpaid. During this time, after the economic reset, sabbaticals may seem like a cost firms simply can't afford. Yet companies like General Mills have actually introduced the benefit to reward those who have served effectively and loyally during a time of profound economic uncertainty.

Through their company, YourSABBATICAL.com, Barbra and Elizabeth Pagano, advise for-profit and not-for-profit organizations on how to structure time off so that both the employee and employer benefit. They note that a lack of definition around a benefit such a sabbatical can quickly lead to it being a fad with no staying power. Yet, they conclude that the companies that have built it into a powerful benefit have at least four aspects. First, the program must have unambiguous objectives that define why the company is doing it. Second, top management must sustain and support it. Third, the sabbatical program must have a well-crafted policy, and fourth it must have structured support and clearly defined communications. As we have seen, think time and reflection without a supporting architecture tends to be less valuable to the individual and the organization—even when it's given as free benefit to the employee.

Since technology follows employees everywhere, the Paganos caution against such connections with the company during the sabbatical. They say, "People are numb from all the technology, the 'doing' and the 'busyness.' A sabbatical is a disconnection from all of that. You may have your laptop and PDA with you while on vacation, but a sabbatical should be different. Some companies with sabbatical programs realize this and have a 'no contact' policy while a person is away on sabbatical. The sabbatical-goer benefits from disconnecting by having space to think and reflect and recharge. And the sabbatical-goer's work coverage team grows because they have to figure things out on their own."[8]

YourSABBATICAL.com's research reveals a compelling list of benefits that companies derive from having sabbatical programs, including:

- Talent is measured and leaders are developed. When a person goes away on sabbatical, it puts their previous work into a context that reveals needs and gaps within their teams.
- Succession planning occurs. The forced time off means that those in waiting must "step up" and have their work take on new significance. People can actually take on a "stretch role" for a short period of time.
- Cultures of collaboration and trust are built. While employees are away teams develop new approaches that may not have existed before and may continue once the person comes back.
- Opportunity to live their stated core values. Companies with stated values linked to such time off get the chance to "walk the talk."

- Customers actually love it. Evidence suggests that people like to buy from companies that nurture their employees in such a holistic way.
- A company's brand is strengthened. A sabbatical program can be a strong indicator that a company is a "great place to work," thus helping attract and retain top people.
- A boost for employee engagement. Sabbaticals allow for the integration of personal goals (desire for time away from work) and corporate sustainability. Highly engaged employees outperform their disengaged colleagues by 20 to 28 percent.

The physical and emotional detachment that comes from "unplugging" from a company, even for a few weeks, frees people to think and reflect upon every aspect of their work and personal lives. As people are increasingly "burned out" from the stress and uncertainly of the economic reset, it's too simplistic to just return to basic vacation policies, doing little to introduce meaningful distinctions between home and work. When the workday rarely ends, given technology's ability to engage employees any time and anywhere, sabbaticals offer a refreshing moment to simply pause. Sabbaticals lead to people stepping back to see their work and creativity through a different lens. The "breaks" described below imply that something deeper is happening when one is allowed to detach from the incessant nature of work. We discover that individuals benefit from time away, but so does the employer; sometimes the employer can even structure what looks like a sabbatical in order to launch big and distinctive ideas.

As the economy stabilizes and the pressure and stress of work and life change, employers must consider how sabbaticals can lead to new outcomes for employees and the company. Three diverse examples emerge to highlight the costs, and unlikely benefits, derived from sabbaticals and structured time away from the day-to-day workload. The world's largest restaurant chain, a top New York designer, and managers from a retail technology chain reveal there is no one-size-fits-all approach when it comes to sabbaticals and paid time away from normal routines and demands.

Bragging Rights at the Golden Arches

Founded in 1955, McDonald's Corporation is one of the world's largest restaurant companies, with more than 32,000 stores in

117 countries—and counting. The scope of the company is staggering. Every day, 60 million people have a meal at McDonald's. The *Economist* magazine has even created an informal currency index to measure the relative purchasing power across countries over the sale of a single "Big Mac." A fast-food restaurant like McDonald's appears to be an odd place to go in search of reflection considering the fast pace of their services. Yet, their dedication to long-serving employees through their sabbatical program stands out.

Now in his seventh year with McDonald's, Richard Floersch is the Global Chief Human Resources Officer, whose job ranges from setting compensation policy to developing talent among the nearly 500,000 employees. Floersch is in the office by 7:00 a.m. and asks his assistant not to book meetings until 8:30 a.m. During this uninterrupted time, he maps out the day and the rest of the workweek, steps back to discover patterns that are emerging within the business, and thinks about key critical projects, meetings, and big decisions that are upcoming.[9]

As the head of human resources, Floersch is often on long flights across the Atlantic or en route to Asia. There is high scrutiny of a job at the senior levels of any organization, and when you are in a senior executive role of a publicly traded company it is difficult to find the time to be alone to reflect. Floersch says, "At my level, people watch every single thing that you are doing. Where you spend your time and whom you meet with sends out important signals about what is important to you." For him, the many flights he must take are his chance to close the computer and simply think and get energized about what the company is taking on. He said, "Plane rides are always a great opportunity for me to reflect. I come off of those flights with clearer thinking about what I ought to be doing. It's just a wonderful opportunity to get out of the clutter."[10]

Since 1978, McDonald's has had a policy of granting sabbaticals to managers based on years of service to the company. Their sabbatical program allows eligible employees (including restaurant managers) to take a paid eight-week sabbatical for every ten years of service with the company. Eligible staff includes full-time corporate employees, restaurant management, certified swing managers, and primary maintenance employees. Employees can actually add their annual vacation allowance to the eight weeks for a total of three months off if they choose. Floersch says, "It's an outstanding benefit. It's a differentiator. Only 2 to 3 percent of companies provide paid time off for sabbaticals, and we do not put any restrictions at all on it. Whatever you want to do. Some companies say that they want you to go out and learn the next way to look at some R&D project, for example. For us, it's totally open ended." Since the program's inception, tens of thousands of McDonald's employees have gone on sabbatical and hundreds more qualify each year.[11]

The benefits to employees from sabbatical time include freedom from the controls imposed on the workday and the ability to direct their time to think and act on whatever they choose. McDonald's does not expect employees to report back in during their time off. Before he worked at McDonald's, Floersch was at a company that didn't offer the benefit. He now marvels at the stories people have shared with him. Employees have volunteered their sabbatical time in moments of national crisis, like the Katrina Hurricane, and others have set such goals as to climb Mount Kilimanjaro. "I have seen people the day before they leave, and I have seen the same people on the first day they come back. They are energized about going on sabbatical, and they are re-energized about coming back to work at McDonald's. They have had a great opportunity to clear their head. If you think about it, we are all trying to balance everything. Here is a wonderful opportunity for eight to twelve weeks to be able to say, 'What do you want to do with *your* time?'"

The benefits to McDonald's of the sabbatical program are threefold. First, employees take time to think and reflect about what is important to them, thus promoting a positive relationship between employee and employer. Second, McDonald's is also conscious of the nature of conversations employees have when answering the question, "So what company do you work for?" As employees discuss the sabbatical policy, people are often surprised by the benefit. Floersch notes: "We want people to have bragging rights for why they work at McDonald's. Sabbaticals create a bragging right." Finally, the sabbatical employee's absence creates a moment for others to step into new roles on a trial basis. Within the eight- to twelve-week period, others take on and learn their work. Floersch says, "It's a great opportunity to see someone rise to the occasion. It gives them great confidence to be able to do that job. It gives you a peek at some talent that you may not have known existed before."[12]

Tara Handy is a senior manager with McDonald's, working in their communications department. In 2009, she was put into one of the "step-up" situations that Floersch describes above. The company's vice president of corporate communications, Walt Riker, announced his sabbatical timeframe and gave Handy the unprecedented opportunity to step up and act as the emcee for the annual shareholders meeting. This high-stakes and unpredictable meeting entails working with dozens of news outlets like Bloomberg, Reuters, Chicago Tribune, Associated Press, and the Wall Street Journal. Handy would speak in front of thousands of shareholders as well as work directly with the most senior leaders of the company as the meeting evolved. While Riker ultimately wound up attending the meeting because his timeframe for sabbatical shifted, he did not want to deny Handy the opportunity to lead. The meeting went well—no major difficulties and good press coverage for the company. Handy shared with me that, "This was a tremendous opportunity to prove to myself and others that I could do the meeting and Walt was able to witness it." She continued, "I liken the experience to a dad standing on the sidelines at a child's baseball game. I knew I did well."[13]

It's intuitive for McDonald's to think about letting people step up on a temporary basis, as the company's grounded in another reflective internal business process: McDonald's leaders spend a significant amount of time thinking through succession planning across all levels of the organization. This entails managers meeting to analyze and talk about the bench strength of their people and who is capable of filling new roles, whether it's a normal job opening or an employee on leave. Floersch used his own job as an example: "Let's say that my job opens up over time. There are probably eight or nine people at this company that can do my job. But, right now, there are probably one to two people that have the capacity to do it as good, if not better than me. Whenever we think about filling a job at McDonald's, we use that criterion: Is the candidate pool going to be as good, if not better than the incumbent? If every time that you fill a job you meet those criteria, your organizational capabilities are improving over time. When someone moves on to another role at McDonald's, we have got to make sure that that person coming in behind them is going to be strong, if not stronger than that person. That's how you keep getting better."[14]

In 2007, McDonald's faced new accounting rules that could have threatened the continuation of the sabbatical program. Floersch thought to himself, if McDonald's was in the 2 to 3 percent of companies granting sabbaticals, then would they be willing to continue with a benefit that 97 to 98 percent of companies don't even offer? Instead, he was never called to a single conversation with McDonald's finance department or senior management about the viability of the program. "Sabbaticals are a part of our culture now. It will be one of the last things standing," he said.

"Sameness Is Overrated"

Stefan Sagmeister runs a very successful design studio in New York and has created iconic imagery for CD covers for musicians like the Rolling Stones and Lou Reed. He also develops design identities for businesses and product packaging for high-end consumer product companies. He attacks each client's problem in a different way so that he retains originality. Sagmeister told me, "Strategies to solve a problem vary, as one might expect, with the problem. We go about designing a CD cover differently than when we create an identity system. For the former, I meet with the musicians, talk about why they recorded a new album, where the music came from, influences on the sound, etc. Then we listen constantly to the album (at that point only available as rough cuts)." He continued, "For the latter, we look at the company and its competitors, and talk with the leadership and employees. Then I might forget about all that information and try to start working from a completely unrelated starting point to ensure that I don't design something that everybody else also thought of."[15]

In order to maintain a fresh perspective on design, Sagmeister has adopted a very different approach to thinking about work and his eventual retirement. He told a packed audience at the Technology, Entertainment and Design (TED) conference that every seven years he closes his company for a full year in order to pursue "some little experiments, things that are always difficult to accomplish during the regular working year." He continued: "In that year we are not available for any of our clients. We are totally closed. And as you can imagine, it is a lovely and very energetic time." Sagmeister sets a different context for how he looks at his career. He stands the notion of retirement on its head. "We spend about the first 25 years of our lives learning. Then there's another 40 years that's really reserved for working. And then tacked on at the end of it are about 15 years for retirement. And I thought it might be helpful to basically cut off five of those retirement years and intersperse them in between those working years."[16]

The diagram below depicts what he does.

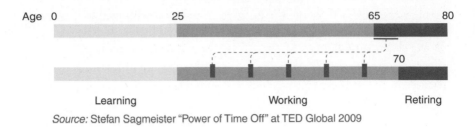

Source: Stefan Sagmeister "Power of Time Off" at TED Global 2009

Sagmeister shared with me that the mechanics of taking a year off every seven years, when you are at the top of your professional game, are somewhat complicated. Can you imagine actually shutting your company down and running the risk of losing clients in order to take a full year off? Can you imagine enabling your employees to stay behind and even launch their own company in your absence?

Here is how Sagmeister actually does it. He messages all his clients three years in advance of the year-long sabbatical. As he nears the day before he begins the year-long sabbatical, his goal is to have ensured that no project or client is left hanging. As far as his employees are concerned, it was different for the two sabbatical years he has taken. He notes, "At the beginning of the first client-free year, designer Hjalti Karlsson (who worked with me at that time) opened his own studio with Jan Wilker, who was a design intern with us. They are now running a successful design studio and we are still good friends. During the second year, another designer, Joe Shouldice actually stayed in the New York office and kept a low-level profile, finishing up some jobs. But we did not take on any new work."[17] Sagmeister means it when he says that he walks away from work, as he revealed that the Obama campaign asked him to design a poster for the then-senator's presidential campaign. He declined their request.[18]

While design remains his passion, Sagmeister noticed throughout many years of work that what he was creating for clients started to look the same and that he was increasingly bored by some of his assignments. He benchmarked the time spent on sabbaticals based on interspersing them every seven years. He thought about how companies like Google and 3M give their employees 15 to 20 percent of their workweeks to focus on what the employee wants. He concluded that a one-year sabbatical taken every seven years across 40 years of work amounts to only 12.5 percent of his total career time.[19]

To derive the most benefit, he advises that one be prepared for, and structure, the time off. Looking back at his first sabbatical, he recalls that the first part of the year off was "rather disastrous." He told the TED conference that without a plan he discovered he was wasting time. He was determined not to squander the time and so immediately added structure. He recalls, "I very quickly made a list of the things I was interested in, put them in a hierarchy, divided them into chunks of time and then made a plan, very much like in grade school." Reflecting back on his first year off he concludes, "What came out of it? I really got close to design again. I had fun."[20] Sagmeister believes the work he did for clients upon his return was dramatically improved and possessed higher quality, such that he was able to command higher prices, thus recapturing much of what was lost financially.

For others thinking of emulating his approach, he advises that the length of time off is not as important as planning out that time and sticking with what is important to the individual. Fully aware that few people will follow his model, he notes that his approach can even happen on a microlevel. He told me, "Somebody who works 40 hours a week could plan two two-hour sessions per week where she pursues her own interests and tries out new things."[21]

The greatest benefit Sagmeister sees to the sabbatical is that after 20 years in business he is not burned out and still loves design. He also concludes that the work he takes on after he returns from the sabbatical is at a higher level of quality and differentiated. While some people value work products that are the same and are repeatable, Sagmeister finds that uninspiring. He says, "Most importantly, everything we've done in the years following the first sabbatical year came out of thinking derived during that time off. One of the strands of thinking I was involved in was that 'sameness is so incredibly overrated.' This whole idea that everything needs to be exactly the same, works for very few companies."[22]

At the root of executing such a radical departure from the "always-on" work life is the courage to follow through on his vision. Sagmeister readily admits he was fearful of losing clients and even of being forgotten, but all the fears proved untrue.[23] After his talk at the TED Conference, he recalled that many people came up to him and said he had inspired them and that they would emulate his model. Skeptical that many would take up his example, he shared with me that the responses became rather boring. He said, jokingly, "If half of them actually go on sabbatical, the GDP of the country is going to go down." I then shared the statistics on how few companies even offer sabbaticals, and he was surprised the number was as high as 3 percent. He said, "Trying to do something like taking a year off every seven years requires guts. Most companies are just not gutsy."[24]

Of Reflective Capacity and Think-or-Die Projects

Imagine you are a top performer and have a hunch for a new business venture that might be a moneymaker. In fact, you have never built a business before and don't quite know where to start. Your idea has merit, but the immediacy of day-to-day needs precludes you from ever getting the time away to prove the concept and so something about your idea. Some companies allow employees the space to rapidly explore new ideas relevant to the employee and the company. While its not a sabbatical in the traditional sense, it is paid time off where the employee has the ability to think within a very different setting.

Electronics retailer Best Buy already had success following the launch of their in-store "Geek Squad" technology services team, so they wanted to find new ways to innovate and create new businesses. Best Buy engaged John Wolpert, a veteran of IBM's Extreme Blue incubator to work with several chosen employees in a unique ten-week session. If these businesses had merit, Wolpert would teach Best Buy employees what questions they had to ask and how to quickly prove to upper management that it was a viable concept worthy of investment. "Companies are challenged to maintain reflective capacity into the really hard times,"[25] Wolpert asserts. Yet, at the beginning of the financial crisis, Best Buy still went forward with the pilot to determine if ideas from their employees could live as new and viable businesses.

Wolpert explained to me, "Just like Extreme Blue at IBM, what we learned is that to bring out that reflective capacity in people you must have them live together. For Best Buy, we secured apartments in Hollywood, California, at a large housing complex. For ten weeks the employees chosen to participate had to be committed to living their idea and seeing if the concept made real business sense. The physical space was modest, as it wasn't a vacation away from work. It was time away from the day-to-day that would actually move at a pace even faster than the normal work day."[26]

One of the ideas that surfaced through Wolpert's facilitation process came from an employee who thought Best Buy should start a new design and Website service called Best Buy Studio. Jeremy Sevush was the employee who hatched the Best Buy Studio idea. Wolpert immersed himself in a West Hollywood store, where Sevush worked. The consultant and business advisor interacted with customers and got a feel for Sevush's work style during the course of a normal workday. Wolpert recalled Sevush had "half of a business plan in his pocket for two years and didn't know what to do with it."

Sevush approached Wolpert on the retail shop floor and said, "I heard that you can help me start a business." Wolpert explained to me, "To be totally honest, I wasn't too sure about the idea, but I got to know him and I believed in his ability to do something to make it come to life." Wolpert then went to his "virtual boss" at Best Buy (as he was still a consultant) and shared the idea as well as his intuition about Sevush's overall potential. In less than two weeks, Best Buy decided to back Sevush and allow him to be joined by two more junior people in the company to work with Wolpert in animating the Web studio concept. The only way to find out if the idea had potential was to think it through within a framework and allow the individual to rise to the moment; that could not happen while Sevush was selling flat screen televisions at his local store. Wolpert told me, "Whatever happened, even if the idea had no merit, Jeremy was going to be better off for it at the end of ten weeks." Wolpert believes in focusing attention on developing the person behind the idea versus getting lost in the fog of sometimes-endless debate around the relative merits of an idea.[27]

The employees then went through the process of designing a detailed business case with Wolpert driving daily conversations and interactions. The days were long and the pace rapid. A set of mentors supplied by Best Buy watches over the outcomes from the time spent outside normal retail business. The conversations focused on asking and then answering tough questions that forced the team to prove the merits of the idea without asking Best Buy for outrageous amounts of start-up money. Best Buy's senior management told Wolpert the business case had to provide evidence the Web site concept was thought through. Questions included: Who are the target customers? How quickly can this generate positive cash flow? Who are our competitors? What assets does Best Buy have that can be reused in support of this initiative? Within the ten weeks, the team built out small-scope "proofs of concept" for the Web business in order to overcome technical objections that it could be a viable business for the product retailer.[28]

Wolpert was paid by Best Buy to coordinate the whole exercise, including securing the physical space for the teams. While participants were actively encouraged to reflect on what happened within any given day, the pace was rapid and more reminiscent of a start-up. Wolpert told me, "With only ten weeks to build a real business, you don't have a lot of time to think and yet oddly it is all about think time. It's about exploration and rapid experimentation. It's about refactoring, throwing away, and then starting again. Think time happens organically. You think or die."[29]

In the case of the Best Buy Studio, the idea had more merit than Wolpert had imagined. The team overcame many objections and difficult questions and the project was brought to life in a half dozen stores in California. Wolpert reports the project is already generating positive cash flows and Sevush is now charged with managing its future growth. Reflecting back on his experience, living away from his family and animating his idea for ten weeks, Sevush recalled the impact of the community atmosphere and its ability to drive innovation through teambuilding. He said, "You learn very, very quickly what would take two or three weeks of meetings; trying to gauge each other and figure out where you can step and not step. That happens in the first two hours as soon as someone is putting their stuff in the bathroom and you say 'Hey, hey...this is my space! Team building happens immediately.'"[30]

Conclusions and Applying Ideas

As demonstrated by the diverse examples above, sabbaticals and time away from the day-to-day routine are evolving. Such time away reinforces meaningful distinctions between home and work that are now permanently intertwined. It also demonstrates that the company takes a holistic approach to how it interacts with employees. Think time and refection can become a benefit given back to employees for their own use or structured to hatch an idea important to them. Using sabbaticals or structured time off implies many things for companies to consider beyond the obvious costs of such programs.

1. The economic reset has forced millions into moments of involuntary time off. As the economy recovers it's unlikely these

employees will look at their jobs and careers in the same way. New mental models are embedded within them based on the forced time off. Employers must discover what this is and realize the narratives that have been planted—oftentimes with a negative edge. Companies must ask themselves how they can engage in an open dialogue about the forced time off and not look at it as a stigma for the employee—given the absence of a job. This forced time off involved thousands of hours of think time that has likely altered the employee's time horizons for retirement and also the overall work ethic. What new models of work time and down time can be developed to address the human side of the economic reset? Ignoring this issue will likely come at a cost in terms of productivity and long-term employee morale.

2. We are now emerging from one of the most shocking and stressful times ever experienced by American workers. Their responsibilities and productivity has been unprecedented but not sustainable. How many of these people need real time away from the company to simply recapture a meaningful distinction between home and work? How many have envisioned new ideas for companies they want to start—away from the ones they were forced to cling to during the downturn. As Best Buy did by nurturing ideas with its employees, leaders should consider stepping back from the flow of day-to-day and engage in dialogues that push new ideas to the surface—the ideas that match the mission should be elevated to a new platform.

3. Sabbaticals are a benefit that, at first glance, imply just costs. Yet, the benefits to the employee and within the company can be significant. The impacts of the unrelenting pace on workers result in vacation and downtime being undervalued, as one's "busyness" implies one's relevance. Researchers like Oriel Sullivan suggest that being busy is also linked to social status.[31] Employers must redefine a narrative that correlates busyness to one's actual value and worth to the company. As does McDonald's, the sabbatical policy allows loyal and hard-working employees to use time outside the firm to pursue what they want—and in the process they think in a new way about their relationship to the company.

4. Taking a sabbatical implies much more than time off for an employee. The structure of that time matters as much as does having the time itself. Within weeks and months, employees can

be exposed to new places and experiences that disrupt the patterns of thinking that have built up within the frenzy of day-to-day activities. New reference models can create new dialogues within teams where creativity has become stale. Companies must structure, not only the policy on sabbaticals, but even the experience for the employees themselves. As Sagmeister teaches us, downtime for people who have never experienced it can result in wasted time. Downtime should be directed, and its outcomes become clear to the individual.

5. Time away from the company can also be powerfully directed at creating new ideas that can positively alter the company's cash flows. It can also allow an employer to take a high-potential employee and give him or her the intellectual freedom to explore what they are capable of, likely going well beyond what has been observed in their daily work. Top performers yearning to demonstrate their value will find themselves newly engaged, as the Best Buy examples demonstrate. (Ideas hatched in the minds of employees may require an outside facilitator to get their initial definition.) This time away from the daily routine represents the atypical application of the "no-break" and "always-on" mindset, and can differentiate the companies that pursue it. It can also help grow individuals professionally—even faster than they thought possible.

9

Reflection and Extreme Situations

From Commander's Intent to Finding the Middle Ground

Reflection is often thought of as a luxury afforded only under circumstances where time is plentiful and immediacy is at bay. Yet, I have discovered it exists inside situations and settings involving crisis, conflict, and entrenched parties. With the speed of markets and the global movement of information, organizations find themselves in circumstances that rapidly deteriorate and seemingly remove moments for true reflection. Leaders will always face instantaneous decision making involving poorly understood tradeoffs. However, when we go inside the three very pressure-filled and consequential situations described below, we quickly discover methods for embracing reflection employed by resourceful people. From the night before the invasion of Iraq, to the near-eruption of gang violence in Chicago, leaders are finding novel ways to help others rethink their assumptions and maintain their composure while facing unimaginable circumstances. Reflection plays a critical role.

As you read these three seemingly detached stories, consider that there are a few core things happening. You will discover that emotion, fear, and vitriol rapidly steal away our ability to think clearly. As we have seen in other chapters, think time and reflection play critical roles in generating real dialogue and ensuring a balanced analysis of problems; but that's nearly impossible in the presence of fear and angst. Reflection must be deliberately referenced within such settings in order for new insights and outcomes to emerge. With all the uncertainty and continuing shocks to stability the world is experiencing, leaders must use innovative methods like those below to get the most entrenched and irrational to come back to the table. What you will discover is that when people are at a dangerous extreme, breakthroughs can emerge that pull them back as the problem is reframed and sometimes resolved. You will see that epiphanies can sometimes occur, but they only do so when fear and uncertainty give way to the possibilities of a new path forward. In all the examples below, leaders are saying: "Think with me." Think through the worst of what can happen and you will get through this. Fear can't be conquered but it can be held back and managed in the moment, so clarity reemerges. Reflection trumps fear and anxiety.

A Commander's Intent

For nearly a decade our country has been at war, and there is little evidence it will soon end. This has fatigued the families and the war fighters themselves; thousands have given their lives in service and many have served multiple tours of duty. The methods of military training to adapt to the environments of twenty-first-century warfare reveal many insights about helping soldiers and marines to think, even in the midst of an intense firefight. While unintuitive to most of us, such extreme circumstances require novel methods for helping individual servicemen and women deal with fear and fatigue across sustained periods of time. Embedded within the techniques described below are think time and reflection that are rapidly converted into dialogues and blunt story telling.

I asked General Petraeus, now in charge of Afghanistan operations and former commander of the Iraq conflict, to describe what it's like to be in an actual firefight. Can it even be put into words? He reminded me that what we see in the movies is very deceiving. Training methods employed within the military today help soldiers envision what battle will be like before they actually face one. Petraeus told me, "You must remember that we had mock suicide car bombers at Fort Polk, Louisiana, in the Joint Readiness Training Center, well before we encountered them in Iraq. We did it to help our soldiers envision what the chaos might be like, what the demands might be like, and what the sensory overload might be like." He continued, "People watch a movie and they think you can actually shout and have someone hear you even in the middle of a firefight. In reality, nobody can hear anything."[1]

General Mattis, now in charge of U.S. Central Command and the man who led the First Marine Division during the ground invasion of Iraq, told me, "The more you fight, the more you realize that you really must have an institutional cohesion that allows you to implicitly trust those under your command. [Instilling trust is] still difficult because war has so much fear and fatigue associated with it. The veneer of civilization gets rubbed off."[2]

Within the chaos of war, soldiers must at all times have a connection back to their leadership, even when formal communications are lost. Therefore, generals spend a significant portion of their time expressing what is called "Commander's Intent." It's really a thinking tool born after long hours of the commander's reflection time. General Mattis succinctly defined Commander's Intent as, "helping subordinates to understand the larger context of their part of the action." He went on to say, "It helps to achieve harmonious subordinate action when fleeting windows of opportunity appear on the battlefield and when communications with the remote commander are not possible or would slow the tempo." He noted that by providing the purpose of the mission (the "why?"), Commander's Intent creates unity of effort throughout a far-flung force.[3]

Commanders sequester themselves and draft communications in order to express their "intent" related to the actions and mission about to be undertaken. They are tools aimed at helping soldiers have a permanent window into their leader's mind. Within the chaos of a hostile environment, the language and ideas presented will echo in the thinking of the soldiers so it constantly informs the many decisions they will make. The commander knows fear is an omnipresent factor a soldier must face. Through words that succinctly convey intent, war fighters face fear with fidelity to the mission, even if they are faced with the most shocking of situations. After distributing this communication as an individual letter given to everyone in their command, generals interact with soldiers and marines in smaller settings so dialogues emerge as they further acknowledge the reality of what they are about to face. Such intentions can't be conveyed in pithy "good luck" emails. Intention is a slow, deliberate, and reflective concept to deliver.

In the days before the ground invasion of Iraq, Mattis had dozens of conversations with many of the 20,000 soldiers and marines placed under his command. It took an enormous amount of his time to have multiple question-and-answer sessions that accompanied the letters given to each war fighter. The reality of war was about to begin, and he wanted to encourage them to think through its worst elements so they could still perform. One of the more famous letters Mattis wrote expressing his commander's intent was distributed to troops in the days before the invasion. In March of 2003, Mattis wrote, "You are part of the world's most feared and trusted force. Engage your brain before you engage your weapon. Share your courage with each other as we enter the uncertain terrain north of the Line of Departure." He closed with, "Demonstrate to the world there is 'No better friend, no worse enemy' than a U.S. Marine."[4]

Mattis told me how he messaged to them about the possibility that Iraqis might use chemical weapons during the ground invasion. "We'd talk about what it was going to be like if they got what we called 'slimed' or coated with chemical weapons. I told them, 'When you get hit by gas, just keep fighting.' You're going to have to fight what we called 'dirty' for 24 hours. It means, to put it very bluntly, you will pee and crap inside your suits. But you just keep fighting." He then shared with them the actions that would be taken after such shocking events unfolded. He let them know they would come off the battlefield and that everything they were wearing would be taken off, put in a pile and burned. "Then I would tell them that we're going to clean you and your vehicles. We're going to give you all new gear, and then we're going to send you back to kill the people who did it to you." He told them there was going to be life after being gassed and it was going to be ugly, but then it would get better.[5]

Petraeus explained to me that part of Commander's Intent involves preparing war fighters for the circumstances they are going to experience set inside the larger political context facing the Iraqi and Afghan people. He shared with me copies of several letters he wrote and distributed to the troops throughout his time in Iraq and his new assignment in Afghanistan, including a letter in which he addressed some of the moral consequences of war fighting, reminding troops of their actions when seen within an historic context. Petraeus wrote, "Some may argue that we would be more effective if we sanctioned torture or other expedient methods to obtain information from the enemy. They would be wrong. Beyond the basic fact that such actions are illegal, history shows us that they are also frequently neither useful nor necessary.... What sets us apart from our enemies in this fight is how we behave. In everything we do, we must observe the standards and values that dictate that we treat noncombatants and detainees with dignity and respect. While we are warriors, we are also human beings."[6]

Through a stunning turn of events triggered by an article in *Rolling Stone* magazine that led to the dismissal of General Stanley McChrystal, President Obama asked General Petraeus take over in Afghanistan and successfully execute the strategy they had coauthored months earlier (described in chapter 3). Petraeus shared with me the reflective letters and revised "counterinsurgency guidance" that he composed within the first days and weeks of his arrival in Afghanistan. While he commanded Iraq with great success during the "surge," he immediately grasped that the situation and context within Afghanistan was different. The documents are written in first person and convey in simple sentences how Petraeus wants all who serve with him to see the situation. Several passages stood out as they demonstrate his persistent guidance to all under his command to take the time to think (sometimes long and hard) before they act.

Through clear expressions hatched in his mind while alone and in a deep state of reflection, Petraeus refuses to allow the immediacy and fire power of a weapon to become the singular default for a soldier thinking through the downside and unintended consequences of their actions and behaviors. The revised counterinsurgency guidance was issued within 30 days of his arrival in Afghanistan in the summer of 2010. His advice reminds the troops that counterinsurgency involves interactions with the native people and that nuance, symbols, gestures, subtlety, and the simple things are also prerequisites for their success. As you examine what Petraeus is writing here, consider the thoughtfulness and clarity of his expression. As a leader, ask yourself how often you create language that succinctly conveys your most deeply held ideas and beliefs that you want to share with employees at the highest and lowest levels of your organization. At the same time, think about what the absence of such direction means as people flounder for context and guidance given the mental and physical exhaustion wrought by the protracted economic crisis and recession.

In a comprehensive letter, Petraeus tells the troops to foster "lasting solutions" and advises them to "think hard before pursuing initiatives that may not be sustainable in the long run." When it comes to projects, small is often beautiful." He later notes: "Situational awareness can only be gained face-to-face, not separated by ballistic glass or Oakleys." Relationship building involves far more than a cursory interaction between a U.S. Soldier and local Afghan leaders and civilians.[7]

Petraeus demands that the Afghan people be treated with respect. Again, he asks these tired military men and woman, many of whom are in Afghanistan for a third or forth rotation, to engage their minds first. He says, "Think about how we drive, how we patrol, how we relate to people, and how we help the community." He wants them to consult and build relationships even with those who don't seek to engage with troops. Soldiers must be curious and ask questions. He says, "Inquire about social dynamics, frictions, local histories and grievances. Hear what they say. Be aware of others in the room and how their presence may affect the answers you get . . . Avoid knee jerk responses based on first impressions. Don't be a pawn in someone else's game. Spend time, listen, consult and drink lots of tea."[8]

Petraeus's final piece of advice reveals that his intentions and guidance can and will take soldiers into situations for which there is no reference point. Self-direction and an individual's thinking will drive key outcomes; soldiers must exercise initiative. He says, "In the absence of guidance or orders, figure out what the orders should have been and execute them aggressively."[9]

For all the value and human connection achieved through the Commander's Intent mechanisms, the enemy is keen to disrupt the flow of communications between leaders and their subordinates. In an electronic world, modern enemies have many means to interfere in the midst of battle. Enemies don't want the intent to soak in; but let chaos and confusion overpower reflection and they may win. General Mattis wondered if the future might entail even more reliance on the decidedly lower-technology methods of communicating he and Petraeus routinely employ. Clarity of words and unambiguous language will matter most. Mattis told me, "My (admittedly biased) view is that such communications (letter, verbal, message, etc) will need to become more used in the future because the electronic means to do 'command & control' (C2) are going to be subjected to enemy jamming, disruption, and deception." He continued, "Commander's Intent messages will have to give the commander's aim or purpose and the outcome the commander's desires (in the broadest possible terms), done by giving the least possible information so the main points stand out."[10]

Out of Your Intellectual Comfort Zone

While Commander's Intent is a powerful tool that helps troops manage fear and ensure alignment with the mission at all times, many other techniques are employed by the military that help forge adaptive thinkers. Another element of training to help war fighters involves removing them from the battlefield in order to give them new reference points. General Mattis once was briefed by a psychologist about what was termed as "dramatic instance fallacy," or making assumptions based on one's limited experience. He worried what its potential impact could be on young officers, as this was their first war. He explained to me, "The only wars they have fought in are, generally, Iraq or some have served in Afghanistan. If they think that's all that war is, that one war experience becomes their 'fallacy.' So if you don't pull them out and go to War College or to Harvard—to think, write and reflect while talking to others, then they will actually be worse, for all their experience." He concluded, "They'll be great technicians; they will not be good thinkers."[11]

General Petraeus has long espoused the value of such diverse training and experiences; he explained to me what it was like to get his PhD within the 'civilian' school environment at Princeton. "In the military we don't pause and look up enough because we don't have the time. Particularly for our commissioned officers, we try to provide them with 'out of their intellectual comfort zone experiences.' For me, the biggest of those experiences was civilian graduate school." He continued, "I learned that there are really exceedingly bright people with extraordinary academic credentials, who have very different assumptions about basic concepts than I do. They had very different views about policies and reality than I did."[12] Petraeus believes this experience helped him to better think through the many problems posed by the wars in Iraq, Afghanistan, and increasingly conflicts in Pakistan. He is able to think from political and diplomatic viewpoints, as well as from macro and microeconomic viewpoints, as so much of the mission is helping to reconnect these countries—within their own borders and into the fabric of globalization.

Even if an officer doesn't go to graduate school, the global nature of military operations today requires an understanding never before demanded by the military. From the influence of religion to the latest technology, officers and enlisted personnel must consume and comprehend extraordinary amounts of content. At one point, General Mattis had a personal book collection of over 3,000 volumes. He would have moved his beloved texts with him at each change of command. Today, he has a required reading list for all those who serve under him. The titles cover a diverse range of thinking, from militant Islam to the Battle of Thermopylae in 435 BC. He expects his marines to carve out time to read and reflect, as the nature of modern war demands it. Mattis believes devaluing think time and reflection in the military is coming at a cost. He told me, "I only have so many hours in the day. Sometimes it's the right thing to do just to yell at a bunch of marines nearby to hit the deck. But most of the time you can leave that to a lance corporal, and as a general you can be more reflective and less connected to the here and now. "He continued, "There's a saying in the marines that was passed on to me: 'You can make captain on a good set of legs, but by the time you make major, we expect you to be able to really think.' That's reflection. But the saying goes on: 'by the time you're a colonel, or a general, we expect it to be more of a spiritual journey.' And that's where you really get the results of reflection."[13]

All these approaches are adaptations the military employs to enable war fighters to think and evolve along with an enemy who continues to do the same. No approaches are perfect substitutes for handling the mental and physical exhaustion of battles and workdays that often extend for 14 to 16 hours a day for weeks at a time. The generals are seeking thinkers first, followed only then by soldiers and marines taking the actions afforded to them through modern weapons and communications. Once in battle there are few natural breaks, as the body synchronizes to meet the extreme dangers of the situations around it. But then a moment arises and the generals teach the war fighters yet again how to make the most of it. Mattis told me, "I can remember, after a rather physical and fearful period in Iraq, a bunch of us got into a house and were sitting and leaning against a wall for a couple of minutes. We just sat there. As I collected my breath and myself, I could see more clearly what needed to be done. And I'd come into that room with no thought of what to do. Yet, once under cover, I could actually think. And after a while, you somewhat remove yourself from what's around you. Your body will actually slow things down and just block out certain stimulus."[14]

In all the above examples, we see the military adapting to meeting their dangerous mission through think time and reflection. Most

business professionals will never be faced with the life-and-death decisions of war fighters, but none of us is immune to the fears and anxiety
that have accompanied the economic collapse and uncertain prospect
of recovery. Leaders and organizations can learn many things from
what the military is doing. From taking the time to forge crisp, clear
expressions of intent, to ensuring that we encourage managers to get
out of their intellectual comfort zones, we discover fear can be managed and reflection can reemerge.

Reflection and Think Time Aimed at Deterring Violence

Far from the battles of Iraq and Afghanistan, a war rages inside
America. The proliferation of guns and gang violence in cities like
Chicago continue to grab headlines and ceaselessly take thousands of
lives each year. There are no generals and soldiers in these nightly street
battles. There are few heroes and many innocent victims. The situations surrounding much of the violence are often rooted in accusations
and misunderstandings that quickly escalate into violence and death.
In Chicago, we meet up with a former street hustler, Tio Hardiman,
and an epidemiologist, Dr. Gary Slutkin, who have formed an innovative not-for-profit that brings brief and powerful moments of reflection
into even the most desperate of situations.

Hardiman proudly describes himself as a "community organizer."
He grew up on the south side of Chicago, where he observed street violence early in life. When he was 16 years old and on his way to the
grocery store, Hardiman was violently attacked by an older man. Days
after the incident, Hardiman watched as his relative found and killed
the man who beat him. That moment set in his mind the belief that
violence should be responded to with violence. Thinking back on the
incident, he said, "It made me feel damn good to see that guy get shot.
I felt vindicated."[15] Hardiman floundered for much of his youth and
became addicted to alcohol. Yet, his life would one day turn around,
and he would form a new mental model for looking at violence.[16]

Hardiman's grandmother raised him to always listen before he spoke
and take moments out for himself each day to think and reflect—especially before making any big decisions. One simple story she told him
sits in the back of his mind during the many hours he spends trying to
reframe the thinking of gang members with whom he interacts. The
story taught him the value of framing a problem and thinking through

an answer before reflexively responding with an obvious answer. "My grandmother told me about three frogs sitting on a log and one of them made a decision to jump off the log." She then asked him, "So, how many frogs were left on the log after that?" He continued, "I said, "two of them were left sitting on the log." She replied, "No, you're wrong, Tio! All three of them are still sitting on the log. One just made a decision to jump. He hadn't actually jumped yet."[17]

Hardiman met an epidemiologist, Dr. Gary Slutkin, through meetings at The Chicago Project for Non Violence. Their interactions would eventually help forge CeaseFire, an innovative and lasting Chicago-based program that attempts to treat violence as a disease. Hardiman explained to me that, "Homicide is the leading cause of death for African-American youth between the ages of 1 and 34 years old. I just became sick and tired of it; somebody had to step up and do something." He told me, "Don't get me wrong. Early on it was kind of rough for me because I didn't really believe in peace. But it began to really grab a hold of me and I had to go on a mission." He continued: "I want people to recognize that violence is an illness, a sickness. People don't want to be associated with words like illness, sickness, disease, and epidemic, but that's what it is."[18]

An independent report explained the scope of the program: "The behavior-change goal of CeaseFire was very tightly defined: their direct clients, other young men and women on the street, and gang members and leaders with whom they were in contact, were called upon to stop shooting." The report continues, "CeaseFire did not make larger demands upon them; there was no expectation that the often inadequately educated and underemployed young people they largely dealt with would—or could—"go straight" without a great deal of investment in turning their lives around."[19]

While directed solely at stopping the violence, the results achieved by CeaseFire have been impressive. A recent Department of Justice independent report, looking back over 17 years of data from seven sites in the Chicago area stated that, "As a direct result of CeaseFire, shootings decreased 16 to 28 percent in four of the seven sites studied. The researchers called this decrease in gun violence 'immediate and permanent' in three of the sites and 'gradual and permanent' in the fourth site."[20]

Hardiman conceived of adding credible people to potentially violent situations, people who would "interrupt" the violence, before it reached a deadly tipping point. The *New York Times* described who these people are and how they join CeaseFire: "In addition to outreach workers, they also hire men and women who had been deep into street life, and…began recruiting people even while they were in prison….The new recruits, with strong connections to the toughest communities, would focus solely on sniffing out clashes that had the potential to escalate. They would intervene in potential acts of retribution—as well as try to diffuse seemingly minor spats that might erupt into something bigger, like disputes over women or insulting remarks."[21] These violence "interrupters," as they are called within CeaseFire, are paid about $15 an hour. They also get basic health benefits from the University of Illinois at Chicago, which helps administer the program.

From Teddy Bears to an Interruption

The following story illustrates the power of the interrupter concept. It never made the news and was known only to those who took part. Hardiman told me about it on the very day he was involved. An eight-year-old girl, "Lisa," in the southwest side of Chicago had received a teddy bear as a present from the school principal as a reward for her good work at school. The present was too big for Lisa to carry, so she had a teenage friend, "Mary," help carry it to Lisa's home. Mary had no intention of doing that and went another direction and eventually to her own home. Meanwhile, Lisa went home in tears and immediately told her mother and 14-year-old brother, "Tom." Tom immediately went to Mary's house and demanded she give the gift back to his little sister.[22]

As Tom was demanding the present back, Mary's three teenage brothers and a cousin came out the front door, put him on the ground and punched him, breaking his front teeth. Tom struggled home and told his cousins what had just happened. They then moved to confront the boys who had just assaulted Tom. More people gathered, until there were over 30 people involved in a confrontation that arose because a little girl was given a gift. Hardiman said, "It turned into a big, big problem in that community. Mary's granddad had heard about CeaseFire and called in a request for us to get involved." Hardiman dispatched former gang member Ameena Matthews to insert herself into the situation and defuse the situation before it went any further. Matthews is paid by the state and trained in the many mediation techniques espoused by

Hardiman and Dr. Slutkin. She has credibility with people in the community, since she had lived through moments like this one and she isn't the police. No one called the police, and by the time Matthews moved out on her assignment, she was facing a situation that seemed likely to result in the death of several people.[23]

Hardiman explained how the actual violence-interruption worked. He told me, "Ameena began to talk to one side and she had to call in other violence interrupters to quickly talk to the other side. She got down to the root cause of the problem. It was all about the gift, but it had started to turn into a gang war. People got beat up. People lost their teeth but nobody got shot because Ameena was there to present a solution. She made people realize this was all about a gift and nothing else." The violence interrupters must think quickly on their feet and use common street language that can and does mean the difference between life and death. I asked Hardiman what types of things would be said in order to move people's thinking away from violence. Hardiman explained, "To be graphic with you, there are a lot of times where we have to cuss people out. We say things like 'Look here, motherfucker! You know this is some bullshit you're trying to do.'" He continued, "You shouldn't be doing it because there is no method to this madness. And I know about it, and everybody knows about it so that may mean the police know about it. Think about your kids, think about your grandmother, who doesn't have anything."[24]

CeaseFire has several site locations throughout Chicago from which it runs programs meant to further strengthen its relationships with the community and, where possible, supply mentors to those who have never had them. Some sites employ a group-facilitation session called "Reflections." These discussions force moments of self-reflection that are important to enabling young people to see their lives in a different context. Hardiman explained to me, "We had a training session today on the power of healing from the inside out. One of the assignments was to write daily about who you think you are and what your family means to you. Then we ask them to reflect on a lot of positive statements (quotations) from people like: Nelson Mandela, Gandhi, Dr. King, and Malcolm X." Hardiman continued, "These leaders are people who went through transitions in their lives, through trying times they were confronted with. And we all agreed today that the majority of us haven't gone through anything close to the things they went through." He then shared with me that they employ a technique often associated with the renowned author Steven Covey, where these young people must write out what they envision the end of their life to be. Hardiman said, "We ask everyone at the sessions to write and reflect on what their life would be like between the year they were born up until if they died today. They reflect on how they wouldn't want to just leave earth without contributing anything to society."[25]

Back at home on the south side of Chicago, Hardiman each day employs meditation and other moments sitting quietly alone just to take stock of his life and all he observes in his unique line of work. He told me, "I grew up on the streets. I know how it is out here. But no one killed me today. If you die, you never get a chance to know what you could have achieved in your life. To me, reflection is about taking an in-depth look at my life on a regular basis so that I can help steer myself in the right direction." He paused a moment, then continued, "For 30 minutes every day I don't do anything. I just sit in my basement with all the lights off and I just relax and meditate. I do an introspection of my day and my week. I want to make sure that I'm not making some of the same mistakes that I've made in the past." He concluded, "If you're too busy just bobbing and moving all the time, you begin to miss out and overlook little simple things in life that mean more than anything."[26]

Facilitating Middle-Ground Solutions

Each day, we are presented with conflicts both big and small. We may be in a meeting and someone publicly disagrees with us. We may get direction from a supervisor via an email message that we recoil from. As we saw in earlier chapters, debate and dissent are critical to ensuring that we don't just think through the upside of things. When bankers and regulators failed to think through the downside of risk, we watched in horror as the global economic marketplace nearly collapsed. What we learn from all this is that entrenched positions never move a team forward to breakthrough thinking. We also learn that organizations must get better at encouraging thoughtful dissent that never gets bogged down by immovable factions. Below, we meet an attorney who uses moments of reflection in order to allow for the most entrenched parties to come back to the table to reach a conclusion. Kenneth Feinberg teaches that when you demonstrate the ability to listen to both sides with dispassionate understanding, then vitriol can be left behind and reconciliation can happen. What seems like a lost cause can be remedied, but only through the resolution of awkward moments to allow each party to come to a new awareness of what is possible.

Ken Feinberg is an expert at mediation. When he is not carrying out atypical assignments, as he did while administering the 9/11 Victims Compensation Fund or as President Obama's "Pay Czar," he can be found in the middle of difficult negotiations between entrenched parties. His latest assignment is to act as the "claims czar," independently administering an unprecedented $20 billion fund established by BP to compensate the many people effected by the Deepwater Horizon disaster. Although he once considered acting as a profession, his parents pushed him to go into law, and he received his JD from NYU. In 1984, his law career evolved into mediation. Brooklyn Federal District Judge Jack Weinstein asked him to settle a prolonged dispute between a group of Vietnam War veterans who had been exposed to Agent Orange and the chemical companies that manufactured this product for use by the military. While he had no experience in mediation, Feinberg got both parties to settle the dispute for $180 million. The judge later told the *Washington Post* that he was impressed by Feinberg's ability to grasp "how people acted and why they did what they did."[27] Feinberg has since been involved in settling high-profile cases related to product-liability claims, including asbestos and defective heart valves. You call Ken Feinberg in when years of acrimony have built up and the costs of maintaining the status quo are higher than an uncertain payoff that may never come.

Feinberg explains that while one side will usually make the initial call to him, both sides need to agree to his involvement. He told me, "I usually get called in after the lawsuit has been filed and is getting ready to go to trial. By this point, the lawyers have been banging away at each other for at least a year or so." Feinberg's impact is most felt through how he controls the information flow between the two fighting parties. Both parties will brief him so he understands the impasse and their positions. Then he brings both together to discuss the case for about an hour. Then the two parties go into separate rooms, not to face each other again. Over the course of two days, each party will convey offers, demands, and counter-offers though him. He told me, "I essentially control the communication flow, the information going back and forth. As the only one who has heard from both sides, I try to meld a middle ground solution."[28]

During that one-time face-to-face meeting, Feinberg drives the conversation. He insists the actual parties be in the same room and not just their attorneys. They must each hear the setup, so everyone is on the same page. Following whatever awkward introductions are exchanged, Feinberg begins the process of having the parties go at each other in the joint session. He told me, "I will say, 'Party One, can you please tell Party Two why you're going to win the case?' After Party One finishes, I say, 'Party Two, now please tell Party One why *you* are going to win the case.'"[29] Blood pressure is high as entrenched positions and worn out arguments are once again voiced—with each warring party facing the other. Once both parties have had equal time and all the vitriol is on the table in the open, he dismisses them to separate rooms. There they may consider, alone, what was just discussed. He uses the alone time to his advantage. These moments of downtime and reflection allow both sides to discover a possible new outcome.

"Shuttle diplomacy" is the key, with the participants in different rooms, so Feinberg controls the information flow. He floats between the parties like a honeybee pollinating their minds so new ideas can finally bloom. He sits with each side and offers short bursts of his thinking for the parties to chew on once he closes the door. He directs his comments at both the client and their attorneys. "Attorney, you may lose. Client, here is your choice: I can get you $3 million in this mediation. You'll have the money. You don't have to wait for it. You can put it in the bank and let it collect interest. There is no more uncertainty. No more risk." In some cases, he reminds the parties that they may have an ongoing business relationship with the other side that's being damaged by the dispute. He will say, "It's poisoning the well. By resolving the dispute, you reaffirm your business relationship on friendly terms." Within the mediations, he often makes a proposal designed to give the parties an opportunity to respond rather than "lead with their chin." He explained, "I might also suggest that one party condition its offer/demand on whether or not its adversary moves to a certain range designed to minimize differences and narrow the gap."[30] While often only with their attorneys, the warring parties begin to reexamine their core assumptions in the case and they ponder what Feinberg suggests as potential outcomes. Think time slowly gives rise to more rational decision making. The impulse for revenge is replaced by the awareness of what could be lost—should the matter linger or come to trial and they lose.

At the end of the first day of negotiations, Feinberg actively encourages people to go home, have a nice dinner, get a good night's sleep, and mull over all he has said that day. He explained to me, "I want people to think about it so that the next day they come back creative, ready to negotiate, and take into account what I've said." In other words, Feinberg ensures the reflection continues throughout the night as new paths are explored and some semblance of concession enters one's mind. Logic is a big part of his method, but so is the psychology. He told me, "I find it fascinating when you begin day one of the mediation, the parties are sitting with their arms folded across their chests and they are immovable. Yet, by the end of that day, they actually have a vested interest in getting the mediation done. By the end of day one, they don't want it to fail. I'm devoting two days to its success, a settlement, and I don't want it to fail." He continues, "On day two of mediation, everyone agrees to quit around 4:00 p.m. Usually by 3:40 or 3:50 p.m. they settle. The parties usually settle in the last ten minutes before we adjourn. It's the end game they know at 4:00 p.m., BING! Feinberg is out of here."

As he moves between the two parties in their separate rooms, Feinberg poses questions that force them to step back from their entrenched views. Sometimes he directs his comments at the attorney, who then echoes what he has said, even though Feinberg has left the room. Feinberg envisions what the lawyers might say to their clients after he offers a reframed way to look at the problem: "Did you hear what he said back there? Listen to Feinberg. He has credibility. You guys have a 60 percent chance of losing this case. Don't you think your offer should reflect a 60 percent risk factor?" Feinberg explained that the whole process acts like a sort of verbalized decision tree. He will go into the room and say things like, "A 60 percent risk factor? You want $5 million. I've looked at your numbers and its really not $5 million. You really want $4 million but you have got a 60 percent chance of losing. At least reduce your demand by half. Isn't your $4 million actually $2 million once you reduce it for a roll of the dice in the court room?"[31] The entrenched parties think with Feinberg about the downside of holding on to their positions. They can lose everything.

Sitting back in his office chair after explaining the methods he employs to bring reflection into moments of impasse, Feinberg takes pride in reporting that his approach settles about 94 percent of the cases he is brought in to mediate. Yet, mediation and alternative dispute resolution are not likely to become the dominant method for settling, given the ingrained litigiousness of the American judicial system. The bias toward legal action will not diminish, Feinberg suggests, as it's as old as the republic itself. He told me, "After Alexander de Tocqueville came over to the United States from France in 1840, he traveled around our country for a year and wrote the book *Democracy in America*. He wrote that one of the strangest things about America is that it's so litigious. Every important issue in America ends up in the court room." Feinberg continued, "The American litigation system is such an ingrained part of the American fabric, the American constitution, and the republic system, that it will never change. It is a part of America, joined at the hip to the separation of powers and governmental principal. And anybody who thinks tort reform, reform of the courts, reform of the civil-justice system, alternative dispute resolution, mediation, arbitration, is going to become the dominant problem-solving vehicle in our society, does not understand our society."[32]

Applying the Lessons from These Atypical Situations

The above examples demonstrate that think time and reflection are powerful tools even when emotion, stress, and irrational behavior are involved. Reflection plays a critical role in allowing new ideas to form in minds that have wandered into the dangerous places. There are multiple ways to apply them:

1. Leadership and intention. The use of Commander's Intent demonstrates that a leader's reflection time can translate into the immediate thinking of their subordinates—even within the chaos of war. Such language must then be conveyed through face-to-face contact where the intent is translated into descriptions of the furthest extreme of what the organization may experience. Intention also comes down to the written expression of key ideas that are memorable and sticky. Such realism on display helps those with little-to-no experience to see the context of what is about to unfold. When was the last time you created such a clear statement of the intention behind a strategy or project? How much time do you spend walking people to the edge of their anxieties while ignoring the many uncertainties and risks that are a permanent part of solving big problems? How can you teach managers within your organization to carve time out to replicate this behavior so those

working for them understand the intent of what is being placed before them?

2. Intellectual comfort zones. Having people toil away for years in the same roles can quickly breed stale thinking that levels performance. If even the military shows the capacity to be monastic and insulated at times, can you be sure your organization is open and integrated? How much does your organization encourage people to get out of their intellectual comfort zones so new thinking can emerge? What structures exist to encourage people to unplug in order to see the larger context of their role and their eventual maturity within the organization? Do you model the behaviors you seek to be emulated by those around you?

3. Virus and antibody analogies. The CeaseFire program is far from the mission of many organizations, Yet, the model and analogy of disease and antibody response it employs is very powerful. Slutkin and Hardiman looked at the problem and suggested new methods and language meant to attack a problem that had persisted for years. How can we "interrupt" the addictive behaviors we observe involving the incessant use of technology, all the way to the spreading of false information through rumor mills? The great lesson of the CeaseFire program is that reflection can be brought to bear upon minds so that the downside of decisions are understood before violent actions are undertaken. Who within our organization has the credibility to intervene to make a difference by forcing people to rethink what they are doing and its downside impact on the organization?

4. New ways to resolve disputes. The shuttle diplomacy methods of Feinberg can be employed in resolving conflicts between deeply divided factions. He forces people to step away from entrenched thinking by introducing reason and probability and then silence in order for them to ponder new outcomes. Sometimes we must intervene within our organizations as factions and silos between divisions can harm collaboration and information sharing. Over time, this can harden the positions such that defending the status quo becomes a permanent barrier to change. No organization is immune from conflict and, yet, when allowed to fester it can destroy a company through lost time and the cost of holding on to vitriol. Feinberg shows there are no such things as lost causes

and even the most entrenched can be reached through structured moments of reflection. He allows the warring parties to come to new conclusions as he remains above the fray and listening. Organizations must discover who their "Feinbergs" are. Such people can drive powerful, cross-organizational conflict-resolution so critical to managing through the complexity and uncertainty we face.

10

The Future of Think Time and Reflection

From Sovereign Debt to Subway Performances

The AMC cable television show, "Mad Men," has rapidly advanced to cult status in the few years it's been on. The show dramatically portrays the culture and happenings within the New York advertising agencies of Madison Ave in the 1960s. The drama grabs attention as it supplies a portal into a time that has long since passed, where cigarette smoking and alcohol consumption were widely permitted and even encouraged in the course of a workday. The show also demonstrates how societal norms have changed in regard to seat belts, car seats for children, and prenatal care (two or three martinis while many months pregnant, for example).

As the show's characters think through the next ad campaign for companies like Kodak and Hilton Hotels, conference rooms are filled with plumes of smoke that everyone inhales multiple times an hour. With the seemingly sophisticated and evolved set of rules we obey in our home and work lives today, watching "Mad Men" can sometimes give you a sickening feeling as you pass judgment on past behaviors and social contracts. You will find yourself asking, "How could they have worked that way? How did anything ever get done?"

So, now project into the future. It's the year 2055 and let's imagine a television show that, like "Mad Men," peers back into the behaviors of people working inside a service company in say the year 2011. The camera pans to a scene inside an office, somewhere in a major U.S. city, with dozens of desks amassed in open spaces. Employees sit quietly hunched over their laptops, switching among tasks such as checking reams of new emails, searching the Web, talking to the colleague at the next desk, text messaging through their cell phones, reading and responding to personal emails, scanning the many short blurbs of the fifty people they follow on Twitter, instant messaging to nine different colleagues in different offices around the world, and working on a draft PowerPoint presentation for a meeting with a major client that will happen in less than three hours.

Later in the show, the characters assemble in a boardroom with a beautiful pull-down screen that features the PowerPoint slides projected in clear images and words. Nine people attending the briefing bring their own laptops and cell phones so they can check in or out of the presentation depending on its subjective relevance to their workload. Distraction and fragmented thinking partially wrought by technology addictions are analogous to what smoking was inside companies in the 1960s. Few rules govern the use of technology in the context of our behaviors toward one another in professional settings—just as for decades there were few rules governing smoking within the workplace.

Lots of comments are given to the presenter who diligently makes notes. Some raise opposition to a few core concepts he wants to present, but among all the tasks they are doing during the meeting, they never enter a real discussion in which any one of the presentation's fundamental assumptions or conclusions are deeply questioned or even reversed. Dissent is a pithy subjective comment. Dialogue devolves into a fragmented verbal meandering through a topic requiring a group's collective concentration and disciplined review of the down side of the potential strategy. Will people watching a show like this in 2055 have the same sickening feeling we get today from watching "Mad Men"? Will people ask, "How did anyone ever work like that?"

It's perilous to project a view of the future, given all the uncertainty we face, so I won't make any specific predictions. I will make some assumptions, however, and offer several guideposts that can help organizations better recognize and reward reflection—even when immediacy is all we see and must contend with. As I said at the start of this book, I don't lament the speed of work and life; it's an unstoppable constant. Rather, it strikes me that this period we are all living through—as technology drives our behavior as much as we push the technology—is creating significant waves of nonproductive churn and anxiety we must reconcile.

I employed two lenses in considering what will become of reflection and think time: namely, the aftermath of the financial crisis and the role of education in shaping future generations to better embrace reflection. I close with one last example I couldn't resist sharing, as well some parting advice.

Aftermath of the Global Recession:
Our Immediate Future

Kyle Bass, the skeptical global investor from Dallas we met in chapter 6 compared the international response to the fiscal crisis (involving massive fiscal stimulants and the coordinated printing of money) to watching dozens of drug addicts all overdosing at the same time. Bass believes global leaders and finance ministers—in an effort to "ensure liquidity"—failed to properly describe the problem they were called on to solve. "This wasn't a liquidity problem; it was and remains a solvency problem," Bass told me. He believes the printing of money added to the mounds of debt already racked up by countries through years of overspending, unregulated banking, and failing to maintain reasonable debt-to-taxation revenue ratios. Bass told me, "Once the initial euphoria wears off on a drug addict, we all know they face a painful withdrawal."[1] His point: the world is now in the first few hours of what will be a prolonged and painful withdrawal that will last for years to come.

In the aftermath of the crisis, we can watch countries like Iceland, Greece, Hungary, Spain, and the United States wake up to realize that avoiding going off the cliff involved taking painful fiscal medicine with lasting side effects. Tens of thousands of disconnected decisions over generations have brought the world to this time of financial crisis. It did not just begin with a few bankers on Wall Street. The crisis that seemingly should be short may linger for years and involve the reshaping of national identities, as each country looks anew at its balance sheet and assesses the real consequences of declining populations disinterested in "austerity measures" to remedy massive budget gaps. This all matters, as the next several decades will be spent dealing with the repercussions of unprecedented assumption of sovereign debt against a backdrop of demographic trends that are unavoidable.

Iceland was one of the first Western countries to seek IMF support as it essentially declared bankruptcy. Its bankers indulged in risky ventures that exposed the country and its taxpayers to obligations that were 33 times the annual tax revenues of the country. Bass explained to me, "At the height of what just happened before the financial meltdown, countries were agnostic with regard to the size of their banking systems. So when their banking systems hit a bump in the road, the countries themselves are unable to solve the problems. Countries let the problem get so big that they themselves can't handle the problem."[2]

Trillions of dollars were spent to prop up a weakened global finance system in order to ensure the world avoided a global depression. Such spending has dramatic consequences that we are just now coming to understand. For many countries this was not their first hit of heroin, either; debt had been piling up in many developed countries as budgets were out of balance and spending was at all-time highs. It will be a country-by-country reconciliation with consequences for every business and citizen. Pensions that were assured, no longer are. Workdays and career lengths are now permanently elongated. Career time horizons have been reset. The destruction of personal wealth will ripple through each community, and every family touched by the global decision to prop up the banking nervous system. Newly minted college graduates, saddled with heavy student debts are slowly entering a workforce that is resistant to letting them in. Each painful choice by one country is interconnected to all others through the promise and persistence of globalization. Companies and leaders must be ready to think in a context far beyond the parochial; risk management does not begin to describe this moment and the unknowns to follow. How many can honestly say what year they hope to retire in? What are the implications of this reset? We are just beginning to discover them.

What will it mean to work in a world where country after country faces painful domestic choices that impact millions of people across years of uncertainty? As this is being written, Greece is under huge pressure to get its fiscal house in order so that it does not default on its debt obligations. A default would expose European interdependence resulting from the European Union and the Euro, and could create a cascading set of defaults since countries like Spain, the United Kingdom, Ireland, and Switzerland are all in somewhat similar positions to that of

Iceland before it defaulted. Are the bailout packages that seem to save the day just a salve or a real solution? Where is all this money coming from, because most countries are in poor positions to post collateral against another's obligations?

Living through a wave of defaults on sovereign debt is akin to skiing blindfolded down a tree-covered mountain. You might get down the hill in one piece. You might also never get off the mountain alive. When the Greek people were briefed on the "austerity measures" required to allow the country to remain solvent, reactions were sometimes violent and irrational. The financial crisis exposed a profound lack of financial and strategic planning within dozens of countries. Problems that have been punted downfield for generations are now too big to ignore. Solving them will require unprecedented intra-country collaboration; but only if there is a willingness to think together beyond political and social identity.

While the world looks at China and India as the engines of the future, it becomes easy to forget that countries like Japan have deeply entrenched global connectivity that impacts all of us. Embedded in Japan is a painful reconciliation of how it finances trillions of its currency against the background of anemic economic growth and too few taxpayers paying into their system. They also have an aging population that is presenting waves of new costs that must be paid at some point. Japan is the second largest economy in the world behind the United States in terms of its Gross Domestic Product. For well over a decade, Japan's economy has not grown, as it watched almost every asset category—from stocks to real estate—devalue or stagnate, while the cost of living has gone up. The only asset class that has held its value is Japanese bonds. Bass has once again placed some big bets against what he sees as the next wave of opportunity. He believes it's only a matter of time before the world watches as Japan goes through the largest economic reset of any country in the history of the world. Of Japan's woes, he told me, "Japan has a secular inexorable population decline going on. It's clear as day if you just put pen to paper. By 2013, they will sell more adult diapers in Japan than they will sell children's diapers."[3] While Greece may be a country struggling with debt, Japan is no Greece in terms of its relationships, people, and global impact. If Japan defaults on debt (that its people largely own), can anyone actually predict what that means for all the goods and services it's responsible for globally? If the Greek financial crisis sent shocks around the world, what will it mean if a country like Japan or United States begins to convulse under the weight of its debt and a confluence of other shocks?

For well over a decade, David Walker has been warning anyone who will listen inside America that spending for entitlement programs like Social Security and Medicare is unsustainable, given a host of colliding factors. Walker is the former comptroller of the United States and has served in various senior government roles for three U.S. presidents. He suggests America is approaching a tipping point, where unthinkable things like a downgrading of U.S. debt and even sovereign bankruptcy of the United States are actually possible. Walker has attempted to get the United States and its policy makers to reflect and "wake up" to the fiscal realities facing the country. He told me, "Unfortunately our society tends to focus on today and not worry about emerging challenges until they reach crisis proportions. In addition, most politicians don't want to make tough choices until they have to because they want to keep their jobs." Kyle Bass agreed with Walker and said, "The only way that reflection winds up happening in the United States is for it to be forced. A catastrophic event must happen in order to create reflection."[4]

In the hyperbolic and nonreflective partisanship of today, the U.S. seems far from being able to create a coherent strategy for the country as we face the twenty-first century. In fact, there is no mid- or long-term strategic plan for our country in terms of overarching goals, objectives, and outcomes that are transgenerational and fiscally rational. There is no national reference point that all parties agree upon based on the simple idea that doing so is in our "national interest." To get to such a moment will take years and involve new methods and models that few are prepared to even consider. Walker told me, "Any comprehensive reform effort must involve an extensive public education and engagement effort with representative groups of the American people in different parts of the country. This citizen education and engagement effort should also leverage the Web in new and unprecedented ways. These efforts should be supplemented by various public and private engagement efforts with key leaders in Washington." He continued, "In the final analysis, the overall effort needs to result in a range of recommendations that should be the subject of public hearings in Washington and would be assured of receiving a vote in congress."[5]

It's safe to say there are no political candidates who even have the language in their stump speech to embrace what Walker advises. There is no incentive to think horizontally. There are countries like Canada and Australia that have such plans and have forced the think time and consensus. Yet, countries like the United Kingdom and United States operate from short-term political platforms where macro-level trends are constantly pushed aside. Countries have lost the capacity to have true and generative dialogue that assimilates many ideas and allows people to think as groups within some framework of consensus. While technology can play a dramatic role in facilitating such dialogues, online citizen engagement tends to be issue-driven and polarized; online dialogue is often an expanding echo chamber of sound bites.

As we have seen throughout this book, when true dialogues emerge and time is given to think, benefits arise. We marvel at America's Founding Fathers for their wisdom in assimilating so many concepts and thinking through such a lasting political architecture. Their concepts were grounded in the countless hours many of them spent reflecting and assimilating the ideas of Europe's great thinkers. Only then were they prepared to enter the debates and dialogues that were some of the most generative moments in human history, as we defined a vision and political architecture for a country unlike any other. Today's sets of problems demand the capability to hold simultaneous national dialogues enmeshed within a tapestry of global conversations. The complexity can't be dismissed. We must ask ourselves, "With all the technology we have deployed, are we rising to think deeply through this extraordinary moment or are we drowning in data and diversion?" What matters more: data or meaning?

In all of this, valuing think time and group reflection through dialogue will become behavioral and cultural imperatives. Technology will play a critical role in hatching the dialogue but it will not be the key means for driving consensus. Human contact and face-to-face discussion will be required to codify new structures and methods. Organizations with ingrained, reflective, and adaptive problem-solving habits will flourish. As the great recession appears in the rearview window, we are facing a set of unknowns and interconnected problems that will require sustained periods of transgenerational thinking at institutional, national, and global levels. Organizations and nation-states that devalue reflection as a core organizational skill set will rapidly find themselves in the unsettling reactive posture that signals their rapid descent. Only the most reflective will survive.

Trust is the intangible currency of all business interactions. Trust is often driven by perception, especially when complexity and inter-connectivity mask the true underpinnings of what a company is involved in. When trust is gone, so is the firm. We all must ask ourselves, "Can we trust an organization that acts boldly without any architecture that forces it to consistently step away from the core assumptions that drives it?" In addition, we must all be curious about the incentives that push people in organizations to do what they do. If there is no incentive to dissent, except at a board meeting with overworked executives, who only have cursory insights into the future of the company, this may be one of the greatest weaknesses inside a firm. With all the examples we have discussed in the book, you now have ways to do something about it; it starts with valuing think time.

From No Question Left Behind to Vespers Revisited

When a crisis hits and immediate lessons are revealed, eyes quickly turn to how we are educating the next generations so they don't repeat the same mistakes. The future is altered by what we do or don't teach today. The current generations of students, across all levels, are immersed in technology in ways that make my childhood look like the Dark Ages in terms of technological advancement. Students are termed, "digital natives" as, unlike myself, they are growing up with the Internet and all its connectivity as standard and ingrained; not something that one day swept upon them.

Yet, once again, my survey reveals a few examples of educators help-ing students to step away from the speed and immediacy of the moment as they attempt to introduce them to the benefits of thinking together in groups or alone. These educators aren't dismissing technology; rather, they are encouraging what is in fact more important—the ability to use one's brain capacity to think. Their goal is to create a permanent reference point for reflection as a powerful capability that can carry students through the most challenging moments of their adult lives.

Kristina Sullivan is a grade-school teacher at the American Community School in Beirut, Lebanon, who had a 20-year career in the United States teaching sixth graders. As the mother of two digi-tal natives, Sullivan is aware of the pace of technology and its impact on children. She is also aware there is value in children learning to be alone—even for a short period of time, given that technology connects us all the time. What drew me to Sullivan was an article she wrote over a decade ago about the power of reflection as applied to children. She laments the lack of time for life (living) itself and considers what impact this is having on children in classrooms and how it will affect their adult lives. She points out that many teachers today bombard children with dozens of questions per hour with little to no time left for in-depth assessments and forcing connections. The rapid pace of questioning in the classroom becomes more important than allowing time for actual thinking. Sullivan proposes a different route. She writes, "We must pose 'five minute questions' or difficult questions there are no answers to. Furthermore, if we want children to be reflective, we have to be so ourselves. We must provide a classroom environment that is conducive to thoughtfulness." In the same article she concludes, "We must give children an opportunity to discover the world through their own lenses. This all takes time. When we ask ourselves what we can give to the generation we have given birth to, time would be the best idea yet. Unqualified, unstructured, 'lifetime.'"[6]

One of the curriculum milestones for her sixth graders is to undertake somewhat lengthy writing assignments; ones that force them to look at their lives in a much larger context. Students write a "memoir"— even at the young age of ten. Sullivan shares her own memoir with them and how as a child she loved to roam the hillsides alone. She even reads aloud from her biography and shares the story of a very scary day when a man pulled up alongside her and asked her to join him for a ride in his car. She ran away and made it home safely, but her students connect for the first time with the reality that she wasn't always an adult—in fact she was a kid just like they are. She told me, "I see my time spent alone as a child as really valuable. I thought about who I was. I thought about what I wanted to be. I believed that there were possibilities beyond what I could imagine. By being alone, kids have the time to tap into the inner wilderness and make some vital connections with themselves that sustain them." She concluded, "The challenge for teachers today is to create a thoughtful classroom environment." She said, "Information abounds. Our students need to synthesize and become empathetic with one another. For teachers, this is far different than delivering a fact-driven curriculum."[7]

On a cold winter night in 2009, in Columbia, Missouri, the Midwest, the president of Stephens College attempted to introduce digital natives to the concept of simply being alone. President Dianne Lynch asked

75 undergraduates to join her in the campus chapel to participate in an hour-long exercise called, "Vespers: Stephens Unplugged," which draws on an older tradition at the college simply called: "Vespers." Students voluntarily came to the session that was not about prayers, as the once-Baptist school is women-only and secular.[8]

At the beginning of the inaugural 'Vespers: Stephens Unplugged' session, Lynch announced, "We are all here together, but we are all alone. At the end of this conversation, I hope you leave here with an understanding that being alone in solitude has value." Students were asked to turn off their cell phones and place them in baskets far away from their hands and from the impulse to text their friends just across the chapel. As part of her doctoral work, Lynch spent five years studying digital natives who have never known a world without constant connectivity. Unplugging is not intuitive for them. It will never be unless it's seen as something valuable. The inaugural session of silence would last only 15 minutes, and Lynch warned students that at times it would be uncomfortable. At the start of the session, she asked everyone attending to trust her. After an initial talk and introduction (which can be heard online, as the school recorded the session), her last words to the students were: "So...go." And those in the room sat and attempted to silence their minds, even while finals were looming and most had never in their lives experienced such a detached moment.[9]

Stephens College estimates U.S. college students spend approximately $6.5 billion a year on technology and an average of 12 hours a day engaged with some type of media. Lynch put the vespers program into context: "Learning to be self-reflective, quiet, and focused is as important a part of becoming a successful, centered, and healthy adult as many of the subjects that are a common part of college curricula. It's a life skill, and students today—who live in a world of constant static—need it more than ever before."[10] Stephens College coordinates and advertises the moments of silence through the "Stephens Unplugged" Web page on Facebook. One recent posting promoting a follow-on Vesper night said: "Off they go!...The gadgets that is, as you power down, quiet down, and get down to pondering life's big questions at Vespers."[11]

Blame Games and Business Schools

The financial recession has forced all organizations, including institutions of higher learning, to reconsider how they help students prepare for, and think through, crisis and uncertainty. As the global economy nearly collapsed, millions have flocked back to school, many in pursuit of a masters degree in business administration (MBA). Business schools have been singled out following the crisis. Critics have posited that even top schools graduated thinkers unable to manage the risks that underpinned the collapse. But did these schools fail to teach the critical skills that could have prevented the collapse? Are they failing to teach the next generation? Was greed, hatched inside unethical classroom settings, at the core of what drove so many bad decisions on Wall Street? Such questions oversimplify the still-unwinding tale of the financial crisis.

Business schools certainly played a role in the financial crisis, and several are taking a step back to reconsider their missions and what they could have done better. More importantly, they are asking what within the curriculum should change? Tom Cooley was dean of NYU's Stern School of Business in the run-up and through the financial crisis. He engaged the Stern faculty to immediately publish a book that summarized the institution's best ideas for addressing the crisis and the regulations and rule sets that would inevitably arise in its wake. With the arrival of the Obama administration in January 2009, Cooley wanted Stern's thinking to have an impact on the future. He saw the school's response as critical, given their deep connectivity to Wall Street and their positioning as a top research institution. Cooley told me, "We were deconstructing what happened and explaining it to the world. What should change? What proposals do we have to better structure the financial and regulatory system? If you don't have proposals, then we need to talk about relevance."[12]

Cooley is also a realist, who doesn't believe past management practices are the best ways to train for the future. He said, "People are constantly navel-gazing about business education...questioning what business education is all about. What are we doing right and what are we doing wrong?" He continued, "Business education can be very backward-looking. You don't always want to know what the best practice or past practice is. What you want to know is how do you think through unforeseen technologies or unforeseen events? You need analytical capabilities that will help you to prosper in a career that will last 30 or 40 years."[13]

In other words, Cooley is saying it's how the mind is trained to think through ambiguous problems that matters more than studying a single management trend. Cooley concluded, "If you look at the extent of technological change in the world economy and the structure of relationships over 30 or 40 years it's staggering. There's nothing you can look at in the world of current practice that would prepare you for that. The only thing that can prepare you is a forward-looking mode of thinking and an understanding of how you acquire new knowledge and the ability to adapt."[14]

Harvard's Moment of Self-Reflection

Few schools are as synonymous with the acronym MBA as is Harvard Business School (HBS). When Jay Light took over as dean of HBS in 2005, he formalized an annual review process that would allow the school to ensure it remains relevant, given the constant changes in business. Light agreed with Cooley about the backward-looking view of business schools, at times, and said, "Usually the bullet that gets you isn't the one you planned for. You know how French generals always plan for the last war? My guess is we do a little of that, too. We condition our students to really figure out how they could have avoided the last crisis and it's hard to know if you are doing a better job of getting them through the next three crises. The next three will be importantly different than the last three." Annually, 25 to 30 percent of the curriculum rolls over, as courses are constantly changing. For example, now taught in the immediate wake of the financial collapse are case studies on Citibank and Lehman Brothers. The case methodology approach at HBS ensures new content and business practices are being continuously introduced.[15]

Dean Light commissioned a case study that chronicled the potential changes that would take place within the school in the context of changes happening globally. Light explained, "I tried to make it a self-reflective organization. In most years, it doesn't lead to a whole lot of change. Some years, when a real crisis occurs, it does." In January and February, Light gets together for dinner with faculty members in groups of about six, focused on a single topic relevant to the school and its overall mission. Over these lengthy dinners, Light opens up the entire curriculum for discussion and debate. The topics are intentionally broad in scope. There are no simple answers. He told me, "Dinners may feature a discussion around how HBS should become more global, what's going on in the world of organizational change, or the character of our research agenda and its appropriateness for the problems of the world." The results of the discussions are reported to what Light calls the "Dean's Management Group," and findings are incorporated into a case study for internal consumption.[16]

Light shared with me one of the case studies written in April 2009. With the exception of the word "confidential" stamped across the top, the case resembles the thousands produced by HBS about other organizations. One passage acknowledged criticism facing HBS. It reads:

> As the economic crisis deepened, many sought a culprit, and public sentiment turned against business in general and Wall Street in particular. Large bonus payouts at high profile firms, including Lehman Brothers and AIG, became a focal point for widespread anger. "It was a short leap to question the role business schools had played in training the leaders of those firms," said Professor Carl Kester, Deputy Dean for Academic Affairs. "And a number of pieces began to appear in the press. While the headlines clearly were intended to provoke—including 'Blame It on Harvard: Is the MBA Culture Responsible for the Financial Crisis?' and 'Harvard's Masters of the Apocalypse' (*Sunday Times* 1 March 2009)— some of the stories raised important questions, truth be told."[17]

After the Enron and WorldCom scandals in early 2000, Harvard reflected on what it was not teaching its students and decided to add a new and mandatory course on ethics. During the recent financial crisis, some argued within HBS that there was need to revisit ethics. Light and others did not see ethics as the core problem to be addressed. He explained, "What in fact we opted for was more of a bottoms-up process. We decided that the lessons of this last crisis weren't so much about ethics, albeit we did have a Bernie Madoff or two; it was more about risk management. It was more about people who meant well— who weren't looking at the kinds of risks their organizations were taking. They just weren't thinking about what the downside was."[18]

Light pointed out that in the 1970s, HBS had a course called "Risk Management." Over time, it disappeared from the curriculum as student interest waned. Light, who taught at HBS, recalled the uncertainty facing the country during that time. He said, "The 1970s was a time when we had a number of rocky episodes and we were all much more conscious of the downside of things. The 90s and 2000s were such a wonderful period of growth that we just got out of the habit and mindset." He admits HBS did not do enough to encourage graduates to think with equal passion and rigor about downside risk. "It's good to focus on opportunities and it's good to focus on growth, but the more you start making decisions you must consider the magnitude of the downside," Light explained. He continued, "It's easy to lose sight of the fact that one of the principle functions of a leader is to manage the downside and to make sure that the organization is thinking about it, analyzing it, and monitoring it." Risk management is back on the curriculum at HBS and taught within multiple courses that are often oversubscribed.

Light stepped down as dean of HBS in the summer of 2010, but will remain on the faculty and focus again on research and new management models. He is no longer in the hot seat. I asked him to score his performance during his tenure as head of one of the most iconic schools in the world during a time of significant economic uncertainty. Light didn't hesitate and said, "I would give myself an 'incomplete.'"[19]

Evidence and Guideposts

With all the trends and permutations of the future, what has become clear to me after studying reflection inside organizations today is that a necessary, and often unspoken, element underpins organizational success and/or failure. Well beyond simply paying attention, reflection is a capability that allows for problem solving amidst a constant onslaught of distraction and data. Throughout this book, I have given examples of what some leaders and organizations are doing to prioritize think time and reflection over constant action and speed. I have not discovered one company or leader with a codified set of skills that prove it is the "most reflective in America." But I do believe this will be a title of distinction one day. It will be celebrated, as reflection becomes a capability that defines the viability of an organization. Our greatest blind spot is the ingrained belief in the stability of the status quo and in cyclical solutions to complicated problems. Consultant and author Bruce Piasecki describes the world today as "swift and severe." In such a point in time, leaders must ask themselves how often can they afford not to pull back from a problem and reframe it, as well as reframing the entire strategic context around the organization.

Following are five guideposts to look for as you seek to discover reflection in your organization. These guideposts provide evidence that reflection is valued. You can use them to begin some critical conversations.

Guidepost 1: Technology Versus Human Capacity

One of the key villains stealing away time for thinking and reflection is technology, the same thing that helps bring so much good to life through its ability to parse and move data. Connectivity and the narrative of responsiveness afforded by technology drive often-addictive behaviors. Constant connectivity and persistent disruption quickly evaporate obvious gains technology brings. Organizations that question technology's role in the context of routine human behaviors reveal evidence of reflection. The absence of any questioning also tells you a lot. Technology's greatest bottleneck remains the single-tasking human brain.

Guidepost 2: Real or Masked Dialogues

Organizations that demonstrate the ability to engage in uninterrupted dialogues that are generative of new thinking will be the most relevant and lasting of this century. Reflection isn't just an alone thing—it happens in small group settings, but only if people have the awareness of what thinking together actually means. Even with policies and core behaviors in place to push back against technology and its incessant connectivity, business still comes down to people moving problems to closure through dialogue, discourse, reporting, and decision making. Leaders and organizations must protect, nurture, and encourage dialogue—perhaps for the first time.

Guidepost 3: Dedicating Time for Thinking

Organizations that offer and celebrate think time, both inside and outside the workday, will prove to be the most innovative. Instant decision making often remains a must; but addressing chronic problems and nurturing big ideas can't be done in an instant. Organizations that sustain think time across months and years, preferably within a defined set of predetermined gates, will produce atypical responses to previously unforeseen problems. Devaluing reflection while expecting constant growth and innovation is nonsensical. It's only when we step away from the onslaught of the day that a new direction arises (good or bad). By never stepping away and, instead, insisting on constant connectivity, you can't be sure if what you are working on will prove you to be relevant in the future.

Guidepost 4: Leaders who Walk the Walk

Building reflection into the habits and routines of an organization will not happen if the senior-most executives don't lead from the front. When CEOs crave connectivity and fragment their day through worshipping busyness, they send powerful signals that action and immediacy matter most of all. An email sent by a leader at 1:00 a.m. sends a powerful signal to all working for them that the firm's social contract involves being online at anytime. Such behavior will be aped within the organization and reflection will be consumed in its wake. We have also seen that when leaders force think time and reflection into their own routines, others imitate such behavior, resulting in busyness giving way to controlled and sustained thought.

Guidepost 5: Cultures of Dissent and Deep Thinking

When discussion is stilted and cultures can't actually engage in constructive debate, fundamental assumptions are not questioned, and the wrong problems get solved. Intellectual products of reflection are born only after many hours of constructive debate. Embracing paradoxical thinking and pushing back (without recrimination) amidst rapid decision making indicates a culture that values reflection over immediate response. Managing risk is not a proficiency relegated to a small team that is authorized to step back and ask awkward questions. Downside risk assessments must be considered within the exuberance of creating new and promising projects. Dissent doesn't indicate one is not a "team player"; it's more indicative of a mind that will not rationalize away dissonance.

Final Thoughts and Music at a Subway Station

For most of my adult life I have called the Washington, D.C., area my home. It's a city where well-educated people are constantly on the move, pushing ideas and political agendas. Writer Gene Weingarten of the *Washington Post* wondered what would happen if a very talented violinist, playing a 300-year-old, priceless Stradivarius were to don a baseball cap and play in the D.C. subway. Would people stop? Would there be crowds to control? Shouldn't people stop? Or, are we all just too busy to even notice?

Weingarten convinced Grammy award-winning violinist, Joshua Bell, to do just that. Bell played complex pieces by Bach and Beethoven. He would not shortchange the morning commuters as they came out of the elevators atop the L'Enfant metro station. He picked difficult pieces to play. In summarizing the results of this unique experiment, Weingarten wrote: "In the three-quarters of an hour that Joshua Bell played, seven people stopped what they were doing to hang around and take in the performance, at least for a minute. Twenty-seven gave money, most of them on the run—for a total of $32 and change. That leaves the 1,070 people who hurried by, oblivious, many only three feet away, few even turning to look."[20]

Three years after this famous experiment, Bell told me he still gets emails and comments from people who have read the article or watched the clips of his subway performance that are available on YouTube. Bell admitted he was curious about the experiment, but not surprised by its results. He understood why few people stopped to listen to him. Engaging in classical music required a commitment few people on a morning commute are willing to make. When Bell performs at a classical music venue, attendees are there to focus on what he is playing; they have paid to make the time to soak in the music. They think their way through his performances. That's not the case for a busy commuter on the way to work.[21]

What surprised Bell was how people perceived the results of the experiment. He marveled at how the story spread virally on the Internet. It's become the most watched video ever on the *Washington Post*'s Web site—over 1.8 million views, including hundreds of thousands of derivative downloads on YouTube. Bell told me, "I haven't heard the end of it, and it's been three years already." He continued, "I think that what people took from the experiment is that we don't appreciate the beauty that is around. I think that's why it struck a chord. I think everyone feels in his or her heart that we are in a rush. I am not sure that the experiment necessarily showed that, but I think that's what people got out of it." Weingarten had his own conclusion, expressed in his Pulitzer

Prize-winning article: "If we can't take the time out of our lives to stay a moment and listen to one of the best musicians on Earth play some of the best music ever written; if the surge of modern life so overpowers us that we are deaf and blind to something like that—then what else are we missing?"[22]

People have emailed Bell from around the world, many touched by what they saw on the video and read in the article. Some told Bell they would change their behaviors; they would pause more—slow down. As he looks to the future, Bell is concerned that it takes time and thinking in order to have appreciation for the music he plays. He told me, "One of things that scares me about the future of people listening to classical music is that they are less and less taught the value of using our brains for think time. Even music itself is now about consuming while you are on the go, or only dancing to it only when it's very loud. It really doesn't promote thinking or contemplation. It's all about the visceral reaction it." He continued, "For classical music to have its effect you have to be completely focused on it. As a listener, you must engage your mind and let yourself just think. It's a beautiful thing when it happens, but it takes practice."[23]

If you never buy a ticket to hear Joshua Bell play Vivaldi, or stop the next time you think you are hearing beautiful music on a street corner, just realize that meaning is out there. Ideas are out there. Insights and innovation await us only if we are capable of stepping outside the frenzied worlds of data and distraction that wash over us. Unlike any other time in human history, technology allows for the assembly and visualization of data that has the potential to inform solutions to problem sets. We must remember that technology is not the destination.

The power of reflection lies not in how much time we allocate to it. The power of reflection lies in how we choose to use that time and what structure we bring to the fleeting disjointed moments we are afforded. The organizations and leaders who can sustain thinking upon the right problems, while they absorb the unknowns that will inevitably arise, will prove the most relevant and lasting. There is much innovation to come, and the ability to embrace reflection, as a critical tool, will become one of the primary determinants of corporate, and even national, success in the twenty-first century. New methods and incentives will be found whereby leaders will value detachment and think time as much as connection and speed. We are a resourceful species. Failure to force think time and reflection into habits, routines, and processes is no longer a blind spot and topic of lament. Time for reflection is an open invitation to discover what awaits us; it's an opportunity we all can take advantage of as data and connectivity compound, and the tempo increases. The choice is ours: to permanently raise and reward the importance of reflection or simply meander through our next 10,000 emails. The consequences of that choice are also ours.

Notes

Introduction

1. Author's interview with Dr. Robert Bea.
2. CBS News, *60 Minutes*, May 16, 2010, "Blowout: The Deepwater Horizon Disaster."
3. Ibid.
4. Ibid.
5. Ibid.
6. Ibid.
7. Van Wishard, *Between Two Ages: The 21st Century and the Crisis of Meaning* (Bloomington, IN: Xlibris Publishing, 2000), p. 20.
8. Testimony to Congress: Statement of Dr. James H. Billington, Librarian of Congress, before the House Subcommittee on Legislative Branch, U.S. House of Representatives, March 20, 2007.
9. Dana Wachter and Lisa Stark, "Tired? Study Says Americans Need More Sleep: CDC Report Finds 70 Percent of Adults Don't Get Enough Rest," ABCNEWS.com, February 28, 2008.
10. Suzanne Choney, "'Millennials': An Always On, Texting Generation," msnbc.com, February 23, 2010.
11. David Brown, "Scientists Create Cell Based on Man-made Genetic Instructions," *Washington Post*, May 21, 2010.
12. Term derived from Tom Peters and Robert H. Waterman Jr., *In Search of Excellence* (New York: Grand Central Publishing, 1988).
13. Michael Bar-Eli, Ofer H. Azar, Ilana Ritov, Yael Keidar-Levin, and Galit Schein. "Action Bias among Elite Soccer Goalkeepers: The Case of Penalty Kicks," 2005, available at http://ideas.repec.org/p/pra/mprapa/4477.html.

1 The Human Need for Think Time

1. "Obama on Vacationing and Time to Think," The Associated Press, July 27, 2008, www.nytimes.com/2008/07/27/us/politics/27CHAT.html?_r=1& scp=1&sq=obama%20vacation&st=cse&oref=slogin.

2. Remarks by President Obama at Hampton University Commencement, May 10, 2010, www.whitehouse.gov/the-press-office/remarks-president-hampton-university-commencement.

3. "New British PM Bans Mobile Phones at Cabinet Meetings," Agency France, May 13, 2010, http://news.yahoo.com/s/afp/britainpoliticstechnologyoffbeat.

4. "Cameron's Coalition: Mobile Phones Banned from Cabinet," BBC News, May 13, 2010.

5. Author's interview with Thomas Barnett.

6. http://www.psych.utah.edu/lab/appliedcognition/publications/supertaskers.pdfntline http://www.pbs.org/wgbh/pages/frontline/digital nation/interviews/nass.html.

7. "Supertaskers: Profiles in Extraordinary Multitasking Ability," http://www.psych.utah.edu/people/upforreview/watson/2.pdf.

8. "Solitude and Leadership: If You Want Others to Follow Learn to be Alone with Your Thoughts," *The American Scholar*, Spring 2010, http://www.theamericanscholar.org/solitude-and-leadership/print/.

9. Author's interview with Ken Anderson.

10. Author's interview with Maria Bezaitis.

11. Author's interview with Darryl V. Poole.

12. Author's interview with Robert Shumsky.

13. Ibid.

14. Author's interview with Robert Shumsky.

15. Author's first interview with Admiral Thad Allen.

16. Ibid.

17. Ibid.

18. Ibid.

19. Ibid.

20. Press Briefing by Press Secretary Robert Gibbs, Admiral Thad Allen and Assistant to The President for Energy and Climate Change Carol Browner, May 24, 2010.

21. Author's second interview with Admiral Thad Allen.

22. Ibid.

23. Ibid.

24. Ibid.

25. Ibid.

26. Ibid.

27. Ibid.

28. Transcript Whitehouse Press Briefing, May 24, 2010. http://www.whitehouse.gov/the-press-office/press-briefing-press-secretary-robert-gibbs-admiral-thad-allen-and-assistant-president/.

29. Apollo 13 was NASA's third mission intending to land on the moon for exploration. The ship was successfully launched toward the moon, but the

landing was aborted after an oxygen tank ruptured severely damaging the spacecraft's electrical system. The crew aboard and NASA leadership had to improvise with available technology and resources on board the space ship in order to successfully bring the astronauts home safely.

30. Authors interview with Admiral Thad Allen.
31. Author's interview with Joshua Bell.
32. Author's interview with Joshua Bell.
33. Secretary Robert Gates's remarks read during award ceremony June 26, 2008.
34. Author's interview with Jeb Nadaner.
35. Anthony Stoor, *Solitude* (New York: Free Press, 1988), p. 60.
36. Author's interview with Professor Edward Watkins.
37. Ibid.
38. Author's interview with Susan Nolen-Hoeksema.
39. Author's interview with U.S. Marine Corps General James Mattis.

2 Forcing Think Time

1. Matthew Pinsker, *Lincoln's Sanctuary* (New York: Oxford University Press, 2003).
2. John C. Waugh, *Reflecting Lincoln: The Battle for the 1864 Presidency* (New York: Crown Publishers, Inc. 1977), p. 82.
3. Ibid.
4. Author's interview with Erin Mast.
5. Author's interview with Matthew Pinsker.
6. Tom Wheeler, *Mr. Lincoln's T-mails, How Abraham Lincoln Used the Telegraph to Win the Civil War* (New York: Harper Collins, 2008).
7. Michael Burkhimer, *One Hundred Essential Lincoln Books* (Nashville: Cumberland House Publishing, 2003), p. 34.
8. Sherry Turkle "Always On; Always on You: The Tethered Self," 2006. Available online at http://web.mit.edu/sturkle/www/Always-on%20Always-on-you_The%20Tethered%20Self_ST.pdf.
9. Author's interview with Tom Wheeler.
10. Ibid.
11. Mr. Linclon's T-Mails, How Abraham Lincoln used the Telegraph to Win the Civil War, 183.
12. Author's interview with General David Petraeus.
13. Author's interview with General Jack Keane.
14. Rob Guth, "In Secret Hideaway, Bill Gates Ponders Microsoft's Future," *Wall Street Journal*, March 2005.
15. Todd Bishop, "43 of Microsoft's Biggest Thinkers Try to Replicate Bill Gates' Brain," 2009. Available online at http://www.techflash.com.

16. Steve Ballmer on How to Run Meetings." WSJ.com leadership videos http://online.wsj.com/video/digits-ballmers-ipad-envy/40F77A6F-7CC5–437E-8C81–5E91D435B9D0.html?KEYWORDS=ballmer.

17. Author's interview.

18. "Steve Ballmer's Management Rx," wsj.com, June 16, 2009. Available at http://blogs.wsj.com/digits/2009/06/16/steve-ballmers-management-rx/tab/video/.

19. John Medina, *Brain Rules: 12 Principles for Surviving and Thriving at Work, Home and School* (Seattle: Pear Press, 2009) p. 163.

20. Sam Walton with John Huey, *Sam Walton: Made in America* (New York: Doubleday, 1992), p. 117.

21. Author's interview with Andrew Belton.

22. http://www.google.com/trends/hottrends.

23. Phrase was actually coined by Linda Stone and defined on: http://lindastone.net/.

3　Thinking Out Loud

1. Author's interview with Joe Raelin.

2. Author's interview with Van Wishard.

3. Author's interview with Fred Collopy.

4. Author's interview with Doug Bennett.

5. "Dick Cheney: Stop 'Dithering' over Afghanistan," Associated Press, October 22, 2009.

6. Peter Baker, "How Obama Came to Plan for the 'Surge' in Afghanistan," *Washington Post*, December 5, 2009.

7. Foreign Policy Magazine. Fred Kaplan's interview with Secretary Robert Gates, August 2010. http://www.foreignpolicy.com/articles/2010/08/13/robert_gates?page=0,5.

8. *Washington Post*.

9. William Safire, "Groupthink," *New York Times*, August 8, 2004.

10. Author's interview with Dr. Mitchell Reiss.

11. Ibid.

12. Ibid.

13. Ibid.

14. Ibid.

15. Ibid.

16. Joseph A. Raelin, *Work-Based Learning: Bridging Knowledge and Action in the Workplace* (Hoboken: John Wiley and Sons, 2008).

17. Adam Bryant, "Xerox's New Chief Tries to Redefine Its Culture," *New York Times*, February 20, 2010.

18. Ibid.
19. Author's interview with Sandy Linver.
20. Ibid.
21. Ibid.
22. Ibid.
23. Ibid.
24. The framework was taken from Joe Raelin, "'I Don't Have Time to Think!' versus the Art of Reflective Practice," *Reflections Magazine* 4(1).

4   Promoting Think Time

1. Content compiled from archivist from Jim Henson's company and also cited in *It's Not Easy Being Green* (New York: Hyperion, 2005).
2. Ibid.
3. Ron Schmidt "Are Incentives Sufficient?" November 19, 2009.
4. Ibid.
5. Please note that each time Whirlpool is referenced within this chapter it is actually referring to Whirlpool Corporation.
6. Google US Jobs. Available online at http://www.google.com/support/jobs/bin/static.py?page=about.html&about=eng.
7. Gary Hammel, *The Future of Management* (Cambridge: Harvard University Press, 2007).
8. Melissa Mayer, "License to Dream," lecture at Stanford University, 2006. Available online at http://ecorner.stanford.edu/authorMaterialInfo.html?mid=15.
9. Author's interview with Jim Brickley.
10. Bharat Mediratta, "The Google Way: Give Engineer's Room," *New York Times*, October 21, 2007. Available online at http://www.nytimes.com/2007/10/21/jobs/21pre.html.
11. Paul Buchheit, "Communicating with Code." Available online at http://paulbuchheit.blogspot.com/2009/01/communicating-with-code.html.
12. Ken Auletta, *"Googled: The End of the World as We Know It"* (New York: Penguin, 2009).
13. Ibid.
14. "Google Searches for Staffing Answers," *Wall Street Journal*, May 19, 2009. Available online at http://online.wsj.com/article/SB124269038041932531.htm.
15. Ibid.
16. Jessica E. Vascellaro, "Google Searches for Ways to Keep Big Ideas at Home," *Wall Street Journal*, June 16, 2009.
17. Ibid.

18. Vindu Goel, "How Google Decides to Pull the Plug," *New York Times*, February 15, 2009. Available online at http://www.nytimes.com/2009/02/15/business/15ping.html?_r=1.

19. Louis V. Gerstner, *Who Says Elephants Can't Dance?* (New York: Harper Business, 2002) p. 182.

20. Ibid.

21. Nancy Tennant Snyder and Deborah Duarte, *Unleashing Innovation*, Foreword by Jeff M. Fettig (Hoboken: Jossey-Bass, 2006), p. viii.

22. Author's interview with Nancy Tennant.

23. Ibid.

24. How Whirlpool Defines Innovation, Bloomberg Businessweek, March 6, 2006. Available online at http://www.businessweek.com/innovate/content/mar2006/id20060306_ 287425.htm.

25. Ibid.

26. "The Government's New Breed of Change Agents," Daniel P. Forrester, 2006.

5   Taking a Step Back

1. Sue Shellenbarger, "A Day without Email Is Like...," *Wall Street Journal*, October 11, 2007. Available online at http://online.wsj.com/public/article/SB119205641656255234-tmvyaC6sQRWh4D2UINHEAJlbWdU_20071109.html?mod=tff_main_tff_top.

2. Author's interview with Jonathan Spira.

3. John Freeman, "Not So Fast," *Wall Street Journal,* August 21, 2009. Available online at http://online.wsj.com/article/SB1000142405297020355060457435864311740778.html.

4. Leslie Perlow and Jessica Porter, "Making Time Off Predictable and Required," *Harvard Business Review*, October 2009. Available online at http://hbr.org/2009/10/making-time-off-predictable-and-required/ar/1.

5. Ibid.

6. Ibid.

7. Ibid.

8. SSM website and interviews with key staff.

9. Author's interview with Sister Mary Jean Ryan, all subsequent quotes are from the same interview.

10. Author's interview with Bill Thompson, all subsequent quotes are from the same interview.

11. Author's interview with Harry Hertz, all subsequent quotations are from the same interview.

12. Atul Gawande, "The Check List," *New Yorker*, December 10, 2007. Available online at http://www.newyorker.com/reporting/2007/12/10/071210fa_ fact_gawande.

6   Too Big to Think?

1. Author's interview with Brooksley Born.
2. Ibid.
3. Ibid.
4. Frontline, "The Warning," PBS.com. http://www.pbs.org/http://www.pbs. org/wgbh/pages/frontline/warning/etc/script.htmlwgbh/pages/frontline/ warning/etc/script.html.
5. Author's interview with Brooksley Born.
6. Ibid.
7. Ibid.
8. Ibid.
9. Robert Hotz, "Get Out of Your Own Way," *Wall Street Journal*, June 27, 2008.
10. Carol Tavris and Elliot Aronson, *Mistakes Were Made (But Not By Me)* (New York: Harcourt Books, 2007) p. 13.
11. Ibid.
12. Testimony by Lloyd C. Blankfein, Chairman and CEO, The Goldman Sachs Group, Inc., before the Financial Crisis Inquiry Commission, January 13, 2010. Available online at http://www.fcic.gov/hearings/ pdfs/2010–0113-Blankfein.pdf.
13. Ibid.
14. Ibid.
15. Ibid.
16. Ibid.
17. Ibid.
18. Commodity Futures Trading Commission, "Over-the-Counter Derivatives," May 6, 1998. Available online at http://www.cftc.gov/opa/ press98/opamntn.htm#issues_for_comment.
19. Acceptance Speech by Brooksley Born, May 18, 2009. Available online at http://www.jfklibrary.org.
20. CNBC, "House of Cards."
21. Imre Karacs, "Bremer Vulkan Joins Germany's Casualty List," *The Independent*, February 23, 1996. Available online at http://www.inde- pendent.co.uk/news/business/bremer-vulkan-joins-germanys-casualty- list-1320596.html.
22. Author's interview with Kyle Bass.

23. Ibid.
24. Author's interview with Carol Tavris.
25. Author's interview with Kyle Bass.
26. Ibid.
27. Ibid.
28. Ibid.
29. Ibid.
30. Ibid.
31. Tavris and Aronson, "Mistakes Were Made."
32. Author's interview with Kyle Bass.
33. "Testimony before the Financial Crisis Inquiry Commission Hearing on the Financial Crisis," January 13, 2010. Available online at http://www.fcic.gov/hearings/pdfs/2010–0113-Bass.pdf.
34. Ibid.

7   Rapid Contemplation

1. Author's interview with U.S. Army General David Petraeus.
2. Author's interview with U.S. Army General Jack Keane (ret.).
3. Ibid.
4. Ibid.
5. Insight derived through author's interview with John Nagl.
6. Author's interview with U.S. Marine General James Mattis.
7. Ibid.
8. Iraq Study Group Final Report, December 6, 2006. Available online at http://media.usip.org/reports/iraq_study_group_report.pdf.
9. Ibid.
10. Author's interview with Sarah Sewell.
11. Workshop Summary Report: Counterinsurgency in Iraq: Implications for Irregular Warfare for the U.S. Government, Carr Center for Human Rights Policy, October 2005.
12. Ibid.
13. Lt. Colonel John A. Nagl, "The Evolution and Importance of Army/Marine Corps Field Manual 3–24, *Counterinsurgency*," in *The U.S. Army/Marine Corps Counterinsurgency Field Manual* (Chicago: University of Chicago Press, 2007), pp. xiii–xx.
14. Ibid.
15. Ibid.
16. Ibid.
17. Author's interview with Dr. Conrad Crane.
18. Ibid.

19. Ibid.
20. Ibid.
21. Ibid.
22. Ibid.
23. Ibid.
24. Ibid.
25. Ibid.
26. Ibid.
27. Ibid.
28. Ibid.
29. Ibid.
30. *The U.S. Army/Marine Corps Counterinsurgency Field Manual.*
31. Ibid.
32. Author's interview with General David Petraeus.
33. Author's interview with Conrad Crane.
34. Ibid.
35. Ibid.
36. John Nagl, *Learning to Eat Soup with a Knife* (Chicago: University Of Chicago Press, 2005), p. 115.
37. Ibid.
38. Author's interview with General David Petracus.
39. Ibid.
40. Thomas Ricks, *The Gamble* (New York: Penguin Press, 2009).
41. Ibid.
42. *The Fourth Star* (New York: Crown Publishers, 2009), p. 220.
43. Author's interview with John Nagl.
44. Author's interview with Conrad Crane.

8   Outside the Day-to-Day

1. "Spiritual Leadership as a Paradigm for Organizational Transformation and Recovery from Extended Work Hours Cultures," *Journal of Business Ethics*, 2008.
2. Author's interview with Rakesh Khurana.
3. John Medina, "Brain Rules: 12 Principles for Surviving and Thriving at Work, Home, and School" (Seattle: Pear Press, 2009) p. 187.
4. "From Marriott to Ernst & Young to General Mills, Why Some Companies Excel," *Christian Science Monitor*, December 8, 2009.
5. Samantha Gross, "Laid-off Wall Streeters Take Stock, Start Fresh," Associated Press, December 16, 2009.
6. Joseph Schumpeter, *Economist*, October 10, 2009.

7. Author's interview with Barbra and Elizabeth Pagano.
8. Ibid.
9. Author's interview with Richard Floersch.
10. Ibid.
11. Ibid.
12. Ibid.
13. Author's interview with Tara Handy.
14. Author's interview with Richard Floersch.
15. Author's interview with Stefan Sagmeister.
16. "The Power of Time Off" Stefan Sagmeister, TED Global Talk 2009, http://www.ted.com/talks/stefan_sagmeister_the_power_of_time_off.html.
17. Author's interview with Stefan Sagmeister.
18. Stefan Sagmeister, "Designer on Sabbatical," Printmag.com, February 2009.
19. Ibid, TED Talk.
20. Ted Talk.
21. Author's interview with Stefan Sagmeister.
22. Ibid.
23. Ibid.
24. Ibid. Author's interview with Stefan Sagmeister.
25. Author's interview with John Wolpert.
26. Ibid.
27. Ibid.
28. Sources: (1) Ibid Wolpert Interview & (2) "Companies Corral Staff for In-house Brainstorming," Bloomberg Businessweek, March 12, 2009, http://www.businessweek.com/magazine/content/09_12/b4124042082382.htm.
29. Author's interview with John Wolpert.
30. Youtube, Best Buy Corp., http://www.youtube.com/watch?v=7Q7bmmjskFU&feature=related.
31. O. Sullivan, "Busyness, Status Distinction and Consumption Strategies of the Income Rich, Time Poor," *Time and Society* 17(5); 2008, pp. 5–26.

9   Reflection and Extreme Situations

1. Author's interview with General David Petraeus.
2. Author's interview with General James Mattis.
3. Ibid.
4. James Mattis, Commanding General's Message to All Hands, First Marine Division (REIN) March 2003.
5. Author's interview with James Mattis.
6. Letter from General David Petraeus, May 10, 2007.

7. COMISAF'S Counterinsurgency Guidance letter written by General David Petraeus on August 1, 2010.

8. Ibid.

9. Ibid.

10. Ibid.

11. Ibid.

12. Ibid.

13. Ibid.

14. Ibid.

15. Danny Fenster, "Sweet Home Chicago," June 2, 2008. Available online at http://gapersblock.com/detour/taking_a_stand_against_guns/.

16. Author's interview with Tio Hardiman.

17. Ibid.

18. Ibid.

19. Wesley G. Skogan, Susan M. Hartnett, Natalie Bump, and Jill Dubois with the assistance of Ryan Hollon and Danielle Morris, "Evaluation of CeaseFire-Chicago," May 2008.

20. Nancy Ritter, "CeaseFire: A Public Health Approach to Reduce Shootings and Killings."

21. "Blocking the Transmission of Violence," *New York Times*, May 5, 2008. Available online at http://www.nytimes.com/2008/05/04/magazine/04health.

22. Author's interview with Tio Hardiman.

23. Ibid.

24. Ibid.

25. Ibid.

26. Ibid.

27. "Special Master Kenneth Feinberg Is a Mediator's Mediator," *Washington Post*, January 14, 2010.

28. Author's interview with Kenneth Feinberg.

29. Ibid.

30. Ibid.

31. Ibid.

32. Ibid.

10   The Future of Think Time and Reflection

1. Author's interview with Kyle Bass

2. Ibid.

3. Ibid.

4. Author's interview with David Walker

5. Ibid.

6. Thinking about a Child's Need for Reflection," From Now On The Educational Technology Journal, April 2000, Kristina Sullivan. http://www.fno.org/apr2000/reflection.html.
7. Author's interview with Kristina Sullivan.
8. Sources: "College Asks Students to Power Down, Contemplate" ALAN SCHER ZAGIER, Associated Press, December 25, 2009. Also, Stephens College: http://www.stephens.edu/photofeatures/2010/unplugged/, also content reviewed by Dianne Lynch.
9. Ibid
10. Ibid.
11. http://www.facebook.com/StephensUnplugged.
12. Author's interview with Tom Cooley.
13. Ibid.
14. Ibid.
15. Author's interview with Jay Light.
16. Ibid.
17. Case Study: Harvard Business School and the Global Economic Crisis, April 2009.
18. Ibid.
19. Ibid.
20. Pearls Before Breakfast by Gene Weingarten, Washington Post, April 8, 2007.
21. Author's interview with Joshua Bell.
22. Ibid.
23. Ibid.

Index